Xenia – A Memoir

GREECE 1919–1949

Xenia – A Memoir

Mary Henderson

WEIDENFELD AND NICOLSON · LONDON

First published in Great Britain in 1988 by
George Weidenfeld & Nicolson Ltd
91 Clapham High Street, London SW4 7TA

ISBN 0 297 79252 0

Printed in Great Britain at The Bath Press, Avon

Map drawn by Technical Art Services

*To Alexandra
for
our grandchildren Benjamin and Garrett
who are a quarter Greek.*

Contents

Illustrations

(Unless otherwise stated all photographs come from the author's collection.)

Between pages 108 and 109

Phanariot grandparents with their children.
Mother.
Father.
Father's Heidelberg fencing friends.
Uncle 'Nonda', Epaminondas Cawadias, Admiral of the Fleet.
In Greek Red Cross nurse's uniform.
Brother Constantine, 'Costaki', after he had escaped from Greece.
Mother in Alexandria in Bedouin costume.
Athens, 12 October 1944. Frank Macaskie and Archbishop Damaskinos lay a wreath on the tomb of the Unknown Warrior. (*Reproduced by kind permission of Hutchinson & Co. Ltd.*)
Liberation Day, 13 October 1944. George Jellicoe, Archbishop Damaskinos, Frank Macaskie and Shan Sedgwick.
The abduction gang. (*Reproduced by kind permission of Harrap Ltd.*)
German Victory Parade in Athens at the tomb of the Unknown Warrior, May 1941. (*Reproduced by kind permission of A. & C. Black Ltd./Lindsay Drummond Ltd.*)
Sitting with Aunt Helene in her Byzantine salon.
US officer briefs the press.
Setting out with the Greek army from Komotini for a night patrol.
UN officials in Florina talk to a fourteen-year-old peasant boy, Nicolas Sinos.
Marcos Vaphiadis, the Communist military commander-in-chief of the Democratic Army, the ELAS forces, 1946–9.
Scenes from the Civil War.

Acknowledgements

I wish to thank the editor of *Time* magazine, Henry Anatole Grunwald, for allowing me to publish my reports sent during the Greek guerrilla war (1946–9), and for the assistance I received from the *Time-Life* London office. Although this does not attempt to be a history book, such are the complexities and mire of Greek politics that I have felt bound to include a brief historical note which I leave to the reader either to read first, last or not at all! (see pp. 205–11). But the brief historical sketch may lead to a better understanding of my book since it covers the events which not only overshadowed my life but the life of all Greeks during those sometimes glorious and often tragic years between 1919 and 1949.

I have occasionally drawn on the personal experiences of authors, most of whom I knew and who were in Greece when I was there. Their eyewitness accounts have often jogged my memory and I am indebted to them for this, since I did not keep a diary. I have listed their names and their works on p. 226.

I have also included descriptions of certain events which I did not personally experience. These are the experiences of some British officers in Greece during the German occupation. Although I was unaware of their operations at the time and only learnt the details when Liberation came, they are an important part of Greek history and Greek life and they fill in the gaps throughout the years I am describing. I therefore wish to thank Lord Jellicoe, Paddy Leigh Fermor, Nigel Clive, Xan Fielding, Sir Derek Dodson and Alexis Ladas for their help.

I am particularly grateful to the Hon. C.M. Woodhouse for so carefully reading my manuscript. To have his knowledgeable and scholarly view and assistance has been invaluable.

Finally, I would like to thank Judy Mooney for her rapid and helpful deciphering of my manuscript. Fearing the post, she not only happily collected my copy but also personally, speedily returned it, beautifully typed; and to my amazement and admiration held it safely in the bowels of her word-processor for the ease of further changes.

'And with regard to my factual reporting of the events of the war I have made it a principle not to write down the first story that came my way, and not even to be guided by my own general impressions; either I was present myself at the events which I have described or else I heard of them from eye-witnesses whose reports I have checked with as much thoroughness as possible. Not that even so the truth was easy to discover: different eye-witnesses give different accounts of the same events, speaking out of partiality for one side or the other or else from imperfect memories. . . . It will be enough for me, however, if these words of mine are judged useful by those who want to understand clearly the events which happened in the past and which (human nature being what it is) will at some time or other and in much the same ways, be repeated in the future.'

Thucydides, *History of the Peloponnesian War*, Book I

Foreword

'Imagination and Memory are but one thing ...'

Hobbes *Leviathan*

I have chosen to call these recollections *Xenia* although it is I who am looking back, because throughout my life I have experienced the disturbing imbalance of being a foreigner, and Xenia which is my second name is Greek for 'foreign' (an abridged version of Polyxenia, which means 'very foreign'). Was I Greek or was I British? This recurring question was always hard to answer. Both my parents were Greek but later became British subjects.

I did not keep a diary, and this is not meant to be an autobiography – although events I describe are accurate, were witnessed by me, were part of my life. But memory plays tricks, chooses, forgets and enhances certain events and feelings. And then everyone is really two people, the person one knows and sees in a mirror and the other person that people think they know and see as one walks into the room. Today it is as though I have an untidy pile of old photographs before me waiting to be stuck into a book marked 1919–1951; most of them were taken in Greece, but there are English ones too. Some of the pictures as I look through them are blurred, foggy and faded but others are sharp and clear – they reveal every detail. Some are missing.

I was born in Athens on 29 March 1919 – I am told it was in a snow storm, which is unusual in Greece. (By strange coincidence, Nicko my husband was born in London a few days later, on 1 April 1919 in a snow storm too – though snow is of course not so unusual in Britain.) My parents moved to England in 1924 when King George of the Hellenes abdicated. My father was the King's doctor and head of the largest teaching hospital in Athens, the Evangelismos. Just before the outbreak of World War II I returned to Greece on holiday, and remained in Greece throughout the German occupation. I was a Red Cross nurse during the Greco-Italian War in Albania, I ran a soup kitchen for children during the famine and later was arrested by the SS and condemned to death for assisting the Allies. Liberated by the British in 1944, I served as a nurse in a British hospital during the Civil War in Athens. From 1946 to 1949 I covered the Communist guerrilla war as *Time* and *Life* correspondent in Greece.

During those turbulent and tragic years, during the war and the civil strife, without knowledge of politics, with scant schoolgirl knowledge of history, unprepared and fortuitously – I found myself involved in a major political conflict – first with the Germans and then with my own countrymen. I suffered too the agony of divided love and divided loyalty, experienced by so many people in occupied and post-World War II Europe. But the life I describe is in fact the everyday life of a person as it runs parallel to dramatic and historic events. War is not glorious; being condemned to death when one is young is not so frightening. Civil War is the deepest wound.

Background Note

Both my parents were Greek but later they became British subjects. My father (Professor A.P.Cawadias, OBE, MD, FRCP) was half Cephalonian and half Cretan – a tough mixture. He came from an academic family with little money but much pride. His father was a distinguished archaeologist and his ancestor the heroic Archbishop of Cephalonia who had cast aside his cassock and fought the Turks during the Greek War of Independence (1800–33). As a young student my father studied medicine in Heidelberg and Paris and I remember how later he regaled my brother Costaki (short for Constantine) and me with Heidelberg fencing songs and Proustian salon conversation picked up *chez* Mme Guermantes. He had an imposing personality, serious dark brown eyes and a very long forehead which we, as children, presumed was packed with brains. But it was when he spoke that his whole countenance came to life – he had a special way of accentuating words and forcefully stating his view – often with firm hand gestures and a twinkle in his eyes. He was a gifted orator and his medical students crowded into his lectures sometimes even spilling out into the street. His fame in Greece, where he headed the large teaching hospital the Evangelismos, was so widespread that peasants from distant mountain villages and islands would come to Athens to seek his care. I recall the long, pathetic queues of peasants outside our Athens home. There were sick babies with watering encrusted eyes, yellow-faced malaria – and typhus-ridden young men and women and frail, gnarled old grandfathers and grandmothers leaning on their sticks. I must admit that at that time the sight terrified me and often at night those agonized faces and staring eyes would haunt my childhood nightmares.

Although as a child I saw little of my father, I can still today picture his huge desk cluttered with books. Medical books – with passages underlined – which shared the space with the Greek classics – Plato and Demosthenes, and English paperback thrillers in Tauchnitz editions – Edgar Wallace and Agatha Christie. There was too that giant round ashtray in the shape of a coiled snake always brim-full of cigarette ends. The untidy bulging bookcases, the framed Hippocratic Oath, the busts of Socrates, Hippocrates and Napoleon completed the scene. He always worked late into the night, often getting up from his desk, pacing the room, reading aloud encircled in a cloud of cigarette smoke. When I was brought in to kiss him good night it was his prickly skin and smell of tobacco that remained stuck in my mind.

My mother, Sophie Constantinides, was born in Alexandria where her parents were wealthy cotton landowners on the banks of the Nile. They were descended from the Phanariots, those aristocratic Greek families who lived in the Phanar quarter of Constantinople after the Turkish conquest. My childhood recollections of Egypt, however, were limited to the frightening noise, the gesticulating crowds and to being carried off the boat – which had brought us from Athens – in the arms of a tall, erect, dark-skinned man in bedroom slippers, wearing the most beautiful gold and blue striped dressing-gown. This was Abdul, the head man in my grandfather's house.

My mother's education was entrusted to a stern English governess and a French seamstress. Miss Upjohn, the English governess, taught behaviour, manners and principles never to be forgotten; the seamstress taught my mother how to copy Paris dresses in other fabrics and so save money. Throughout her life Mother was chic, neat and pretty; and I will always remember a trip to Paris with her – just before the London season. On that first night I was lying in a big brass bed – in the Hotel Regina on the rue de Rivoli – when there were several furtive knocks on the bedroom door. When Mother opened it, two buxom ladies carrying balloon-like parcels stumbled into the room. They were Mother's *copieuses* – dressmakers and hatters who during the daytime worked for the leading fashion houses and at night came round with copies of the latest fashions which they would make up for their clients at half the price. Mme Bertin, the hatter, delved into a huge paper bag and produced hats for Ascot. These she placed firmly on Mother's head – always at an angle and well, well over one eye. Mme Josephine, the dressmaker, brought out her *toiles* (patterns of half a dress in unbleached cambric) and draped these round my mother, explaining in a non-stop monologue how the new line emphasized the moving figure and how this unpromising bit of linen would be made up – transformed – into the most gorgeous beaded ball-dress.

Mother had large, sunken, heavy lidded black eyes, a quizzical smile, and carefully cut, flat-waved auburn hair. (It was cut in Paris by the famous hairdresser, Antoine, whose customers' heads at that time were all turned out by him with auburn, flat-waved hair.) She had definite and strict ideas about right and wrong, and as children we were told that her forceful character came from the fact that one of her ancestors had been a ruthless leader in the Greek War of Independence – *Kapetanios Tromara* – Chieftain Terror.

Mother's life was entirely devoted to her family; she had no other thoughts or ambitions and did not understand women who did or thought otherwise. Her house, her husband and her children filled her life. The day the ambulance came for her in Athens – two days before she died of pneumonia – she sternly told them to wait while she curled her hair, chose her prettiest nightdress, prepared my father's breakfast and threaded his cuff links through his clean shirt for the last time.

Until I was four, my mother put me in the charge of a Greek wet-nurse, as was the custom of the day. Despina was her name and she was a large, loving and warm peasant woman who, unused to the cleanliness demanded by my mother, would cross herself in awe before taking her daily bath. I loved her and when she left (I am told), I hid under her bed, refused to come out and suffered an attack of jaundice. Our English nanny, Nell, took over then and she stayed with us until we returned to Athens in 1938 for a holiday just before the war broke out. Although not planned that way, she was to introduce us to England – *her* home – which became *our* home and – our country.

PART I

A Greek Childhood

A Last Glimpse of the Peacock–Blue Room

'Christian children all must be
Mild, obedient, good as He'

Hymn by Mrs Cecil Frances Alexander
1818–95

My brother and I were brought up from an early age to love all things British; to believe that the English (and in particular Byron) were blond Gods who could do no wrong while the Germans were wicked murderers. The reason for this simplistic view was due to the fact that we were entrusted to the care of an English nanny and Nanny Nell was our first touch of England and the greatest influence in our lives. Nell was blonde and petite. She arrived in Athens in a neatly fitting tailored suit with a very short skirt and immediately took over the household, speaking English to the Greek maids and taking it for granted that they understood her. (I suppose I remember the length of Nell's skirt because whilst I was on a short visit to Greece to see the family in 1925, General Pangalos, who was the military dictator at the time, threw women in jail if they wore very short skirts. Policemen stood at bus terminals with yardsticks measuring women's skirts as they alighted from buses or trams. My brother and I were terrified for Nell's safety.)

Nell came to us through Mrs Boucher's Bureau, which specialized in sending nannies to foreign families and she was highly recommended. She was a widow from World War I, and had been married only a week before her husband Cyril left for the front – never to return. The very first things she took out of her suitcase when she arrived in Athens were three carefully wrapped photographs of Cyril in silver frames which she placed in a straight row on her dressing-table. To us children they were like a shrine, a perpetual reminder of the evil Germans.

Smells are things that one remembers, and I remember Nell loved perfume – preferably violets. She had bottles of violet water, cakes of violet bath soap and bowls of violet bath salts. On her day out the bathroom would exude these smells hours after Nell had left the house.

Like the best English nannies Nell was practical. She believed in 'long walks to get the circulation going' and no doubt to keep my brother out of mischief, and 'early to bed' to keep tempers even, and we deduced, to give her time to dress for dances on her nights out and for letter-writing on her nights in. 'Church on Sundays' too (and the Anglican Church* of course), so that my brother and I should learn the difference between good and evil and should feel very guilty when we had been wicked, and angelic when we had been good. Nell also insisted on 'sensible food', meat and two vegetables and pudding. 'None of those foreign dishes soaked in oil.'

I can still visualize Maria the cook, her shiny black hair tightly plaited round her lined face and her white starched apron bulging out over her mountainous bosom, as she took her orders (sometimes translated by me) in sullen disapproving silence. But as she reckoned that this blonde goddess – this 'Mee-ees' – could not be wrong, there were no actual protests.

The picture I have now of our Athens home is patchy. Partly because it is really a combination of early childhood memories – those uncoordinated oddities that spring out of the back of one's mind such as the four pointed *akrotiria* (decorative corner ornaments) on our roof or the pink geraniums in the yard – and much later recollections when I lived one block down the hill during the German occupation. Our address, I recall, was Patriarchou Ioachim 25. Today the house would be described as a classical Athenian nineteenth-century two-storey residence – but most of these have now been pulled down to make way for the crammed balconied apartment buildings in what has become Athens's 'Mayfair' – Colonaki.† Our wooden front door, which intrigued me as a child, had glass panels protected by wrought-iron decorative swirls and it faced the main street. Round the corner the house followed the steep angle of the hill – up towards Lycabettus – that little hill which dominates Athens with its white-washed church and huge fluttering blue-and-white national flag. From our nursery windows, caressed by feathery pepper

---

* As Greek babies we were baptized in the Orthodox church and, in accordance with the ritual, received communion as part of the baptism ceremony. The priest who officiated in the small chapel attached to my father's hospital, the Evangelismos, was British. He was father David Balfour who was Confessor to the Greek Royal family. Later he abandoned the Orthodox faith and joined the Foreign Office. In 1944 he was posted to Greece and as a member of the British Embassy staff interpreted for Churchill during the battle for Athens.

† My Aunt Helene Stathatos's house, a few yards away, is an exception. Dwarfed by the surrounding buildings it stands almost like an historical monument, carefully restored by its new owner who now uses it to exhibit paintings and collector's items for sale.

trees with their trailing pink peppercorns hanging like miniature vines, I could catch a glimpse of a small *cafeneion* half-way up the hill almost right in the middle of the street. There were a few rush-seated chairs and square wooden tables where dark, moustachioed men with shiny tanned faces and glossy black hair sat and played with their tasselled amber beads as they sipped their coffee out of minute, thick white cups and chased it down with glasses of cool water. It was not an elegant café – the smart ones were further along the main street on the square and these sold delicious, sticky cakes and sugar-dusted half-moon almond cakes, *kourabiedes*, which Nell would occasionally allow us as a treat. I also remember the comings and goings in our street and across the square as maids or busy cooks carrying large baking trays of food – moussaka, stuffed tomatoes or thin filo pastry cheese pies – made their way – like an army of aproned ants – to and fro from their houses to the various ovens in the bakeries or cafés which offered this service. Looking back I presume no ovens at home could have been large enough in those days.

When we came into the house after walks with Nell, we were always told to wipe our feet carefully because the ground floor, which was Father's surgery, had marble tiles and was kept spotlessly clean. I remember the smell of ether too – or was it disinfectant? But our part of the house, the main part, was up two flights of marble stairs (marble is no luxury in Greece, every pebble is that pinkish golden white colour) and through a bevelled glass door which opened into the hall-sitting room. This had no windows and was dimly lit; green shades cast ripples of green light over the green damask settees and armchairs and the banks of red, gold and pink silk brocade cushions. There were Turkish rugs on the floor. The dining room, drawing room and the door to our bedrooms all led off this centre hall. Down a corridor the first bedroom was Mother and Father's – decorated in the French manner as was then the fashionable Athenian taste. I seem to recall the pale grey painted furniture included a huge bed and a giant wardrobe. Or did they just seem so large to me? Over the cane bedhead there was a grey painted wreath of roses which was repeated over the mirrored wardrobe. Further down the passage came our day and night nurseries. Our bedroom had two high children's beds – that is how I remember them – as one night Nell was just able to save me from being strangled by Costaki's pyjama cord. He was trying out a noose which he had just learnt and had it round my neck. My only picture of the day nursery was that it had a settee under which we stuffed our toys when told to tidy up. Leading off this room was a 'cupboard room' where Nell kept her 'things' and her trunks. From time to time Nell would shut Costaki up there for bad behaviour. This included throwing a book out of the window – it was aimed at me and he was furious that I ducked – or climbing up on the screen between Nell's bed and ours and falling on top of her. Costaki confided to me though that he did not mind the punishment 'cell' as it gave him an opportunity to nose into Nell's belongings – but he never divulged to his younger sister what these were.

I saw little of my parents during those early years, for at that time, children were kept in the nursery and only brought 'out' to 'say good-night' or to be shown off to guests. But I still remember vividly the grown-up parties in the blue drawing-room where everything was deep peacock blue – the lamps, the carpet, the sofa, the cushions and the curtains. In one corner there was the gramophone which had come from England – a large wooden box with a handle and a huge salmon-pink horn. It was in this room that my parents and their friends danced tangos and the charleston; my mother wore tight-fitting short satin dresses and the noise and laughter penetrated through the nursery door.

But for us children, our real world was Nell's. I would often lie awake at night thinking about – almost feeling – the bombs that had killed Cyril. My lungs seemed to breathe in the poison gas which had damaged Nell's brother's lungs for life. Sometimes, half asleep, I would hum a tune from a new hymn Nell had taught me and then I would feel as if I were being lifted up, up into the blue sky where there were dozens of angels all looking like Nell when she let her blond hair down to brush it with her Mason Pearson brush. At other times I would mouth a hasty prayer, clasping my hands together rather guiltily as I lay on my back – instead of kneeling. It would run something like this, 'Please God, send us to England soon'. After that I would imagine a shopping spree at Boots in the Edgware Road, a store which had been so highly praised by Nell (her enamel butterfly brooch had come from there) that to me it became a glittering palace full of gorgeous, desirable things with doors guarded by braided doormen who looked like an army of Cyrils.

As children we hardly knew anything of the turmoil which was going on in Greece at the time. And I did not know about the disastrous Asia Minor campaign and the humiliating Greek defeat by the Turks, although I think I do remember my father in officer's uniform when he was called-up to tend the wounded. Or is it the photograph I remember? But I knew nothing of the successive coups and counter coups, schisms, mani-pulated plebiscites and elections which were the pattern of Greek politics between 1920 and 1924. I was ignorant of the personal antagonism between the Cretan politician Elefterios Venizelos, who had supported the British and the Entente Powers, and King Constantine, who sup-ported the Germans or preferred to keep Greece neutral. But I often

heard shots in the street and watched angry and frightening demonst-
rations through the delicate screen of the pepper trees which lined the
street outside our nursery window. Yet life in the nursery was calm.
Nell read us fairy stories, sometimes complained about the greasy food,
did a little smocking on my party dresses and kept strict bedtime hours.

Then one day Nell changed. She suddenly seemed to be taking on
a new role – perhaps it was what she had once described as being 'a
pillar of strength'? She dashed about carrying clothes and suitcases and
giving orders to the frightened maids, who mumbled and intermittently
crossed themselves. She made 'a nice cup of tea' for Mother, who was
in tears, and answered the front door bell which rang continuously. She
ushered visitors – my parents' friends – in and out of the house like
a trained butler, but was obviously hastening their goodbyes. I felt in
the way – yet desperately wanted to know what was going on. The
door to the blue drawing-room was ajar and I peeped inside. To my
horror the carpet was up; it looked bare and foreboding. There were
towers of heavy leather trunks with large locks all piled up high, one
on top of the other and a weeping maid was on her knees in front of
a big wicker trunk, filling it with bed-linen. Finally, Nell explained in
her usual matter-of-fact way, 'We are going home, my dear. After all,
the King is leaving and they have shot I don't know how many Ministers'.

Later I was to learn that a revolutionary committee had unjustly blamed
King Constantine for the disastrous Asia Minor Campaign and had called
on him to abdicate in favour of his eldest son George II. At the same
time five senior Ministers and the former Commander-in-Chief were executed. This political murder of six of Greece's leading politicians caused
an even greater rift between Republican Venizelists and Royalists. After
endless political strife King George II left for London pending a plebiscite
which resulted in an overwhelming vote for a Republic.

But to me 'going home' was pure bliss. God had obviously answered
my prayer even though it was sent off while I was lying on my back
instead of kneeling.

The Kennels in the Snow

'I can never remember whether it snowed for six days and six nights when I was twelve or whether it snowed for twelve days and twelve nights when I was six.'

Dylan Thomas *A Child's Christmas in Wales*

On arrival in London, my parents took a temporary flat in Bayswater. It was not too far away from Boots in the Edgware Road, which was of course my imaginary Mecca. And while my mother rather tensely called on house agents to discuss leases (something she did not understand, since not being able to buy property outright with one's money went against her foreign instinct) and while she chose furnishers (here Nell insisted that our house should be done up from cellar to attic by Maples because the Queen always bought her beds there) I was sent off to Nell's parents' cottage in Berkshire. The Kennels, as it was called, was a child's paradise. It lived up to all my dreams – it looked exactly like those thatched cottages on the calendars that Nell had pinned up in our Athens nursery. Nell's father, I remember clearly. He was the Duke of Wellington's gamekeeper and had a long, grey, fuzzy, bushy beard, like a bird's nest; he wore neat tweed knee-breeches and carefully turned-down ribbed woollen socks (knitted by his wife, naturally). He was very punctual – and made a point of this. (Nell told me that this was a quality that every man must possess.) His large silver watch, which hung from a sturdy Victorian chain, was tucked into his waistcoat pocket and he consulted it frequently. Sometimes he showed it to me and allowed me to put my ear to it, explaining that it never lost a minute. Once a week he would regulate all the clocks in the cottage so that they were on time. Nell's mother was plump and comfortably round; she was kind, huggingly warm and very efficient. She did send me to bed early – but I never protested as I loved my cottage bed – it had a puffy, soft, real feather mattress. And I loved the feeling of sinking down, down, right down into those thousands of fluffy things, that kept me tight and warm in their arms at night. My bedroom window was latticed (Nell had told me about those diamond shapes – yet I never really believed such windows existed except in fairy tales) and the wallpaper, which stretched across the ceiling too, was a mass of fat roses and forget-me-nots tied up in pale blue ribbons. The milk in the mug by my bed was real, thick milk and smelt of cows – not that watered-down goat's milk I was used to in Athens. And as a special treat Nell's mother would give me a small square of Cadbury's chocolate – before cleaning my teeth of course.

There were no other children in the cottage, but that did not worry me and I soon made friends with the two carefully groomed black Labradors who were kept on a strict diet. I remember thinking that their glossy coats and Nell's father's boots too were an admirable advertisement for Cherry Blossom boot polish. (There were a number of those pretty tins kept in the shoe cupboard along with a neat array of brushes.) It was in Nell's home, when I wandered out alone in the woods and fields that I first met, saw, felt and lived among squirrels, rabbits, primroses, violets, bluebells and soft green moss – all that very English countryside world. I remember climbing gates and perching on fences. I looked around – surveying the scene – and loved it. Arguing with myself I found that I did not miss the bright blue sky, the scent of orange blossom, the wild anemones or the feathery pepper trees outside my Athens nursery window. Strange as it might be, I felt so very much at home at The Kennels and oh! those puddings, especially those milk puddings, with their thick, sugary burnt skin coating – so much better than Maria's!

At weekends, when Nell came on a visit, she took me shopping and we rode on a green bus to Reading – the birthplace of the biscuits I had heard so much about. We also visited her invalid brother in his cottage, and although I was shy and afraid of him – wondering how he could breathe after being gassed during the war – his courage and jokes soon put me at ease. On Sundays we went to church in the pretty village church decorated with fresh-smelling flowers and autumn berries; I sang the hymns Nell had taught me and did not cross myself as Mother had taught me in the Greek church. And then one day, in answer no doubt to one of my lazy, lying-on-the-back prayers, there was snow! I had never seen snow except on those cards Nell received at Christmas. As I peeped out of my bedroom window one morning I remember thinking that all the angels in heaven were emptying their feather mattresses. I rushed downstairs, put my boots on and ran across the lawn, giggling with delight at the sight of my own footprints. I picked up a handful of snow and watched it melt in my hand – I did not know why it was so painful. And then as I ran back into the house, on the way, I caught sight of a cheeky bird with a red breast perching on the wall. And so at last I knew that the Christmas bird really did exist 'at home' as Nell had said.

3 LONDON 1924

School. A Foreign Pupil Dresses Up

'And one man in his time plays many parts,
His acts being seven ages. At first the infant,
Mewling and puking in the nurse's arms;
And then the whining school-boy, with his satchel . . .'

William Shakespeare, *As You Like It*, Act 2, Scene VII

After a long search, and much soul searching, my parents finally settled on a ninety-nine-year lease on an Adam house – No. 52 Wimpole Street. It was one of those tall, narrow London houses, hemmed in between two similar houses and it had two or three rooms on each floor. The ground floor was to be my father's consulting room, but the waiting room would be used as a dining room at night and at weekends. It is the decoration of this room that I recall so well, since it seemed to me at the time so full of mystery. (It was in fact just gloomy Maples' mock-Tudor style, which was then in fashion.) Mother and Nell had chosen olive-green walls, dark purple curtains trimmed with silver braid and very, very heavy, highly polished carved oak furniture. At the end of the room, between the two long windows that looked out on the street, there was a grandfather clock. In Greece I had never seen anything like it and I often stood outside the door – when there were patients inside reading magazines – waiting for it to chime.

The first floor had two drawing rooms and it was here that my parents entertained the exiled King of Greece. I remember creeping out in my nightdress and leaning perilously over the nursery rails to catch a glimpse of the guests – in evening dress and decorations – as they went down to dinner. The main bedrooms were on the second floor and the two top floors, which had smaller rooms, were our nursery rooms and staff bedrooms. Like most London houses there was a dark, cold basement – a damp rabbit warren of connecting rooms – which housed the servant's dining room, the kitchen, pantry and the chauffeur's room.

There were open fires throughout the house in the elegant marble Adam fireplaces, lots of stairs and coils of shiny banisters which I could slide down when Nell was not looking. A staff of ten was engaged by

Nell, headed by a butler. The hierarchy descended right down to an Irish kitchenmaid who was always handing in her notice. Her mood was usually reported at breakfast time, when an envelope giving the details – spelt out by the irate housekeeper – would be placed on my mother's tray.

Our house was next door to the Barretts' – with such a romantic connection for me – particularly when I thought of their spaniel Flush! It was in the heart of doctor-land and was considered the best medical address. But before taking up his practice there, my father had to re-take his medical degree to comply with British law, and this he did at Durham University. While he was struggling in the north my mother struggled in London with builders and decorators. Nell, however, who always believed in keeping children out of the way in a crisis, promptly arranged for us to start school. My brother went to boarding school and I went to day school – Queen's College in Harley Street, just round the corner.

Growing up is really a process of 'dressing up' and at the time I was dressing up to become a schoolgirl. Before term, preparations for my new life began with a shopping trip to buy my school uniform. The best children's shop in those early pre-war days was Daniel Neal's in Portman Square and, since Nanny Nell always insisted on the best, she and my mother took me there to be fitted out. I tried on shirts, ties, lace-up shoes, a gym tunic and a blazer with a large green-and-silver badge and a black velour hat. I found the whole exercise tiring and frightening, although the idea of school was very exciting.

But looking at my mother's strained face I was worried. The move, the great expense and the uncertain future had made her so much more serious than she had been when she was dancing in Athens in the blue room. Nell, on the contrary, was calm if a little unusually stern. All the same I knew that there were long, serious talks in the nursery after my brother and I had gone to bed. And at night before that comforting curtain of sleep drew across my eyes, I would lie awake straining to hear the conversation, not catching much of it except when my brother managed to sneak up behind the nursery door – and then report to me.

On the first day of term Nell accompanied me to school. I proudly carried my brand new leather case; my initials had been stamped on it and inside a new fountain pen, carefully sharpened pencils and a large rubber rattled together as I walked somewhat haltingly in my new shoes. Perhaps they were too big. As I approached the school building, as I approached the white-columned porch – which looked huge – I felt unsafe. I clutched Nell's coat – but then I let it go. My hand was sweating and I wiped it on my new blazer pocket and ran up the steps.

'I'll pick you up at one – now run along and be a good girl', were

Nell's parting words – or words to that effect. She then vanished through the school's park-green door with its highly polished brass letterbox and doorknocker. I stood alone in a hall which was painted dark green halfway up and then cream. A brown line divided the two colours. This was school – I gathered. I felt queer. Then a pretty blonde girl came towards me. She had grey-blue eyes and long dark eyelashes. I had always longed for blue eyes and had once cut my eyelashes with Nell's nail scissors, hoping that they would grow. They never did.

'Are you new?' the girl asked. 'Yes', I replied. But neither the question nor the answer was necessary as both were obvious. It was, however, an opening, and the conversation continued roughly thus:

> 'What is your name?'
> 'Xenia Cawadias.'
> 'What on earth is that? Are you foreign?'
> 'What does foreign mean?'

I asked, trembling all over as a group of girls moved towards me and suddenly burst into laughter. Luckily the bell rang and the girls ran off to another room. I remember blushing and feeling that I had gone bright red. Nell used to go red up her neck, but that was when she was angry. I was not angry; I was in pain and wanted to cry.

A teacher came up to me and showed me the way to the Hall for prayers and roll-call. During prayers I tried in vain – and I found I could not – reach my familiar vision of heaven. I kept on looking at the girls kneeling on either side of me and wondering whether they were different.

After prayers the Headmistress opened a large book and called out the girls' names. (Nell had told me about roll-call.) The Headmistress's voice was shrill and stern: 'Jane Gubbins, Sarah Wallis, Xenia Caawwaar-diiaaaa ...' 'Present' I interrupted. I could feel my heart throbbing. Was it visible? There were suppressed giggles all round and tears came into my eyes. 'Sorry dear,' the Head said later, 'But it *is* an unusual name.'

I stayed at Queen's for ten years and during that time there were a number of crises. Quite often the Headmistress would send for my father and complain that his daughter was difficult to understand and that she had not learnt 'the value of obedience and self-control'. She explained how on one occasion I had been found downstairs in the long corridor during the hours when this was forbidden. And when asked to explain my disobedience, I had quite simply said that I was trying to find out why it was against the rules – and also what was *there*. Another time I had drawn William of Orange all in oranges and passed it round the history class, causing giggles and disorder. (After that I was banned from all history classes.) And during the French lessons I often corrected the teacher's accent (or 'accident' as I liked to call it*) sometimes backing up my knowledge by bringing the Larousse pronunciation to the teacher's and the class's notice. All this was far from what passed as acceptable British schoolgirl behaviour in those days.

I also suffered tremendously from teasing by some of my classmates and I could not speak about it to Nell because I felt that she would not understand. I remember how once one of the girls said that when I laughed – unlike other girls – there were lines down my cheeks and that was foreign. I believed her and for months I dared not laugh. Another day one of the prefects told me that I looked untidy. I dashed into the cloakroom to look at myself in the mirror and found that, unlike my English classmates, I was bulging out at the top of my gym tunic – the pleats over my chest were wide apart. When I got home I tied a scarf very tightly across my breasts to see if this did any good. The bulges simply moved elsewhere and it was pretty painful. It was, alas, no good.

Lessons were a kind of refuge; I loved them. There was, however, one dreadful occasion when the Latin mistress accused me in front of the whole class of cheating during a test. I was then moved to a separate room – the library – to do the test by myself. My paper – though soggy with tears – when corrected gave me top marks, ninety per cent. None of the rest of the class reached fifty per cent. But the teacher never said anything, never apologized, never put the matter right.

As I grew older I knew that there was a difference between myself and the English girls and I came to know what it meant to be foreign. But in spite of all this I enjoyed school and I made a number of good friends. We used to sit together – usually on the radiators to keep warm in the winter – giggling and discussing life. (I seemed to get worse chilblains than they did – school was incredibly cold but this was considered healthy.) I came to like many of my teachers too – with the exception of the games and gym teachers. I was no good at games. And I loved the new world they had led me into – the world of books, art and poetry; Bacon, Milton, Keats, Wordsworth and Shelley had become part of my private conversations with myself. I had begun to outgrow Nell. And often when she asked me what I had learnt at school I did not reply. I dashed up to my bedroom and lay flat on my back taking off into my private world of nightingales, daffodils and unrequited love.

* I was bilingual at the time. Most educated Greeks were brought up to speak English, French and Greek. I spoke fluent French and English with only a smattering of Greek, having left Greece as a child.

4

ATHENS 1939

First Love then War

'For surely we choose our death as much as we choose our job.
It grows out of our acts and our evasions, out of our fears and
out of our moments of courage.'

Graham Greene, *The Lost Childhood*

Schooldays were over and I was off to Greece with my mother. Although I had passed my Oxford entrance examination to study science and medicine, my father had refused to allow me to go up to university. 'I do not want a blue-stocking daughter – I want you to go out and meet young people and get happily married.' Those were his words and I remember them to this day. I also remember my last day of term – my very last day at school, how I was bubbling over with excitement as I emptied my locker and threw all my clothes and books into my large school trunk. It was over-full and would not close, but my friend Sarah Roberts came to the rescue. We both stood on it, then sat on it and as we wriggled and pushed, Sarah asked, 'Xenia, ducks, where are you going for the hols?' 'Greece,' I had replied with delight. 'Oh! How spiffing – you won't need clothes, just togas!' I did not bother to answer her or to explain that 'draped sheets' had gone out years ago. And, then, why bother? There had been so many painful jabs at school because I was foreign – because I was Greek – and anyway, the trunk was closed and locked.

Clambering up the steep steps of the train at Victoria station I felt grown up at last. I had said goodbye to school and was saying goodbye to Nell. Finally I was on my own. Nell's parting shot was characteristic. In true Nanny form – following beside the coach as it began to move – she said: 'Look after your mum and don't fall in love with the first Greek you meet.' Looking back, I think I did carry out part of her wish – I always looked after 'Mum' and under difficult circumstances, too – but as to love, I fell head first into the trap she had warned me about.

My first glimpse of Greece was from the grimy sleeping-car window of the Orient Express – we had changed trains in Paris. I pressed my nose against the pane of glass, having observed the brass plate notice in several languages about the dangers of leaning out of the window,

I thought it was particularly funny in Italian, *'E pericolo sporgersi ...'*. But the Greece I now saw was not the romantic Greece I had read of and dreamed of – it smelt of coffee, dust and pepper trees. Or did I perhaps recollect those feathery trees outside my nursery window? There were goats, crowds, dryness, noise and a bright blue sky. I felt I knew it all. Somehow it all came back to me and it belonged to me, I belonged to it. I was no longer a foreigner here – I had come home.

We were almost there. My mother was powdering her nose, fixing her hat and screwing her pearl ear-rings in tighter. She turned to me and ran a comb through my hair. It was tangled and she pulled it; it hurt and I cried. 'You have to suffer to be beautiful,' she had snapped. But my tears were not caused just by the physical pain of having my hair pulled, but because I suddenly had a strange feeling – a feeling of being miserably happy. As the train came to a halt mother began to wave; she was waving to a group standing on the platform. They stood together as if on an island. They all looked like her: they were, as I surmised, 'the family'. My brother was there too. He had been sent to Athens a year before to study Greek and take the examination for the Greek diplomatic service. After Harrow he had enrolled at London University; but when he was about to take his finals he admitted to my father that he had never attended any of the lectures. He was in love with a pretty debutante, Virginia, and had spent his time serenading her with his electric guitar.

I remember a lot of kissing on both cheeks at the station – and faces staring at me. 'So this is the little English girl,' my uncle Aleko said, taking a good look at me. 'Does she speak Greek?' he asked my mother. Seeing that I was embarrassed and blushing profusely, he assured me that I would soon pick it up, and meanwhile all the family could speak English.

It was difficult to explain what I immediately loved about Greece. Was it the light, that pink veil that hung over Mount Hymettus, or was it the sea, that clear water that sparkled in the daytime and danced under the moon at night; or perhaps the flowers, those pink cyclamen that pierced the dry, cracked earth and the blood-red anemones that pushed their strong stems through the rocky soil? Was it the brick-red earth, the olive trees, the coolness of the shade, the scorching of the sun? It was probably all of these. Was it perhaps a feeling of love? Later in life I felt it was, because – strangely enough – I only fell in love in Greece.

It was carnival time when I was supposed to 'come out'* in Athens. There were masked balls almost every night. Black-hooded 'Dominoes' – as the masked figures draped in black from head to foot with only slits for their eyes and mouth were called – flitted by me as I danced and whispered in my ear. Their comments were flattering but strange and ran something like, 'You are blonde and not blonde, that is why we love you'. My hair had not yet gone a mouse colour and my eyes are brown. 'You are Greek and not Greek – what are you?' After the dancing was over we all piled into open cars and took off for the seafront tavernas for coffee, fried eggs and fried cheese. I was always chaperoned in the traditional Greek manner by my brother, who found this task very boring, but as I sat there, on the rickety rush-seated wooden chairs, with the soft warm air blowing off the sea, I did not know what was happening to me. What was I doing? Why was my heart thumping so hard that sometimes I thought my dancing partners would notice it? When I danced with one of my brother's friends I felt weirdly dizzy – quite a new feeling. This young man, Costa, was what Nanny Nell would have described as 'tall, dark and handsome'. His hair was tightly curled and shiny, his eyes widely spaced and jet black. He danced divinely and apparently lived in Paris, London and New York. When I was in his arms I wanted the music to go on for ever.

One night half-way through the carnival week, as he was taking me home he asked me to marry him. It was a moonlit night, the air was heavy with the scent of flowering trees. Across the road in the Royal Gardens couples sat closely entwined on park benches, others wandered through the trees rustling the low branches as they went. I know my answer was futile – schoolgirlishly inadequate – something like, 'Yes, of course, I'd love to'. I did not know how to express my feelings. My brother who was at the back of the car, got out. I followed. After a hasty good-night kiss I ran up the stairs and into the house. When the door closed behind me, I felt safe. That night I lay awake wondering, Was this what my father had wanted? Was this life? And did one live happily ever after? Was what I felt when in Costa's arms love? And if it was, why was I feeling sad?

The next morning I told my mother, breaking the news in what I felt was a casual way, 'Mummy, Costa wants us to get married.' Mother gave no immediate reply and showed little enthusiasm. 'I've heard about him but I must find out a good deal more,' she said and off she went to find out more from – the family.

* A familiar term at the time, which meant a debutante being launched into society, attending 'coming-out' parties, meeting suitable young men or 'debs' delights' and hopefully in the end finding a husband.

Mother's report was dampening. She said that Costa was a rich playboy and not really a good match. I did not believe all this and insisted on her calling on Costa's parents to have a cosy chat. Over cups of sweet coffee, sticky almond biscuits and turkish delight, mother discussed our future with Costa's parents. The blinds were drawn down against the afternoon sun; it was very warm. Costa and I were in a separate room. We were talking awkwardly. 'You will like New York', he said. 'Do you get seasick? I have a yacht ... Do you like diamonds or amethysts?' I was over-shy and speechless. I just longed to run out of the house with Costa and get back to the sea. It was a terrible strain; it was stifling.

Finally, to my relief, after what seemed an agonizingly long time, my mother and Costa's parents joined us. They had, it seemed, agreed – on what, it was unclear to me. But it is, or was, a Greek tradition that parents discuss dowries and marriage settlements before officially accepting an engagement. It is a kind of bargain and I knew that there was little to offer on my side – the move to London had been a cruel expense. But in the end there was some embarrassing kissing and congratulations and more sweets and coffee were passed round. Costa's parents set a tentative date for the wedding. It was to be in five months' time.

That night there was the grandest ball of all at the Grande Bretagne hotel. It marked the end of the carnival. I wore my prettiest dress – off the shoulder, pale blue frothy tulle. I danced all the evening with Costa but found it difficult to find anything much to say to him. When the ball was over, we drove down to the sea. There, I had hoped, standing on the sand and looking out at the little fishing boats with their bright lights winking at us as they bobbed up and down, something would bring the right words back to me. Something would break the terrible strain that had somehow grown up between us.

Costa put his arms round me but he seemed a stranger. 'Let's celebrate', he said. 'Let's sleep together tonight.' I looked at his handsome face. I felt cold. Then I remembered my mother's warning and said, 'My mother says that in Greece if you sleep with your future husband before you marry – he does not marry you.' Costa laughed, angrily I thought. 'You don't know how silly you are.' We got back into the car and drove home in silence.

The next day Costa rang me to say that he was going to New York on business and would be back a week before the wedding. 'Anything I can get you?' he asked, and chuckled. I put the receiver down and felt – empty.

Mother, my aunts, in fact the whole family, had busied themselves with arrangements for my trousseau. I was to have my first black dress, my first fitted tweed suit and bright coloured cocktail dresses. Throughout the fittings I felt dizzy and ill. People asked me of news of Costa and I replied that he was fine. But in fact he had not written. After five busy months my trousseau* was ready at last. I remember taking a look at the wedding trunk in which the maid had sprinkled the traditional rice amongst the silk lingerie, amongst the pale-coloured, hand-embroidered nightdresses and petticoats and the embroidered, monogrammed sheets. I picked up a little of the rice and let it slip through my fingers. At that moment I remember my mother coming into my room with a telegram in her hand. 'Darling,' she said, 'Costa has wired that he cannot get back for the wedding as he must stay in New York because of rumours of war. I don't know what to do – would you like to fly out to him? There may be just time – though he does not suggest this.' 'No – it is off!' was the gist of my reply. I waited for Mother to leave the room and then locked my door. I recall reaching for the bottle of pink pills marked 'KININH', Greek for quinine. I had been given these for a fever some time ago. The pills were large and difficult to swallow but I finished the lot. I wanted to end my life. I lay on my bed. My head throbbed, my eyes closed but for a while there seemed to be a deep red light shining through my lids – then nothing.

I can't remember if it was morning or afternoon when I woke, but my eyelids were stuck and swollen; I felt sick. My mother was at my bedside. Stroking my forehead, she said: 'Darling, *do* wake up! War has been declared! Daddy has wired that we should not return to London because of the bombing.' The pills had failed, but now war was to take their place. It settled the course of my life.

---

* A trousseau was an important part of a future bride's life. In villages, peasant girls spent years embroidering and preparing their wedding trunk.

5

Waiting for My War

'They talked with nostalgia about burying bodies during the war.
If there had not been a war, the man used to say, "I wouldn't have
seen nothing. It was an education."'

V.S.Pritchett, *The Sailor*

After Britain's declaration of war the atmosphere in Athens was tense and rumours rife. Then, as time went by, the clockwork movement of daily life ticked over regularly once again. It was only briefly interrupted from time to time by some item of over-dramatized news from Britain or Germany. This was transmitted immediately on single news sheets with giant headlines, specially rolled off the daily newspaper presses. These *parartimata*, as they were called, were then rapidly distributed throughout the capital to the accompaniment of piercing yells from the small, ragamuffin newspaper boys who sped in and out and around the coffee-house tables like slalom wizards before making their way – at full tilt – down the crowded main streets. Thrusting their news sheets into the worried Athenians' hands, they did not bother much about change, but their performance was electric.

Perhaps I was more nervous and jumpy than most Greeks, but then my heart, my mind, were split. As I anxiously followed events in Britain I wondered what Greece would do and when. From my mother's family I learnt that King George II (who had returned to Greece in 1935 after a period of mounting political instability, communist pressures, strikes and a manipulated plebiscite) was naturally pro-British, while General Metaxas*, Greece's Dictator at that time, wanted to keep Greece out of the war and remain neutral. He had obvious close ties with the Fascist dictatorships in Germany and Italy, and had given Germany a dangerous economic stranglehold on the Greek economy in an effort to raise his country's pitifully low standard of living.

But one of the immediate effects of the war on the Greek people was to highlight sharply the intricate facets and divisions in their political thinking, and, for a brief moment they looked outwards and discussed

---

* Metaxas was not anti-British; he had even asked for an alliance with Britain in 1937, but his policies and politics brought him closer to Fascist Germany.

foreign affairs instead of looking inwards and perpetrating their divisive internal feuds. For a very brief moment too, they gave up – what I had been told was their favourite pastime – that of juggling with numbers of votes and prospective political candidates in pencilled sums on the backs of their square white Papastratos cigarette boxes. But their views and arguments – the views of my fellow countrymen – were all very new to me. I tried hard to learn, to pick up threads, to understand them; I listened first to the conversations and arguments among my relations and their friends and then to the gay chatter and views of my own newly-acquired young friends. In the end I found the picture clearly marked out for me on the Athens pavements – in those sprawling pavement cafés.

The main coffee-house, and perhaps the most traditional one, was Giannakis on Academy Street. This appeared to be the 'headquarters' of the well-dressed, serious-looking, middle-aged or late middle-aged Greek men in dapper British cut pin-striped suits and Lock-style grey Homburgs. It was here that the older members of my family and their friends discussed politics and the events of the day. Sipping glasses of clouded white *ouzo*, or golden, clear white wine, they usually had a plate of *mezedes* on the marble-top tables in front of them. This could be small slices of octopus swimming in olive oil, or fried baby squid, cheese and nuts. As I listened to the views of those sombre mustachioed gentlemen, I soon gathered that a number of them had important business ties with Germany or had studied there. It was obvious that most of them were convinced that the Communists – the Bolsheviks, as they referred to them – were a far greater menace than the Fascists. And they found it impossible to understand why Britain had not realized this yet. Then there were others, who had picked up the news of the latest German peace offensives, who sat back calmly, quite confident that the war would end before it had begun in earnest – so not to worry.

For me all this talk was maddening, particularly as I had received news from London describing the air-raid shelters, the distribution of gas masks, the serious lack of air cover and the imminent bombing of towns in Britain. I was, however, happier with the atmosphere I found among my young friends who frequented the newer café Zonars on the opposite side of the street. Unlike Giannakis, it had large, plate-glass windows stuffed with baskets bulging with crystallized fruit and rows of giant chocolate boxes with garish, coloured bows – not in very good taste, it is true. But inside there were trays of delicious sweets: those Greek specialities made with paper-thin *filo*, honey and nuts and called *baklava* and *kataifi*. Outside, fanned by the balmy autumn breeze (and dust!), pretty girls in bright coloured dresses and their escorts consumed ice creams from tall glasses with coloured straws and long-handled silver spoons – or greedily gorged fat chocolate-coated cream buns that were the café's speciality. Dangerously – or so it seemed to me – but adroitly, and no doubt well practised in the art, while energetically gesticulating with their hands – the young men tipped their chairs back so that they balanced on two legs only. In this precarious position they passionately declaimed their political views. Inevitably these condemned their selfish political 'primadonnas' and their politicians in general. But when the conversation turned to Britain, they enthusiastically applauded British courage and were convinced of a lightning Allied victory. In these young circles there was never any ambivalence and no talk of compromise. There was none of that obscure British concept, which I had just heard of in a letter from home – that one should fight the Nazis only and not the German nation as a whole – separating the goodies from the baddies. Young Greeks at that time, from bootblacks to the sons of rich industrialists, were brim-full of the youthful desire to fight and win and even die – all very gloriously, for a just cause.

Throughout those months of political uncertainty, I was beginning to know my country better and my mother thought, quite rightly, that I should learn Greek. For this purpose she engaged the jovial local priest to give me lessons. But, although Pater Ioannis did his best, I found concentration difficult and Greek verbs, nouns and accents impossible. Sometimes my brother joined our lesson and this would bring a welcome light-hearted interlude. For when the black-clothed prelate vainly tried to teach me the various 'e's' in the Greek language (there are five of these and all pronounced 'e'), my brother would interrupt and ask some irrelevant question such as: 'Can Greek Orthodox priests marry?' knowing full well that they could. And, 'Who is the pretty girl who answers your front door?' Pater Ioannis's firm reply, I remember, was 'My niece'. Always, at the end of the lesson, he would put away his books in a battered leather satchel, coil up his long black hair, winding it round his hand like a corkscrew and then neatly catching it under his tall, black coal-scuttle hat. As he left, gathering up his robes he proffered his hand – or rather his over-sized jewelled ring to kiss. I think I just bent down reverently – and forgot the kiss.

Athens was so close to the sea, and as Greece, for the time being was still untouched by war, I remember several pleasant picnics and bathing parties. I loved the white sandy beaches and the scent of camomile as one trod on those daisy-like flowers that grew in bold clumps on the sea front. In the evenings, like many Athenians, I often dined with friends in the small tavernas off the stony streets at the foot of the Acropolis. It always amazed me, as I entered these tavernas, how tempting and beautiful the display of food was and how hard it was to choose. There were usually large pots of stuffed tomatoes – twice the size of those in England – stuffed aubergines, stuffed vine leaves with rings of fresh lemon and golden-topped moussaka. On marble slabs, like a Dutch still-life painting, lay beady-eyed fresh fish and the smallest baby-lamb cutlets resting on bunches of sweet-smelling thyme. The square wooden tables had plain white paper cloths, and in the centre there was usually a handful of paper napkins thrust into a tumbler and two or three carnations in a tiny glass jug. Often, as soon as our party had sat down, musicians with guitars and concertinas would come to our table and serenade us with Greek music – with traditional Greek songs about women, wine, love or war. Sometimes, alas, thinking I was British, because my accent was so bad, they would play 'It's a long way to Tipperary', hoping to please me. I had to pretend it did.

Since there was no petrol rationing as yet, I was also able to drive out to country tavernas with my brother's friends. I remember a favourite small taverna called Demosthenes at Liopesi – whitewashed and surrounded by silver-grey olive trees and promising vines pushing their way through the red earth. One day when we were having lunch in the courtyard there was a large wedding party at the adjoining table. The teenage bride was as pretty as a china doll, with downcast eyes and pale, transparent skin. The bridegroom had a hard, ruddy, flushed face; he appeared to be much older than his bride – but this, I was told, was not unusual in Greece. After a number of toasts a group of musicians struck up a slow dance rhythm and the party stood up, joined hands – holding them high above their heads – and began to sway as they performed the intricate steps of a traditional Greek peasant dance. The bridegroom waved a handkerchief and led the line. He bent down, slapped his knees and shouting 'Hoppa', leapt into the air – a feat he repeated with relish at well-spaced intervals. I wished I had learnt the steps; I wished I knew the words of the songs they sang. My friends did. I felt an onlooker – a foreigner in my own land.

At weekends I frequently visited my uncle Epaminondas Cawadias, who was Admiral of the Fleet at that time. I was particularly close to him, probably because when I was born, my parents were disappointed that I was not a boy – an attitude prevalent in Greece among all classes, where boys are prized and girls tolerated – and they left me in his care while they travelled, concentrating their love and care on my brother. Nonda, as I called him, spoke perfect English and in fact being blond and blue-eyed, he looked every inch an English Admiral. He had close ties with Britain and loved to give large parties for members of the British Embassy or for members of the British Naval Mission. His headquarters

were at Scaramanga, just off the Eleusis road where it dips past the Byzantine chapel of Daphni. There were, I remember, a number of manned
barriers one had to pass through before taking the Admiral's naval launch
to his residence at Nafstathmos. One day, when he was driving back
from Athens, he noticed that his guards were all clustered round a bush
with their backs to his car instead of standing at attention and saluting
him. On arrival at his headquarters he immediately demanded an explanation for this unusual behaviour. But the reply he received was simple
– the sailors had spotted the British Ambassadress – an eccentric lady,
to say the least – bathing in the nude in the naval shipyard. The matter
was dropped, and no disciplinary action taken.

I remember one particularly large party at Nafstathmos in honour
of a visiting British Admiral with members of the Greek royal family
present. Drinks were served and a large plate of fresh sea urchins sprinkled
with fresh lemon juice passed around; a three-course lunch followed.
At the end of this my uncle's ADC came up to him and whispered something in his ear. I watched my uncle's face – it looked strained – and
I immediately presumed that he had received some bad news about the
war. He rose slowly and then drawing himself up to his full height he
looked down the table and said: 'Your Royal Highnesses, my Lords,
Ladies and Gentlemen, I have just been informed – that a screw is missing
from the ice-cream machine. It may well be on your plate. Please take
care!' There were peals of laughter. The screw was never found.

All through those many months which followed Britain's declaration
of war, although I was surrounded by and very conscious of the beauty
and love of my second country, the news from home was grim. Norway,
Denmark, Holland and Belgium had been invaded; after a gallant struggle
Poland was partitioned. British troops had been evacuated from Dunkirk,
and France had fallen. In Britain there were daily massive air raids, severe
civilian casualties and a mounting fear of an imminent German invasion.
As I listened to the BBC late-night news I tried to picture what was
happening. I longed to be there, so longed to be part of it all instead
of being cut off and, in a way, guiltily enjoying my new life. I longed
to join the battle against Fascism. But what part could I play? I longed
to serve my country, but which country?

In Athens, by 1940 there was serious talk of mobilization and the
reorganization of the army. There was also much discussion as to who
was being promoted and who was left out – the old game of Royalists
versus Venizelists seemed to have returned. But I was neither interested
nor could I follow this political sideline. After Italy joined the Axis powers
I noticed that most Greeks thought that they would soon be drawn into
the war. This feeling was heightened when the Greek cruiser *Elli*, decor-

ated with its festive bunting was torpedoed off the island of Tinos on 15 August during the official religious ceremonies of the Feast of the Holy Virgin – the most sacred festival after Easter in the Greek Orthodox Church. Although the attack was said to have been perpetrated by 'an unidentified submarine' everybody knew it was the Italians, and Greeks were livid with frustration and disgust. I felt that too.

It was just two months later, at dawn on 28 October, after a grand reception at the Italian Legation in Athens, which General Metaxas had attended – always hoping to keep up appearances and emphasizing Greece's neutrality – that the Italians handed the General an ultimatum demanding an unimpeded entry into Greece and occupation of strategic points. And at that very moment their troops were crossing the Albanian border into Greece! I remember being told that Metaxas received the note in his dressing-gown. I do not know whether this is true or not, but his reply – which in Greece has now become legendary – was *'Ochi!'* No! And from that morning Greece went to war on Britain's side.

I was relieved, I was even deliriously happy. Looking back, this seems strange, but for me there was no more waiting, no more uncertainty. My two countries were united against a common enemy. Churchill had called it 'Greece's finest hour'. Greece was Britain's only ally at that time. I recall the feeling of national exaltation throughout Greece – a kind of superhuman force reminiscent of what I had heard of and read about the Greek War of Independence*. And now *I* was part of it, swept up by it. How true, how stirring were the words of the Greek National Anthem. They now meant more to me. How glorious war seemed!

---

* The struggle for independence from Ottoman rule, 1820–32.

PART II

War

6

It's Official. I become a Greek Red Cross Nurse

By the length of thy stride,
By the sweep of thy blade,
By thy countenance stern,
I know thee, proud maid.

The bones of the Hellenes
Have hallowed the tale:
As of old thou art standing:
Hail, Liberty, hail!

Withdrawn into darkness,
Shy, bitter, in pain,
The call wast thou waiting
To come forth again...

But now we have risen!
Hark, hark to the cry
Of thy Hellenes determined
To conquer or die.

The Greek National Anthem,
translated by Compton Mackenzie

Quite suddenly my mother became very ill. She had difficulty in breathing and flung all windows open, gasping for air; racked with violent pain, she would clutch her chest and cry. I was desperate. Doctors came and went and in the end, with grave faces they diagnosed – angina. Added to this alarming situation I had begun to realize that we should soon be in dire financial trouble. With Greece now at war it would obviously become increasingly difficult to receive money from my father in London. We could therefore no longer afford the apartment we had rented for what we thought would be a short stay. But a friend of mine, Marina Ladas, unexpectedly came to the rescue. Marina insisted that we move immediately into her aunt Roxane Sedgwick's flat as she and her husband Shan, the correspondent of the *New York Times*, had left for the Middle East. 'You can pay them at the end of the war', I remember her saying gaily – as if this would be in just a few months' time.

The Sedgwick flat was at the top of a corner apartment building in the elegant residential area of Kolonaki. The *retiré*, as those top-floor flats were called in Athens, overlooked the British Embassy – just down the street. It had two large terraces from which one had a clear view of Mount Hymettus and straining one's eyes over the network of gabled roofs and terraces, one could almost see the sea. Honeysuckle, jasmine and roses grew up through the terrace trellising and there were rows of pots planted with aromatic herbs. I was delighted with my new home and my brother immediately bagged the top room as he saw that it was ideal for his radio equipment and electric guitar. (The radio, however, was soon to be dismantled and hidden.)

To save money I dismissed our cook and decided to move into the kitchen, cookbook in hand. I also replaced the electric cooker with a small peasant-type wood-burning stove. This of course made it even more difficult for me as an inexperienced cook; food stuck to the dishes and saucepans burnt as the flames leapt up through the primitive, ill-fitting rings. My brother complained about the food, which I must admit was pretty bad.

One day, when I was working out the accounts and trying to see how I could save even more money, my mother placed her large diamond engagement ring on the table before me. 'This', she said, with her sad, sunken eyes looking even larger than ever, 'should help us along for a while.' I shall never forget the agony of going to the jeweller's shop (one that our family had known in better days) with my little parcel. I was terrified of losing the ring and had wrapped it up in several layers of tissue paper. When I reached the shop the unwrapping seemed to take ages, my hands were so unsteady. The jeweller first looked at me suspiciously and then, fixing his magnifying glass into his right eye, peered at the stone. As he moved the ring from side to side I noticed how it caught the sunlight from the street door and shot out sharp, rainbow-coloured beams. It was so beautiful. Finally the jeweller laid down the ring on the centre of his ruby-velvet tray and turning to me remarked apologetically, 'It is a lovely piece – a *really* lovely piece – but who would buy it now – I mean today? I can only let you have a small price for it. I'm sorry!' With that he handed me some crumpled drachma notes and turning his back on me, he locked the ring away in his safe. That was the last glimpse I had of a ring my father – as a young doctor studying in Paris – had bought with such pride, and which I, as a child, would finger as if it held some magic charm when mother leant over my bed to kiss me goodnight. Somehow it had always seemed grotesquely big for her delicate white hands and in my childish imagination I sometimes believed that some giant must have placed it there.

But we were at war and I was now anxious to take part in the war and could not wait to serve in some way or other. Although my Greek was shaky, I immediately applied to join the ranks of the Greek Voluntary Red Cross Nurses. The task before me was tough. Night after night I sat up working by candle-light as there were power cuts and a strict blackout had been enforced. I looked up words in a dictionary and tried to make sense of the medical books I had to study for my degree. In the end I gave it all up and instead learnt whole passages off by heart, hoping that this would do the trick.

On the day – the examination day – I can still see the scene in my mind's eye – that huge, round amphitheatre at the Red Cross Hospital outside Athens was packed. They were all there, hundreds of student nurses like me in their white piqué uniforms and white veils, and several rows of experienced trained nurses in their navy-blue cloaks. Halfway through the morning my name was called. I remember getting up awkwardly: I was so terrified that I was sweating and my dress had stuck to me. Rather self-consciously I pulled my skirt down at the back and walked unsteadily down the steps. I wondered what they would ask me. As I stood in front of the doctors and nurses of the examining team I went over in my mind the passages I had learnt off by heart. Usually there would have been both an oral and a written examination for Red Cross nurses but now, in wartime – happily for me – the need was so great that there was just one oral test. Finally the question came: and I could do it! I remembered the page and with relief I rattled off my answer – rather like reciting a set poem at school. The doctors and nurses smiled and whispered to one another. I waited. Then the head doctor rose and said: 'Xenia, you have a charming English accent – yet you have passed. Congratulations!' He handed me my certificate and cross. I was now officially a Greek Red Cross nurse.

As I went home, clutching my Red Cross scroll, I passed a truckload of soldiers going to the front. A girl on the pavement threw them up a bunch of pink cyclamen. They caught it and blew her a kiss, then broke into a gay song. At that moment the air-raid sirens started up. I dashed into a doorway but two minutes later the all-clear was sounded. It was a false alarm. My first job as a Red Cross nurse came when I was sent to the first aid station in the centre of Athens. There I spent many hours sterilizing gauzes and surgical equipment and preparing the operating theatre. Though I should have hated to admit it – and should have been ashamed to do so – I was really happy and excited. Yet at the same time I would argue with myself that it was wrong to feel that way; after all, I was waiting for the wounded to arrive – for pain and tragedy – and I *should* feel sad or at least moved. But I did not.

I remember the shrill sound of that first emergency bell. A friend of mine, Nancy Caccia, the wife of a British Embassy official in Athens,* who had hastily trained as a Greek Red Cross ambulance driver, had arrived at the door. I could feel my heart beating fast – here at last was my first patient! The stretcher-bearer brought in a totally immobile British tommy with apple-red cheeks; his arms hung limply as he was lifted up on to the operating table. Then, gently and carefully I undid his jacket to search for the wound. But at that moment the head doctor came in. After a quick but thorough examination he turned to me and sternly ordered – emetics. The soldier was just dead drunk!

Throughout those early nursing days I only dealt with minor injuries. There were a number of British servicemen, soldiers and airmen who were either drunk or had cuts and bruises. They obviously could not take, or had taken too much of that golden Greek resin wine. But there were some Greek sailors too; these were brought in with shrapnel wounds which they had suffered from the Italian strafing of the Greek fleet as it lay in the naval base at Scaramanga. I remember the day I was called into the operating theatre as a Greek sailor needed several stitches for a large gash in his lip and jaw. I was just going off duty but looked in to see if I could arrange for another nurse to take over. As I passed the operating couch I suddenly recognized – my brother, Costaki! 'Hallo Boot', he said with his distorted mouth. ('Boot' was his nickname for me – I don't know why. Perhaps something to do with Puss in Boots?) 'I couldn't stand doing nothing, just waiting, so I got myself accepted as a sailor on the *Averoff*.† Had to hide when the old Uncle went round – ducked under one of the lifeboats. But then the Italians struck. It's not serious, but – I hope you don't mind – I'd rather you didn't do the sewing.' It was not serious and although I had learnt to use that semicircular needle for stitches, I would rather not have done the 'sewing'. But I was glad to have found my brother and to know where he was, as he had suddenly disappeared. Just before I left him in the safe hands of the head nurse, he gave me more details of the Italian raid. Moving

---

* Harold Caccia, now Lord Caccia, GCMG, was at that time First Secretary at the Legation. In 1944 he was appointed Political Adviser GOC-in-Command Land Forces Greece, and in 1945 he became Minister at the British Embassy in Athens.

† The cruiser *Averoff* was the pride of the Greek navy, having served in the Balkan Wars. It was later to sail with my uncle who took the Greek fleet to Egypt before the Germans occupied Greece. In 1944 it proudly transported the Greek government back to Greece on D-Day.

his flapping lips in an attempt to grin, he said: 'Incidentally, we did a lot of fishing after the Italian raid. You know how lousy they are at hitting a target – well, their shells fell all round the boats and as a result a mass of dead fish floated up to the surface. All us sailors had a whale of a time collecting them and taking them to the cooks on board. Dinner will be good tonight if I can eat it!'

After a few weeks I left the first aid station and took up duties in a military hospital just outside Athens. The hospital, formerly a girls' school, the Arsakion – had hastily been fitted-up to receive the casualties from the Albanian front. Although it meant an early bus ride out of Athens in the morning and back at night I was very proud to have been chosen to work in this large and important hospital. On arrival I was particularly happy to find that Marina Ladas had been drafted there too and, as she was a more experienced nurse than I was, she took me under her wing. Together we set to making beds, rolling bandages and organizing wards. We had fun chatting gaily as we completed the preparation of the rows and rows of beds with khaki army blankets all neatly tucked in with those 'envelope corners' that I had practised so often for my Red Cross examination. But what was at the back of my mind all the time, and what I was actually longing for – could hardly wait for – was the arrival of the ambulances carrying the first severely wounded soldiers from the front. Then at last I could be useful, could help – perhaps could even save someone. But when they came – it was not what I had pictured.

'Here we are!' the porters shouted. And hundreds of wounded soldiers covered with mud, sweat and caked blood were carried into the makeshift hospital and left lying on the stone floor on stretchers. There was hardly room for us nurses to walk between the rows of pitiful, suffering, groaning young men as we tried to take down names, addresses and next of kin. '*Adelphoula! Adelphoula!* – little nurse, little nurse!' the cries never stopped. The stench was terrible. The doctors talked of gangrene, of frostbite and immediate operations. For days and nights – it is impossible to remember how many days or nights – but we worked as if our hands were separated from our bodies – separated from our hearts that were drowned in misery. We cut off uniforms as gently as we could, we bathed, washed, gave anti-tetanus injections, we held hands during painful operations, we took temperatures and laughed in order not to cry. It was non-stop.

Most of the wounded soldiers were young peasant boys who had come back from the Albanian front with severe frostbite. They had fought the invading Italians and beaten them back – throwing themselves into battle in an almost holy surge of patriotic fervour which had made them forget that they had no strong boots, no adequate clothing. They had sacrificed their limbs and the future of their lives, for liberty. A great number of them already had gangrene when they reached the hospital and had to have arms or legs amputated immediately. The tragic thing, too, was that often after the operation they did not know that they had lost their limbs and continually begged us nurses to rearrange their bed-clothes so that their legs or arms were more comfortable. But we played the game: we puffed-up pillows, loosened bedclothes. Some of the sol-diers noticed my accent and soon I was dubbed the 'English baby nurse'. I was no baby and although proud of my British upbringing, I was not English.

In the evenings I was beginning to observe, and not without some amusement, that as the house doctor did his rounds on my floor my patients would almost all with one accord begin coughing. What they clearly wanted was the 'English' nurse to rub and cup* them and often the doctor did prescribe this treatment, thinking that they had somehow all caught a chill. I of course always carried out his orders but I knew – and they, the dear, cunning patients – knew too well that it was not necessary. It was only a plan to keep me around longer.

My hospital duties included cleaning out the lavatories, but as peasant soldiers did not know how to use lavatories – had never seen anything like them before – it was a tough job. I had to scrub the whole floor daily and pretend that I did not feel sick and did not mind in the least. Then one day when Marina was helping me in this herculean labour she shouted to me across the partition, 'Well, I never thought you would be able to do this sort of thing. I thought you were a stuck-up British deb'. I was so hurt that I did not bother to reply. I just held my breath and scrubbed even harder. But why was I considered a foreigner, even by my own friends? It had been just the same in England. I realized that the war was now making me feel very British in a way, but my heart – or was it my head? – belonged to Greece.

During this time, when my life was encapsulated in the hospital world, I was not really part of the world outside. My thoughts were always with 'ta paidia', 'the children'. (Perhaps it is because Greeks never entirely grow up that they are called 'children' throughout their lives. The term of endearment bears no relation to age.) I worried about their wounds. Would they heal? Would they need further surgery? Was there any hope of their having artificial limbs fitted or light wheelchairs to take home? And what use would a chair be in their scraggy mountain homes? I

---

* A Greek peasant remedy which entails heating little glass jars and rapidly placing them on the patient's back. In theory they draw out the cold.

also worried about the war. What was happening? In the streets and cafés I had seen a growing number of British airmen – what was Britain doing, I wondered. From the Greek papers, which I skimmed on my bus journey to the hospital, and what I had heard from my relations in Athens, I gathered that Metaxas the dictator wanted the British to keep a low profile for fear of antagonizing the Germans. He felt too, that the help Britain offered was too little and would just end in disaster. Meanwhile the German Minister in Athens, Prince von Erbach, an aristocrat of the old school, was playing Hitler's war game with grace and guile. He repeatedly assured Metaxas that his country would not fight the Greeks, whose past and present they so revered: it was the British they were at war with. And as long as the Greeks kept the British out all would be well. Britain's token force of airmen and officers was acceptable as an act of friendship – just as was his wife's work in the Greek military hospital where she nursed soldiers from the Albanian front. It all sounded plausible to some – but not to others, who watched the German troops massing on the Bulgarian border.

In order not to break any of these delicate diplomatic rules the few British airmen, who flew their Blenheims with the Greek airforce, were forced to fly a very roundabout way. Their mission was to support the Greek army by covering their supply route in Albania and to bomb the port of Valona so as to prevent Italian reinforcements and supplies from landing there. I was very conscious at that time that the Greeks badly needed all the help they could get as most of their own planes were museum pieces and like all Greek machines depended much on string, the Holy Virgin and those blue beads that warded off the evil eye to keep them up. But the Greek pilots were fearless angels and would take off in anything that would fly: I had two of them, badly burnt, in my care.

In my hospital, after the capture of almost the entire 3rd *Alpini* Division and the surrender of hundreds of Italians on the Albanian front, such was the mockery and disdain felt by the patients towards their cowardly enemy that all the walls – in the wards and in the corridors too – were decorated with large, brightly-coloured posters and caricatures of the Italian rout. There were skirted Evzones – the crack Greek unit – leaping across deep mountain crags; there were huge, horned mountain goats eyeing the surrendering Italians as they threw away their arms into the air, and giant red *tsarouchia* – those half-moon-shaped mountain shoes with black tassels on their pointed toes that the Evzones wear – crushing a mass of lilliputian Italian armies. This last poster was a favourite all over Greece as the *tsarouchia* at that time were the emblem of victory, symbols of that kick which would oust the cowardly Italian invader.

Almost everyone had a pair, usually worked in coloured wools or made into an enamel brooch or pendant. They were worn as buttonholes, and Athens taxi drivers proudly dangled them from their windscreens. Even the heavily-laden donkeys from which peasants sold their fresh fruit and flowers sported their *tsarouchia*; sometimes these adorned their foreheads, sometimes their ears or more often they hung from the blue bead necklaces which donkeys in Greece wear round their necks for safety against the evil eye.

On a more sober note, also on the walls of my hospital wards, just above the rows of army beds, my patients' stiffly-posed family photographs, a poignant link with home, shared space with their naïvely-painted and sometimes flaking tin icons of the Virgin Mary. These were often decorated with dry palm leaves from Holy Week or bunches of shrivelled flowers from their mountain villages that had been blessed with holy water by the hospital priest, a symbolic mixture of religious faith and pagan lore. Often, as peasant visitors sat at their sons' bedsides with their touching little knotted cloth parcels of fresh goats' cheese, olives and other country delicacies, the *paidia*, and we nurses – as we perched on edge of their beds – would sing the peasant *Kleftic** ballads, clapping our hands to mark the beat. These ballads dated back to the brigands who had resisted the Ottoman rule; gay, sometimes frightening songs that spoke of revenge, honour, gallantry and love which every Greek peasant child is reared on from birth instead of those cosy English nursery rhymes I learned from Nanny Nell.

Throughout those tragic weeks I remember how my 'children' eagerly followed every political and military move; how they cheered when the first British Hurricanes swept over Athens; how they listened to the radio day and night and avidly scanned the papers. Even the titbit of news that some anti-tank rifles from Britain had reached the front was enough to raise the spirits of my ward. 'They will be *eaten*,' they cried with delight. (The Greek expression for giving a hiding takes it a bit further and uses the word to *eat*!) So moving was Greek faith in Britain's strength and might at that time that my 'children' were convinced that victory was just round the corner. And although I knew that the news coming from the Allied front was far from rosy, I did not have the heart to dampen their feelings. The future in fact was grim.

But I recall the wonderful day when the Greeks took Koritsa – their first major victory against the Italians in Albania. I can never forget that day. I arrived on my ward to find the radio blaring – church music: that Byzantine chanting came first followed by the rhythmic, traditional

* See Appendix II.

peasant war songs. Outside, all the church bells in Athens, in the hills – it seemed to me in the whole world – were ringing. In their narrow iron beds my 'children' were madly waving whatever limbs or bandaged stumps they had left as they shouted deliriously, *'Koritsa! Koritsa! Aera!'** It was so wonderful that tears streamed down my cheeks. One of the soldiers lifted up his arms to hug me. As I bent down he said: 'Don't worry any more, little sister. You will be home soon.' I could not explain that Greece was now my home or that I should be happy to be home in London because at that moment I did not know what I wanted – except to cry. And I was ashamed of that.

But it was a time in my life when I wanted to forget love, being loved or my own personal unhappiness, and so the busy – sometimes comic, sometimes tragic – hospital life was just what I needed. The emotional strain I felt when my legless soldiers had to be stopped from falling out of their beds as they tried to hide beneath them for protection against the planes that thundered overhead or the cold feel in my hand of a stiffening but trusting hand of a dying peasant, acted as a sedative. The pain and danger of war now filled my life. There was no room for anything else.

One dismal January morning as I was coming to the hospital I noticed that all the papers had funereal black headlines. On closer inspection I found that the dramatic news they revealed was that Metaxas had died, and that the King had named a non-political banker, Koryzis, as his Prime Minister. I reckoned that this was perhaps not very constitutional but then, I did not follow the day-to-day political scene. What I did hear later, though – from my uncle the Admiral – was that Koryzis, unlike Metaxas, had accepted Churchill's offer of a British Expeditionary Force which would be backed up by air and naval units and that an important joint battle plan was being worked-out in case the Germans attacked.

Weeks passed by and noticeably more British airmen were to be seen in the streets and more British soldiers and officers too. At the same time daily truckloads of desolate Italian prisoners trundled by our hospital on their way to the detention camp. In Athens impish, pretty girls laughingly sported curly Italian cocks' plumes in their hair – gifts from their boyfriends on the front who had plucked them from Italian *Bersaglieri*† slouch hats. But then all of a sudden the scene changed. The Greek army advance seemed to have stopped and this at a time when there was news of the Germans pushing forward, moving rapidly through Rumania and

---

* Greek for 'wind'. A teasing war-cry used by the Greek *Evzones* as they 'blew' away the Italians, i.e. making them retreat.

† *A corps d'élite* of Italian riflemen.

Bulgaria. 'If they come here, we'll teach them – we'll show them like we showed the Italians!' my patients cried gaily when they heard of the German victories. They never doubted that the German advance through Yugoslavia or Bulgaria if and when it came, would be stemmed by the British Expeditionary Force. History books talk of a 'misunderstanding' at that time between the Greek military command under General Papagos and the British Generals Dill and Wavell. The 'misunderstanding' was said to have been as to where and when the line would be held and by whom and what Yugoslavia would do. But in our hospital we knew nothing of this except that the Germans were advancing and the British and the Greeks were now retreating. Meanwhile the hospital radios gave details of the Greek army's glorious acts of heroism as they withstood the German advance. Whole battalions, they reported, commanders and every one of their men met their deaths at their post. Encircled by the rapidly-advancing German troops, they stood their ground, firing until the last round of ammunition gave out. When one of the commanders called up all his men before the battle and offered those who were married leave, no-one budged. My *'paidia'* shook their fists at the radio sets in anger at all this news, but they still believed in victory.

Just at that time Greece's main daily newspaper, the *Kathimerini**, published a brave open letter from its editor Georges Vlachos to Hitler. It was a vivid and stark interpretation of Germany's duplicity and a historic restatement of Greek defiance and her undying will to fight and die for freedom. This letter was immediately cut out and plastered on our walls. It said everything that all my wounded soldiers felt. The last paragraph read:

> 'What would your army do, Your Excellency if, instead of horse and artillery, we sent to receive them (i.e. the German army) on the frontier our twenty thousand wounded in their bloody bandages? But no, that cannot be. Small or great, that part of the Greek army which can be sent there will stand in Thrace as they have stood in Epirus. They will await the return from Berlin of the Runner, who came five years ago to light the torch at Olympus. We shall see this torch light a fire, a fire which will light *this little nation, which has taught all other nations how to live, and will now teach them how to die.'*

But in spite of glowing patriotism, gallantry and sacrifice the massive German advance could not be stemmed and as the German troops broke through the defences and advanced on Athens we learned that Prime Minister Koryzis had committed suicide and that the King had appointed another banker – this time a Cretan, Tsouderos – in his place. My Cretan patients were elated; they were convinced that the Cretans could do

* See Appendix I for full text.

what others could not. *'Ola ta paidia embros dia tin niki!'* ['All children forward for victory!'] they cried. But now it was clear to me from news from home and from what I had picked up from the British in Athens, that the order for the Evacuation of the British forces to Crete was imminent; a last stand would be made there in an attempt to keep the island as a base.* Meanwhile an army corps commander, General Tsolakoglu, was reported to have signed an armistice with the Germans in Salonica and although General Papagos repudiated this the Germans moved swiftly on to Athens where they appointed Tsolakoglu Prime Minister.

The day the Germans approached the capital my ward were stunned by the news. No-one spoke, or laughed or sang. The radio just blared the truth – every hour like a death knell. Hospital routine, bathing, bandages, injections, medicines, temperature charts etc., all took place as if on another planet. That evening when I reached home there was a brown-paper parcel waiting for me. When I opened it carefully I found a magnificent Byzantine icon – a triptych. In the centre the Virgin holding her baby seemed to smile coyly with tiny upturned lips, but the Holy Child looked serious and old and clasped his mother's hand tightly. The four saints surrounding the Holy Family held prayer books and crosses and one of them held a miniature Byzantine chapel. They were all aged and lined with puckered brows and frowning, almond-shaped eyes. They had huge, jewelled haloes, long white beards and down-turned moustaches, each strand of hair was carefully outlined. Their deep red and green flowing robes stood out like damask on the shimmering gold background. A note was enclosed. It read:

> 'Please keep this safely for me. It is a gift from the Greek Government and I treasure it. You can let me have it back if I return – if not, it is yours. I am leaving in a hurry – sorry – no time to say goodbye – perhaps it is better.'

The icon was Stanley Casson's,† a reader in classical archaeology at Oxford. He was one of the British officers whom I will always remember from those days when I, like all Greeks, was grateful for British support and still believed in victory. [Casson was killed on 17 April 1944 in an air crash over Cornwall on his way to Italy. And alas! his icon is mine. I have kept it safely to this day.]

---

* Crete was expected to fall in a day and in spite of the Germans' airborne invasion – the first ever to be attempted – it held out for ten days and might well have held out for longer if there had been better communications between Cairo and the island. Some of the Allied and Cretan pockets of resistance were still successfully fighting the Germans when ordered to pull out. See also Appendix I.

† Author of *Greece Against the Axis* (Hamish Hamilton Ltd).

As I went to bed that April night the air raid sirens bayed mournfully and witch-like flares lit the sky. Later the frightening muffled thud of bombs being dropped in the distance woke me and from my window I could see flames leaping up into the black sky from the direction of the Port of Piraeus. In the morning I stepped out onto the balcony and saw the last Australian soldier leave. He was carrying a bunch of flowers which a pretty Greek girl had thrust into his hands. Cutting off a bloom, he stuck it in the upturned side of his hat and waved 'Goodbye'. Had he seen me? Then I watched the last British official walk out of the Embassy and saw him lock the huge iron gate behind him. When would it open again, I wondered? I had been offered room on a plane or on a boat but I could not leave as my mother was too ill to move. And then, what had I to fear? No-one knew I felt I belonged to two countries – I would just be considered Greek by the occupying forces.

But it all came back to me. I now remembered Nell's neck getting red and pimply with anger when she described the Germans during the war in which Cyril had been killed. Here they were again, strutting about Athens with the arrogance of an occupying army. They immediately requisitioned buildings, plundered the food shops and gave us orders to empty our military hospitals to make room for their own casualties.

In my hospital the move was traumatic because there was nowhere for the wounded to go. We had orders to send them back home or to relatives in Athens, so our first task was to make sure that they had enough bandages and pills to see them through a few days at least. As I was handing out these meagre supplies a pale, grey-eyed, legless Cretan with a carefully-trimmed dark chestnut moustache called me to his corner bed. I went over to him. 'Little English sister,' he said to me in a conspiratorial whisper, 'will you lift me on to the stretcher! I don't want the Germans to do it.' I looked at his two bandaged stumps. They cruelly set off his handsome, broad, muscular upright body. I did not think I was really strong enough to manage but I saw that he was looking at me anxiously, expecting a reassuring answer. 'Yes, *paidaki mou*' (my child), I replied, 'I will be at your side.' Just as I was putting my arms round him to lift him up he said, 'Take it and use it when you need it – it has done good service. It is under the pillow'. I sat him down again and looked under the pillow. There I saw a huge, antique silver damascened musket, like those I had seen in old prints of the Greek War of Independence. At that moment the two German stretcher bearers appeared at the end of the corridor. I just had time to hide the gun under my nurse's cape. Then I lifted my Cretan 'child' on to the stretcher and walked behind the German stretcher bearers, accompanying him until he was safely in the ambulance.

When I returned to the ward to prepare my other patients a German officer who was in charge stopped me. Clicking his heels and offering his hand – which I did not take – he started: *'Liebe Schwester'* ['Dear Sister']. I cut him off in fluent German, which amazed him. (I had learnt this from my mother's Austrian cook in London, who used to keep delicious cakes for me when I got home from school.) 'I'm busy ... what do you want?' I said, or something to that effect, and I stared at him insolently – or was it with hate? Inwardly I was rather frightened that he might have seen what I was hiding – what was bulging below my nurse's cape. 'Nurse,' he said, 'we want you to stay and work in this hospital for us.'

I remember laughing: it was both a derisive laugh and a nervous laugh. I was relieved that he did not suspect me, but I explained that I did not intend to stay 'a moment after my Greek soldiers had left'. Coming back at this and looking at me sternly, he protested: 'But remember, Nurse, you are a Red Cross nurse, belonging to an international organization'. 'Yes', was my snap reply, and indeed, I was proud to be a Red Cross nurse, 'but', I explained, 'you have moved our wounded soldiers out; they have nowhere to go, no medicines, no care, no food. The Red Cross does not accept that kind of treatment.'

I turned my back on him and mechanically continued my heart-rending work in the wards until all the Greek soldiers had been evacuated. As I left I saw the German orderlies preparing the beds as I had done, not long before. I noticed that a number of the wards had notices reading *'Nerven Krankheit'* [Nervous Diseases]. As a Red Cross nurse I should perhaps have felt sorry or sad – but I did not. I just took a lift from the last ambulance which was going into the town and was dropped off at home. What would happen now, I wondered. What would happen to them, what would happen to us?

PART III

Occupation

7 1941–4

The German Occupation

'... Remember, too, that the reason why Athens has the greatest name in all the world is because she has never given in to adversity, but has spent more life and labour in warfare than any other state, thus winning the greatest power that has ever existed in history ...'

Thucydides, *History of the Peloponnesian War*, Book 11

After the initial shock of the occupation of Athens I remember watching with horror as the German Stukas dive-bombed and strafed the retreating British forces. Helplessly from my balcony I saw swarms of these German planes – which we had never seen or heard of before – taking off like a hideous army of black vultures. They roared up into the clear blue sky cutting into the horizon before nose-diving on Crete. In the streets passers-by looked up in agony – some muttered '*Kriti*', others crossed themselves as they went on their way. I wondered how many of those strong, cheerful, sturdy young Australian and New Zealand troops who made up the greater part of the Expeditionary Force* would be caught? How many of those British and Greek officers in small boats would be killed? There was no way of knowing what was going on. There were rumours – passed on from person to person with a little added to the story each time.

Quite early on during the occupation I recall an evening spent with Marina Ladas (later Marina Sulzberger). It was in her country home at Maroussi, just outside Athens. The house had an enchanting atmosphere: it was usually crammed with Marina's friends, even when there was nothing much to eat or drink and it was always decorated with huge bunches of wild flowers and herbs which Marina arranged so well, pushing them into peasant earthenware jugs as if they had just been gathered from the fields. Yes, Marina loved flowers; her shiny black hair, small, dark head and willowy movements in her crisp white summer dresses were just like a flower. I remember the day her mother had sent her off to Athens to buy whatever food was available. After searching

* The British Expeditionary Force (I learned later) consisted mainly of the British 1st Armoured Brigade, the 6th and 7th Australian Divisions, one New Zealand division and the Polish Independent Brigade.

for a long time – after crawling under semi-closed shutters of shops she knew, hoping that they had some hidden bit of something – she found nothing. As she waited, hungry and desolate at the bus stop she wondered what her mother would say when she returned empty handed. Then suddenly she spotted a small boy with a huge basket, selling daisies. Counting out the money she had been given, she forgot about food and bought the lot, the basket too. When she reached home her mother understood.

But on that particular night that I recall, Marina and I were alone, just the two of us squatting on the floor with our ears glued to the crackling radio which had been brought out of hiding. (We reckoned that at night this would be safe as the Germans rarely patrolled the countryside at night and in those early days of the occupation, I must admit we did not take much care.) A week before, while twiddling with the dials, Marina had, to her amazement, suddenly heard Cy Sulzberger's voice. He was filing a story from Ankara to the *New York Times* and spelling it out as he went. Marina was madly excited, as she had last seen Cy – who had asked her to marry him and with whom she was head over heels in love – when he stepped into a small boat to escape as the Germans advanced. Since then she had not known where he was or if he had survived the German planes which dived low and machine-gunned the small boats carrying those who tried to flee. Somehow through a friend who knew a friend who knew – for that was the way it worked in those days – she had sent a message to Cy in Ankara suggesting that when he was next on the radio he should use a code so that she would know if he still loved her. The code was worked out in such a way that if Cy had changed his mind he could immediately let her know. If he used E for Edgar it meant 'I love you very much but don't think it is a good idea that you should come just now', while E for Ernest meant 'I don't care for you any more'. A for Alexander was what we were waiting for, as this meant 'I adore you: try and come at once'. I remember Cy's voice coming over loud and clear late that night – that unmistakable strong American accent. 'A for Alexander' he said as part of his message. We did not wait for more. Marina called her mother and grandmother, there were kisses, hugs and tears and I believe we celebrated with the last drains of coffee to be had at Maroussi.

The next week was spent planning how Marina would get away. As I spoke fluent German I decided that the two of us – young, dotty girls – would turn up at the *Kommandantur* and just ask for an exit permit. And this we did. I believe the German Headquarters in Athens were on Vassilissis Sophias Street for I remember passing the Royal Gardens. Two bronzed, statuesque *Wehrmacht* guards, bristling with medals, their hands on their machine-guns flanked the doorway. I suddenly felt a bit nervous, but having got that far I did not want to let Marina down. So I pushed my way forward and as the guards barred the door I addressed them in German. 'My friend here', I said, 'is engaged to an American and she wishes to join him in Ankara. She needs a permit.' I think that the guards must have thought us pretty mad – almost the funniest thing they had seen since their arrival in Athens. But as America was as yet not in the war they let us pass and ordered us to go upstairs to the first floor. There we found a blond, curly-haired German officer with child-like blue eyes – rather like a grown-up version of that nursery picture of Bubbles – at his typewriter. I firmly repeated my request and waited for his reply. He just looked at us, smiled, then returned to his typewriter, fed it with a form, and rattled away. Then, handing this to me he said: 'Here is your friend's pass. Good luck! Happy journey. And Oh! do *you* also have a fiancé in Turkey?' he added with a grin. 'No,' I replied, feeling rather like a second-class citizen. We turned tail and quickly left, clutching that precious pass.

Once outside, we decided that we must celebrate this adventure and made for Zonars where we ordered two large ice-creams. (There was no longer much cream in these but to us they tasted delicious.) Our friends who met us at the café could not believe our tale. But now we discussed seriously how and when Marina should leave. We also discussed excitedly how we could make up her trousseau. Since Marina was marrying a rich American – for us at that time all Americans were rich – we felt it was essential that she should go off with a traditional wedding trunk. (In the end, of course, it was just a suitcase.) But none of us had much money and with little in the shops, each of us decided to offer the best we could pull out of our own wardrobes.

Marina* left Greece, having bribed her way on to a German plane leaving for Bulgaria. From there she flew on to Ankara. But just as she was making her final arrangements in Athens she had a curious phone call from a man who intimated that he had an important message for her. He asked her to meet him at a café and gave her precise instructions as to the time and place. She was to sit at a table by the window, reading a newspaper. He would then recognize her. When this stranger arrived he first looked round furtively, then slipped in beside her at her table. After ordering coffee for two he explained in low, conspiratorial tones, that he had a message he wished her to smuggle out of Greece; and handing her an envelope, he told her rather severely – looking straight into her eyes – that she was to learn the contents off by heart and then

* See also *Marina*, ed. C.L.Sulzberger (Crown Publishers, New York).

be sure to destroy the message. On arrival at Ankara she was to relay the contents of the note to the British Military Attaché. Delighted with the idea that she was now a conscripted spy – Mata Hari and all that – Marina took the envelope and stuffed it in her pocket. But she was so excited that when she finally reached Ankara to her horror she found that she had completely forgotten what was written on the secret note. Happily, though, just before meeting the British official, she unpacked her suitcase – and there it was, nestling among her trousseau! Her mother must have found it and carefully packed it. But how dangerous – what would have happened if her luggage had been searched – as well it might have been – by the Germans, the Bulgars or the Turks? Well, it was not, and so the important message about submarines, and about the pipelines that were to be laid in the event of the Corinth Canal being blown up, as well as the exact position of armament factories, was duly delivered to the British Embassy who were more than irate at the way the news had reached them. They even checked with Middle East Command to find out if the bearer of the message was reliable. The person at the other end, who received the query in Cairo, was none other than Marina's brother Alexis Ladas and that was the first news he had had of his sister since he had escaped from Greece.

Although Marina envisaged a gorgeous, romantic wedding in the Church of the Holy Sepulchre in Jerusalem, this was not to be. Since Cy was Jewish and Marina Greek Orthodox they soon found that neither faith would have anything to do with them. In the end a friendly Presbyterian in Beirut performed the ceremony and, in Marina's words, 'Dr Scherer took it upon himself to explain to God that it did not matter what we were as long as we were fundamentally good people.' Marina died too young – at the age of fifty-six. I recall the little Orthodox church in Paris on the day of her funeral. The whole floor was strewn with sweet-smelling rose petals. Wild flowers and herbs, climbing roses and lily of the valley which I had arranged, decorated her bier and covered her coffin. As I left the church in tears a friend said to me: 'Marina would have loved to have seen it – to have been there.'

There are some days, some feelings and events during the occupation that I will remember all my life. Yet it is strange, the pain of those years has almost been erased. Flashes do come back, but they seem as if they were part of another person's life – a passage in a book or a story I am telling. So deep is the wound – the frustration and indignity of life under an occupying power – that as I look back it all seems unreal. Yet today many men and women in the world still live in that cage that I knew so well.

As I reach down into my memory the events I come up with are not always in date order. This is perhaps because during those years bad days, good days and funny days were all telescoped into days when consciously or unconsciously we were waiting – for an end. But one of the most painful and debasing recollections I have is of hunger. All that anybody thought of during the winter of 1941–2 was food. The Germans had requisitioned all the food in the shops and had despatched these supplies out of the country to Italy and Germany. At first some Greek shopkeepers hid their stores 'under the counter' – but when betrayed and exposed they were so cruelly dealt with – either imprisoned or deported – that no-one dared. Fresh food supplies could not reach the capital or the main towns either as the caiques, those small, tall-prowed boats with chugging motors which in the past used to carry food and oil from the islands and from the villages all along Greece's rugged coast, had either been sunk or requisitioned, and most major roads and bridges had been blown up during the fighting. The situation was made even more desperate by the Allied blockade which in the past I had so avidly followed on the BBC news and which had delighted me by the punishing blow it dealt to the Germans. But now, as it prevented food from being shipped into Greece, it filled me with horror as I watched this British weapon inflicting famine and death on Greece – my country.

At that time, I remember, corn bread, coffee made out of toasted chick peas and dandelion-leaf salad were our staple diet. Sometimes a friendly Embassy official (the Rumanians lived in our apartment building and helped many Greeks with food and medicines) would add something to this sparse menu, or rich relatives who had found some delicacy on the black market would invite us to a meal – but in a way all this was humiliating. In an attempt to save at least the starving children in the poorer districts of the capital – there was little one could do for their parents – soup kitchens were set up with some scant supplies from the Greek Red Cross. A friend of mine, Cleo and I, both Red Cross nurses, ran one of the largest soup kitchens in Athens which was organized by Prince Philip's mother, Princess Alice. (I remember she was always clad in grey nun's veil and gown, the habit of a religious order she had founded.) Our soup kitchen was housed in part of the Fix brewery on the road out of Athens towards the sea, *Odos Syngrou*, and it was a long walk from Kolonaki hill where we both lived. But daily as we made our way we walked in silence. Our minds could only think of food. It was degrading, but like all Athenians we were hungry all the time.

Sometimes on our journey we would pass small boys in tattered clothes selling thin fingers of corn bread or what looked like broomsticks dipped in carob honey. At other times passers-by, their clothes hanging limply away from their skeletal bodies, would sway and drop down dead. Their lifeless limbs, sprawled out on the pavement like those of a severed puppet, seemed unreal. We did not stop, nor did others who passed by, as it became such a usual sight – and then, there was nothing we could do. We just mouthed a prayer and hurried on to save our children.

The soup we cooked for the children in large cauldrons over a wood fire was dry bean soup one day and chickpea soup the next. Sometimes we were able to add a bunch of parsley and some onions and the Red Cross supplied us with a little oil. Although the cooks were well-known to us – former devoted servants who had worked for years in our parents' houses – we had to supervise all the weighing, measuring and cooking. Every bean, every drop of oil was checked, such was the temptation of starvation. We also had to enforce strict rules as there was only enough food for the children and not for their parents.

It was forbidden, for instance, to take food out of the building under any circumstances. This was in order to stop parents who often attempted to steal a little soup for themselves by pretending that their children were too sick to make the journey. Second helpings too were out. Yet when some of the spindly-legged children with their overgrown eyelashes framing their winning eyes crawled back under the rope into the queue and turned up with cheeky smiles and empty mugs, I had to turn a blind eye. (The amazing, sometimes beautiful but scary, growth of eyelashes, the prematurely whiskery faces and the blanket of down-like hair on the small children's bodies came from lack of vitamins and food.) If there was any food left over after the children had eaten, we would fling open the doors and the famished, emaciated parents who were locked outside would surge forward, falling over each other, pushing and screaming like wild animals as they battled to scoop up the last dregs.

One day when I was clearing up the kitchen a blond, strong, tall, bronzed German officer – the epitome of Hitler's prized Aryan god – walked in. The Germans had requisitioned the Fix brewery but had given us permission to use part of it for the soup kitchen. When I saw the officer, I was immediately afraid they might have decided to go back on their word. So, thinking it wiser not to take any notice of him, I just went on with my work. Then suddenly I heard a howl; it sounded like an animal in pain and as I looked round, I saw the German officer had collapsed on one of the wooden benches and was sobbing. Lifting his purple, grotesquely swollen face bathed in tears towards me he blurted: 'How can I help these poor Greek children – it is so cruel – I have children of my own ... I can't stand it'. I did not reply. I was locking up: I just asked him to go. There was no way that this one man's pain could end our nation's tragedy.

When the British finally lifted the blockade in 1943 the Swiss and

Swedish Red Cross set up missions in Greece to distribute food and supplies as rapidly as possible. The food was a gift from the US and Canada and was transported through Turkey, but by the time the first consignment had arrived, thousands of Greeks, mainly in the poorer districts of Athens and other large towns, had died. I heard the wonderful news of the lifting of the blockade one night when I was listening to the BBC overseas service. For although the Germans had ordered all Greeks to hand in their radio sets to their local police stations, where the wave lengths were adjusted and then sealed so as to make it impossible to tune into the BBC, my brother had fixed our 'sealed' radio so that it could be unsealed at will. He was a master of these tricks. And even today I can still almost see that useless dangling seal and string – a life line. It was my father's voice, as President of the Greek Red Cross in London, that broke the news and I remember it came on my name day,* 15 August, St Mary's Day, and I also remember that he slipped in a personal message to me – something about thinking of and wishing happiness to those who were named after the Holy Virgin. My father, I learned later, had worked hard to influence the British Government to change its policy. He had appealed to Members of Parliament and written a letter to *The Times* pleading for an end to the tragic famine in Greece. He was greatly helped and supported by Princess Marina, Duchess of Kent, whose mother Princess Nicholas was, like us, in the occupied capital. Yet when we actually heard that the blockade was to be lifted we could hardly believe it – we knew what it meant to us and to all Greeks. And it was hard not to rush to the telephone and pass on the glorious news to all our friends and relations. But we knew this would be fatal, so we just re-sealed the radio and waited to hear the 'official' version over the Greek radio – which was of course censored.

How difficult it is to describe the occupation, and how impossible it is for anyone who has not had the experience to know what it was like. Perhaps because it was not only what one saw but what one felt so deeply that it is hard to put into words. And then today after so many years the ugly creases of hate have almost been pressed out by time. Yet I remember when I watched the arrogant, bronzed, grey-uniformed soldiers of the *Wehrmacht* in their too-short leather shorts – strutting about the town with their Austrian comrades who proudly sported their edelweiss emblems, I knew what Nell had meant when she talked about her feelings towards the Germans. Something that I had not understood at the time. The heavy grip – the stranglehold – of the occupying forces in Athens could have crushed life in the capital

* My name is Maria Xenia.

– but it did not. Life just went its way; it did not hurry or wait. There were always the same number of hours to fill. The sun shone just as brightly and spring flowers came out after a hard winter and filled the air with their fresh, dizzying scent. There were, though, those anxious moments at night, when lying in bed, I heard the clatter of German boots as the army marched past in the street, under our windows; and the sad day when the meatshop on the corner of our street – which had turned into a vegetable shop because there was no meat – had to close down. Now there were no vegetables to be had either, and none of those fresh oranges with their shiny green leaves still on their stalks and which used to smell so strongly of blossom. The Germans had them all. Yet the shopkeeper still stood in the centre of his empty store with his shutters only half-closed.

Every day he greeted his former local customers with a smile as they passed by, wishing them a 'good morning'. Only at closing time at the end of the day, when he went home did his shutters come right down. But it was that feeling of uncertainty – of not knowing what would happen tomorrow – that I recall so well. The Germans would carry out random – and sometimes senseless – searches and arrests. I remember visiting friends one day and finding the front door wide open, the apartment empty; gaping cupboards, empty drawers, papers and clothes strewn all over the place; the usual marks of an ss early morning search. Was it just a case of interrogation or did it mean arrest and deportation? There was no means of finding out; that was what was so debasing and frustrating, to feel helpless and entirely in *their* hands. To feel they could do whatever they wanted with *our* lives.

But the frequent stories of courageous acts of resistance – often picturesquely exaggerated as the details were passed on from one person to another – were stimulating as were the incongruous, unexpected and sometimes even funny episodes and events that made life bearable and human. Sometimes a beautiful poem about the resistance, comparing it to the heroic uprising against the Turks, would be slipped under the door. Or, in the street a British agent – blond, blue-eyed, tall and shabbily dressed would be spotted queueing-up for cigarettes or sitting in a bus – no doubt convinced that he looked like a Greek. And then one day in the cinema, just further down the row from where I was sitting, an obviously British face was suddenly lit up. He had leant forward for a light and a German soldier who happened to be sitting next to him, had obliged – and not noticed. We all breathed again! So many Greeks were hiding British soldiers or agents in their homes that at one time it seemed that everyone that one knew was offering this kind of dangerous shelter. With the exception of agents the British had recruited – such heroes as Charalambos Koutsoyiannopoulos (who went under the pseudonym of 'Prometheus II') and later Gianni Peltekis ('Apollo') – most of those who were engaged in trying to save British lives in Athens were amateurs at the spy game, and in this guise they would often proudly invent naive codes when speaking on the telephone – saying for instance: 'My child is leaving tomorrow to visit his grandmother', meaning, not too discreetly, that an organized underground departure had been arranged.*

This sort of action, like the many spontaneous attempts to help the British, went on frequently just under the Germans' noses. And there were too, the organized and fearless acts of sabotage carried out by young Greeks – the majority of whom were left-wing EAM sympathizers. Operating mainly in Athens, and in the major towns in the early days of the occupation, they destroyed important factories, put railway engines and trucks out of action and blew up ammunition dumps. Daily the news of these daring acts of defiance was passed on to us in Athens by word of mouth. But there was little time to celebrate as at dawn we would hear the rumble of those early morning death trucks taking prisoners or hostages to the firing range outside the city. At first the Germans adhered to what they might have considered to be a semblance of justice. Prisoners were interrogated (usually tortured), tried, condemned to death and executed. But later hundreds of innocent hostages were rounded up and deported or shot. We all knew at that time that the Archbishop of Athens, Archbishop Damaskinos, and his brilliant young legal adviser Professor Gianni Georgakis often intervened successfully with the German authorities and saved many British and Greek lives. Gianni, a young, sharp, jovial lawyer with a round face, a crop of curly brown hair and Byzantine eyes which switched their gaze from love and humour to severity and hate with the click of a camera shutter, had studied in Germany and through his knowledge of German and Germans was able to defend hundreds of prisoners during the occupation. He battled with Herr von Altenburg, the German plenipotentiary, putting the Archbishop's demands in such a forceful manner – knowing well the Germans respected force – that often the Germans gave way. There were of course many poor Greeks who could not be saved and Gianni and the Archbishop tried to visit them in their death cells in the Averoff and other prisons – for a last word, a last blessing. The arrival of the over six-foot tall, grave, regal prelate in his flowing black gowns with his huge, jewelled cross must have appeared like a holy vision to those awaiting execution.

* Although the majority of the British Expeditionary Force had been evacuated in April 1941 some 16,000 had to find underground means of escaping. See Appendix I.

One prisoner, condemned to die on Christmas Day, felt – as he kissed the Archbishop's hand – that at that moment he had reached God. 'With this kiss,' he said to the Archbishop, 'I kiss my mother, my father and God.'*

Often the condemned prisoners left poignant messages on scraps of paper. These they would hand to the Archbishop or Gianni Georgakis – or sometimes just threw them out of the truck which was taking them to the firing range. Every one of these tragic messages – frequently picked up in the street by passers-by and handed on – always stressed that those about to be shot were not afraid and were proud to die for their country. One prisoner was so worried that his shaky handwriting might be interpreted by his family as proof of his agonizing fear, that he explained in detail in his last letter that the truck in which he was travelling was bumping up and down as he was writing to them – hence the unsteady hand. And how calm and brave was the crumpled note left by a nineteen-year-old boy who had worked in an organization which had saved the lives of many British soldiers:

> 'My dear mother, father and sisters,' he wrote. 'This day of June we shall be executed. We die like men for our country. I do not suffer and I do not want to cry ... we are worthy of our ancestors and of Greece. I breathe for the last time the fragrance of the romantic Greek air of the morning. We have had our Holy Communion. I found a little bottle of Eau de Cologne, and I have put it on me. Farewell Greece, mother of heroes.'

In a lighter vein, a more mature prisoner's last message bid his mates not to mourn but instead to 'gather all your friends, offer them a good dinner, read them my letter and drink to my soul. I don't want anyone to cry, old chap, I want you to behave like real men and like Greeks.'†

During the last two years of the occupation the Germans began to shoot such large numbers of hostages that they rarely bothered to publish the lists of the dead. Often when Archbishop Damaskinos asked permission to visit the mass graves with relatives so that they could identify their husbands or sons, the Germans refused. On one occasion the Germans did not have the names of the latest batch of their victims – usually, for some bureaucratic reason which was hard to understand, they did methodically keep lists for their own records. But this time the names were lost and instead the Germans offered the Archbishop a heap of tattered clothes they had removed from their victims. These I was told were hung up on a line in the Archbishop's palace hall. Mothers and sisters who feared that their husbands or brothers had been shot looked

* W. Byford-Jones, *The Greek Trilogy*, p. 53 (Hutchinson & Co Ltd).
† Ibid, pp. 60 and 63.

through the bloodspattered garments – hoping, dreading and then finding and recognizing gory jackets or torn trousers belonging to those they loved. Some women, deranged with grief, wrenched down the garments they believed they knew and lay on the floor hugging them, sobbing and soaking them with tears. Others who could not be sure of the exact identity of bloodstained shirts, torn jackets or trousers punctured with bloody black-edged bullet-holes searched the pockets for that comb they knew, for that handkerchief with an initial or for that packet of cigarettes they had saved up for.

There were, of course, many bright smiling days too during those harrowing years. I remember one brilliant spring day when I was walking in the Royal Gardens in the centre of Athens. Looking up at the sky I thanked God in my mind, or was it my heart? – for all he had given the world: for that balmy, scented spring air, for that bright sunshine, that unique, clear, piercing attic light. At that moment I came across a group of English nannies sitting beneath the flowering Judas trees in the shadow of a ring of tall spiky palm trees. (I knew that a number of these nannies had refused to leave their charges when the Germans came and in fact they stayed on throughout the occupation.) They were sitting bolt upright in a row on a park bench with their large, English, imported prams lined up in front of them – the hoods up so that the strong sun did not shine right into their babies' eyes. And they were all knitting and chatting away quite happily – they could have been in Hyde Park! As a group of German officers passed by one of them took out his camera and was just about to take a picture of these ladies when the most formidable of the group – in grey brimmed felt hat, grey uniform and gold-rimmed spectacles halfway down her nose – moved forward towards him like a battleship. Wagging her finger at him she warned: 'Now now, my dear man – move along – you know you are not wanted here'. The amazed Germans stopped dead for a while, then obeyed the order and moved off smartly. The nannies resumed their knitting.

Often when walking in the streets in Athens I passed the Italian *Carabinieri* who were used by the Germans to patrol the city. Dressed as mini-Napoleons with black tricorns they always went about in twos or threes as they were petrified of being attacked. The Greeks, who so recently had kicked the Italians out of their country, regarded these toy soldiers as a huge joke and openly made fun of them. One day I saw a pretty girl pass a *Carabinieri* patrol and try to stifle a giggle by rapidly clapping her hand over her mouth. But the bullies must have seen her and they turned back. Two of them caught hold of her and held her down as the third knocked her pearl-white teeth out with his bayonet. Marching away triumphantly they left their victim with blood gushing from her mouth. When I recall this scene it is perhaps ironical that I also remember how so many Greek women were later to save Italian soldiers after Italy's collapse in September 1943, by hiding them from the Germans in their homes. It was said they made good lovers.

By 1943 and early 1944 the Allied air raids became more and more frequent and were a great morale booster for us all. Often, just after jazz parties which my brother arranged with his friends and which included George Katsaros – a gifted pianist who would pick up the latest tunes from the BBC on his 'sealed' radio, we would creep out on the balcony. For some unknown reason, but perhaps because I needed extra comfort, I usually carried with me my British mascot – a leggy tommy doll which had been given to me by a friend who was hastily evacuated to Crete and which now shared my waste-paper basket hideout with my wireless. Lying on our backs or as flat as we could, we would look up at the sky and watch the flares cast their eery, bright, white light. They picked out every detail – roofs, walls, streets – transforming the town into the skeleton of a dead city.

Once when I was alone I crawled out onto the balcony just as the Allied planes were coming over. It was essential to crawl as the flares were so bright that if one stood up they cast clear black shadows and the German patrols in the street below would take pot shots at anything moving. On the balcony that night, to my surprise I found a heap of silver tinsel shreds and I was delighted with this unexpected gift from above. (I believe they were called 'windows' and were used to disrupt the radar systems.) But then only a few minutes later my phone rang. It was a call from the head nurse of the Greek Red Cross telling me that there had just been a very heavy air raid on Piraeus, which had caused severe damage. She gave me an address in Athens where the child victims of the raid would be given temporary shelter and asked me to go there at once. The children, who were in a pitiful state, were being transported from the port in ambulances.

Throughout that night as I tried to comfort the miserable, terrified, trembling children, as I cut off the layers and layers of unwashed, matted woollen vests which they wore day and night under their day clothes, and as I bathed them, sang to them, hugged them and put on their fresh clothes – it was hard to be both happy and proud of the Allied raid. It had caused such pain to the already poor and destitute shack-dwellers – mostly refugees from Asia Minor* who had settled round the port.

* After the disastrous campaign against Turkey in 1920–2, Greece took in about a million refugees under the enforced exchange of populations.

Sporadic items of news – probably somewhat exaggerated – of the heroic resistance of armed bands against the Italians, Germans and Bulgarians fired the imagination of my brother and his friends. None of them had had much training for mountain warfare – Costaki, I suppose, had had a bit more than most but that did not amount to much. Apart from a short period with the Greek navy when he passed out successfully (fellow officers said at the time that my uncle, the Admiral of the Fleet, had ordered guns to be trained on those marking his examination papers), his only military training had been the Harrow School's Officers Training Corps (OTC) in 1933. That year was memorable because the OTC went on strike. The reason could have been either in support of the dedicated pacifists of the Oxford Union who had just passed the resolution to refuse 'in any circumstances to fight for King and country', or, more likely, because they wanted to be allowed to parade in 'civvies'. At that time 'puttees' were a must. They were thinly woven bands of khaki mesh which were to be wound round the boot up to the knee. These were supposed to be neat and to meet. In my brother's case they did neither. He was also issued with a 'Sam Browne'* – the name given to an officer's leather belt with a strap over the right shoulder. This had to be highly polished and there was a lot of emphasis on elbow grease. Costaki, however, found that Brylcream – that thick brilliantine – worked wonders and was much quicker. But when the Sergeant Major detected the non-military scent, he had to abandon this method. He then decided to join the band as he had learnt that they were allowed to parade in 'civvies'. He played the clarinet. Finally, much to his surprise, he did obtain his passing-out certificate, though it is true to say that he only just scraped through with the minimum number of marks. But the important certificate gave him the option of being 'considered for a commission in HM's Imperial Indian Army, the Territorials or the Royal Canadian Mountain Police'. The day he took the practical part of his passing-out examination there was a howling wind. None of his commands reached the 'squad', who remained standing at ease. In the written part of his examination he did a little better. He wrote a learned thesis on the placement of latrines. But on the Greek mountains latrines were not a problem. Politics, food and how to keep warm were – as Costaki found out later.

I believe it was in the spring of 1943 that Costaki decided to leave Athens and 'go to the mountains' as was the current Greek expression for joining the resistance movement. He and his friends had contacts, as a number of Greeks had at that time, with resistance groups in the

---

* A 'Sam Browne' is an officer's field belt invented by General Samuel Browne, 1824–1901.

mountains – from their clandestine 'runners' who came in and out of the town, passing messages and enrolling new recruits. They usually met their agents at night in the scented pine foothills of Mount Lycabettus, or in the daytime in smoke-filled, crowded offices or cafés. The Germans were enraged by the ease with which these mountain couriers operated. And this in spite of the harsh and punitive raids which they so ruthlessly inflicted on mountain villages, burning and sacking them, rounding up all the menfolk and shooting them or taking them hostage. Costaki had learnt that the British Military Missions (BMM),* now established with the resistance groups in the mountains, needed more interpreters, and a very unconvincing-looking Greek – an Irishman who had dyed his hair jet black but could do little about his stature and his bright blue eyes – arranged the journey. His name was Bob. (For security reasons Allied personnel were known by Christian names only, and often not their own. It was better this way as the less known about sensitive material – the exact names of agents for instance – the better it was in case of arrest.) There was, however, one last prank that Costaki and his friends wished to play on the Germans before they took off. They delivered two crates to the *Kommandantur*. One was a consignment of light bulbs which were 'fixed' so that when the light was switched on they exploded, and the other a container of several cases of German wine which they had emptied and filled with dirty water.

I remember watching Costaki leaving with George Katsaros, the pianist. I followed them from the balcony until they were out of sight, having climbed into a truck. Costaki was carrying his guitar which he then left on the way with a friend, thinking that it would be safer with him – quite rightly too as it turned out. Both Costaki and George as well as the dozen or so 'passengers' who piled into the truck were scruffily dressed and carried bags and empty tins so as to appear like the standard black-marketeers who travelled in and out of Athens seeking food from farmers in the countryside and then returning to sell it stealthily at exorbitant prices. At a later date Costaki gave us some details of his journey which took him through Thebes, Levadhia and Amfissa in the direction of Delphi, passing burnt-out villages which had suffered German reprisals for Allied sabotage. The old beaten-up truck the party travelled in had

* The British Military Missions (BMM), and later the Allied Military Missions (AMM) when the Americans joined the missions in the mountains, acted as liaison between the Greek resistance forces and Cairo headquarters. The officers attached to these missions were either operating for the Special Operations Executive (SOE), and their task was to organize sabotage and harass the enemy or were agents belonging to the Secret Intelligence Service (SIS), who reported intelligence information. Each of these outfits reported to separate headquarters in Cairo and were the responsibility of different ministries – something which was to cause friction later.

a huge boiler fixed on the back which emitted a trail of black smoke – a contraption described by my brother as being a 'gazogene' conversion. It burnt wood and charcoal – which was important since no petrol was available for civilian transport – and every now and then, when the vehicle came to a grinding halt, a member of the party would get out and collect wood or chop down a tree. On their route to Delphi there were several Italian and German military check-points. The Italians were easy going and not suspicious, but at one German post the truck was stopped and searched. This was towards the end of the journey when the gelignite, hidden under the floorboards, was melting in the heat and was beginning to emit a strong, sticky-sweet smell. A German guard, who had stuck his head inside the truck, sniffed the air and, turning to Bob, asked him in broken Greek what it was. Bob, whose black hair-dye was starting to trickle down his neck and who knew no Greek pointed to the floor where a quick-witted member of the group had upset a tin of honey. The guard nodded with satisfaction and waved the truck on. When they were about two hours distance from Thebes the party abandoned their transport and trekked up through the mountains – arriving at their destination about thirty-six hours later. Costaki's city shoes had lasted for the first three hours only. Bob, he remembered, looked 'as fresh as if he had been on a Sunday outing'.

Eventually Mother and I heard – from a coded note pushed under our door – that the party had reached the BMM post safely; this was early April 1943. The BMM commander who greeted the new arrivals was a Major Brian. The rest of the mission, which included Captain Bob, consisted of George, who was a sergeant and the wireless operator, a tall Australian called Bill who had escaped and avoided arrest after the Allied evacuation, an Austrian deserter, Hans, who was also a cook, and two Italian deserters. The base camp was in the Delphi area – under the shadow of the towering, snow-capped Mount Parnassus where the group of guerrillas operating there were the Communist-led ELAS (the Greek National Popular Liberation Army). They were a bearded lot, decked-out in criss-cross cartridge bandoliers, red hats and khaki kilts, and armed with huge revolvers and curved scimitars – recalling the heroes of the War of Independence. After the new arrivals had been introduced all round, their personal details were carefully taken down, laboriously coded (using selected pages from a Penguin publication*), and then transmitted on a 'suitcase' transmitter to Cairo. Confirmation came back that very evening, and my brother instantly – like the rest – became a Second

---

* Although Costaki does not recall the title he remembers it being 'so dry that in spite of the lack of reading material no one tried to read it'.

Lieutenant in His Majesty's forces after formally swearing allegiance to the British Crown. The new recruits were all issued with battle dress, boots and a black beret; they were handed a tommy gun – shown how to clean and dismantle and operate it and warned not to fire more than one shot at a time to conserve ammunition.

Roughly about three or four months later Costaki and George were separated. George moved to the EAM/ELAS headquarters in the Larissa area, while Costaki's mission moved to the mountains above Thermopylae and set up their base camp within the walls of a crumbling church. Routine daily life, that of translating, collecting information and transmitting this to Cairo was often overshadowed by bitter cold and hunger. Brian believed that shorts and a sweater top were the best turn-out and that nylon parachutes kept one warm at night. The Greek interpreters conformed for a time, but soon reverted to trousers in the daytime and the traditional peasant fleece blankets or *paplomata* at night. But one of the most welcome diversions from this mountain life was a parachute drop. On such an occasion Costaki and a group of men were detailed to wait at a given spot – this was a narrow clearing in a valley hemmed in with tall pine trees where logs had previously been stacked to form the letters of an agreed code – such as X, Y or Z.

At the scheduled time, when the roar of the British plane (usually a Halifax or Wellington bomber) was heard, flashlight recognition signals were exchanged and target recognition fires lit. The plane then flew low – sometimes making three or four sorties before dropping its load of containers to which parachutes had been attached. Blankets though, rolled up in bundles, were just thrown out of the plane door and came whizzing down on the heads of the receiving party. My brother was once knocked out by one of these bundles and thought that it would be ironic to be killed by a blanket! The containers were cylinders about twelve feet long by two feet wide. A smaller, red one was 'first priority' as it contained gold sovereigns which were BMM's only financial means of support. Local villagers and guerrillas knew about this potential bonanza, so BMM personnel had to be quick off the mark. One drop Costaki witnessed provided uniforms, boots, plastic explosives, 'Cape to Cairo' cigarettes, sovereigns and personal mail. To ELAS's disgust no arms were sent for them – it must have been at a time that GHQ in Cairo was beginning to realize that ELAS was using these to fight other rival guerrilla bands instead of the Germans.

The combination of the local ELAS's growing dissatisfaction with the British attitude towards them, and the fear that villagers had of being caught by the Germans when supplying food to the mission, resulted in food supplies almost running out. So one day Costaki volunteered to go down to the villages in the valley and buy food off the peasants with BMM sovereigns. Reverting to his scruffy civilian clothes, and riding a mule with a donkey attached to it by a rope like an anchor, he went down into the valley. At one of the villages, pretending to be a black-marketeer, he exchanged his sovereigns for two large bags of flour and a small piglet. He tied the screeching piglet on to the donkey's back and moved further down the valley where he was told there were warm springs. Before returning to base he wanted a bathe – it was something he had not had for six months. On the way the route crossed a stream and though his mule splashed into the water obediently, the donkey refused to budge. It was only after some lashing and much swearing that they did finally get across and were able to continue their way towards the springs. As Costaki approached the cave he heard loud voices – the German army had obviously also discovered the hot pool. But throwing all caution to the winds he undressed and plunged into the warm water. He was not even noticed by the German soldiers – or if he was, he was taken for an eccentric local, as no normal Greek peasant would bathe naked in a pool. Thoroughly refreshed, he climbed into his dirty clothes, mounted his mule and, leading his protesting donkey with its screaming piglet on its back, clambered back up the mountain, reaching the camp at sunset. The piglet, incidentally, was never eaten – it became the mission's mascot and 'watchdog'.

There were two unexpected arrivals at the mission base camp while Costaki was there. One was an Italian mechanized brigade of the *Pinerolo* Division which appeared after the Italian surrender in September. Brian and Bob ordered them to put water and sand into the fuel tanks of their armoured vehicles, and after they had been disarmed, they were sent off towards the mountain villages of Thessaly which received Allied subsidies – gold sovereigns – for the keep of disarmed Italians.* (Many of these also worked voluntarily for the Greek peasants on their land.) The Italians sought out British or Allied Missions rather than surrender to ELAS. Those who had fallen into ELAS hands, in spite of accepting to fight the Germans, usually had their clothes and boots stripped off and their arms and heavy equipment, mortars and machine guns seized. And this after the unsuspecting Italians had instructed their captors in the use of their weapons.

The other surprise visitors who arrived at the mission came up riding donkeys and mules led by local villagers. They were American airmen who had been rescued by Greek peasants. Their plane had been hit over

---

* The villagers received from AMM one gold sovereign a month *per caput* which was the same allowance as the guerillas. The scheme was controlled by Major Philip Worrall who was decorated by the Italian Government after the war.

the Ploesti oilfield in Rumania but it had managed to fly on to Greece where it finally exploded – giving the airmen just time to bale out near a local village. The peasants, having heard the explosion, looked up at the sky and saw a myriad of parachutes dropping on to their land. They then moved quickly to save the Americans from falling into German hands. The Americans were quite surprised when they met their scruffy hosts and found that they spoke English, and celebrations that night – helped along with a mixture of brandy and ouzo – had devastating results. But happily the Germans did not send up an expeditionary force. The next day the airmen were sent off on a newly constructed air strip, and a grateful airman gave Costaki his Tissot watch.

When I heard that Costaki was with the Communist-led ELAS guerrillas and that his mission's main function was to liaise between EAM/ELAS and GHQ Cairo, I was worried. I remembered how so often, before he had left for the mountains, both he and his friends had had grave doubts about the resistance groups. They had argued over and over again about whether ELAS was a genuine resistance group or just a group of Communist guerrillas – a question which was to be asked over and over again by many Greeks and by the Allies for years to come. But at that time – in 1943 – the Communist-led ELAS forces were the main bands operating in the mountains over the greater part of Greece.

There were liberal, Republican, Royalist and non-Communist bands springing up in other areas too. In the north west, EDES (National Republican Greek League) was the main guerrilla force led by the Republican General, Napoleon Zervas, and among the most important of the smaller bands were EKKA, the 'National and Social Liberation' forces of Colonel Psaros and Colonel Sarafis's AAA (Struggle Restoration Independence). Both leaders of these last two groups were Republicans. Sarafis's band was later wiped out by ELAS, the General himself taken prisoner, brainwashed and escaped death by accepting to join the communist-led ELAS forces and become their commander-in-chief: a switch, which like others in the labyrinth of Greek political allegiances at the time, was hard to understand.

Before the war, under the Metaxas dictatorship, the Communists had been outlawed and many of them had been imprisoned while others formed underground cells in the main towns. These cells sprang into operation when the Germans arrived and let most of the Communists out of jail.* They then formed the underground resistance movement, the EAM (National Liberation Front), which operated in the main towns.

---

* Nicos Zachariadis, the Secretary General of the Communist Party, was, however, kept in German prison camps throughout the occupation. He was flown back to Greece after liberation by the British.

In the mountains the Communists also soon dominated the main ELAS guerrilla bands and their ruthless, dedicated leaders were therefore able to direct and manipulate their forces with a view to seizing power when the Germans left. A political instructor attached to the ELAS unit which Costaki met in the mountains in 1943, spelt out the ELAS doctrine somewhat naïvely though clearly: 'We want peace,' he said. 'When Russia and Communism have conquered the world there *will* be peace.' Fighting the enemies of Communism – as my brother soon surmised – was becoming more important than fighting the Germans. And with the exception of the blowing-up of the Gorgopotamos bridge in September 1942, which linked the Athens–Larissa–Salonica railway line, the main acts of sabotage, such as the blowing up of the Asopos viaduct in June 1943 – also on the main railway line – were carried out by British and Allied forces alone, without ELAS support and sometimes even with some hindrance from ELAS guerrillas. But the blowing-up of the Gorgopotamos bridge, which so successfully cut the German supply line through Greece to Rommel's desert army, was not simply a united action against the Germans by both left- and right-wing guerrillas working with British officers. The ELAS Communist guerrilla leader, Aris Veloukhiotis* – had at first evaded contact with the British parachute mission although they had landed in his territory in order to be near their target. He only co-operated with them when the British officers, waiting in caves for over a month, brought in his rival Zervas, the EDES anti-Communist Republican leader whose territory lay a long march, over 100 miles, away. Fearing that Zervas would become the only Greek hero of this important sabotage action, Aris changed his mind and the dare-devil joint operation was carried out successfully. But after this, Aris used his forces mainly to fight other non-Communist resistance bands and eventually eliminated them all except EDES who (like ELAS) had considerable British material support. But Costaki remembers to this day – and finds it hard to wipe from his memory – how Aris forced him and ELAS guerrillas to stand by and watch him personally butcher a Greek village 'traitor'. The victim, one of fourteen who were tortured to death and who belonged to a non-communist band of guerrillas, was splayed out like a crab and tied to a table in the village square of Mavrolithari. He was then literally – slowly hacked to pieces – blow by blow. The agonizing screams only stopped when Captain Bob pulled out his revolver and put the victim out of his pain. At that point Aris, writhing and shaking with fury, had to be restrained from attacking the British captain. Bob

---

* 'Aris' (god of war) was one of the many names used by this bloodthirsty, flamboyant guerrilla leader.

and Costaki hastily retreated to base camp, posting sentries outside for protection.

I recall that at that time I knew little and cared less about Greek political factions and their rivalries, and the battles in the mountains. The problem of food, medicines for my mother, coupled with the fear for my father's safety in the London blitz were foremost in my mind. Yet I liked to believe that the resistance and acts of sabotage were being carried out by Greek patriotic guerrilla forces who were risking their lives by fighting the Germans and helping the Allies. I was, of course, to learn later that this was not always quite so. But then who can unravel the true motives of clandestine war? Yet I remember how the names 'Chris' and 'Eddy' (Monty Woodhouse's and Eddy Myers's* mountain nicknames) coupled with 'Gorgopotamos' were whispered around Athens. And how I pictured these new Byronic figures working with our brave resistance heroes – moving with them at night – by the light of the moon – sleeping in caves, being fed by gallant peasants on scraps of goat cheese which they so badly needed for themselves – as they struck this major blow at the German supply route. This vision – shared by many Athenians – gave us the renewed faith and courage we needed. Fighting or even the idolized picture of such daring acts of sabotage was so much more glorious than just waiting – which was what we were doing in Athens. But now my brother happily had left.

There was a gap – and for quite a considerable time – I cannot remember exactly how long – before I had news from Costaki again. But I was fully occupied working in the Greek Red Cross offices. A section of the Red Cross had been looking for secretarial help and when I applied and was given the job, I was particularly happy as the pay was in kind – a small bag of flour and one of rice – if I remember rightly. But at first I was in great trouble. In London I had been taught on quite a different typewriter and the one in front of me now was a huge, heavy, black, dusty affair with a kick of an antique cash till. And, to my horror, it had a row of unintelligible – to me – accents and of course a Greek keyboard. But as it was just forms that I had to type, and hundreds of these to accompany the food supplies for the needy (alas! there was no Xerox in those days!) I managed in the end. Of course I did not use the touch-typing method which I had been taught so strictly on my London secretarial course – instead I kept my eyes glued to the keys.

* Hon. Christopher Montague Woodhouse DSO, OBE. Colonel 'Chris' as he was known in occupied Greece, commanded the Allied Military Mission to the Greek guerrillas in German occupied Greece in 1943, while Brigadier Edmund Charles Wolf Myers, CBE, DSO, was Commander of the British Military Mission to the Greek Resistance Forces, 1942–3.

One day when the office was as usual full of cigarette smoke, chatter and pleading crowds and I was hard at work with my head down – trying to concentrate and be more accurate – I suddenly heard a voice behind me say, 'Hallo Boot!' I looked round, and there was Costaki grinning at the start he had given me. My first reaction was one of terror – terror that he might be seen, recognized, betrayed and caught. But he was calm and even bemused by the effect he had on me. He explained that all he had wanted was to give me a kiss before he went 'on his way'. (To Cairo – the name was never uttered.) He said that ELAS had offered Greek petty officers a 'run'. (To Cairo.) Looking back this was just before the Communist inspired mutiny of the Greek forces in Egypt, and no doubt ELAS hoped to infiltrate the Greek navy in Alexandria at that time. Costaki, who knew nothing of this plan, had accepted readily as he wanted to get away from the ELAS-dominated mountain guerrillas. I learnt later that he had left in a caique from Euboea, his fellow passengers being forty Jews. The Jews had been ordered to strip to make sure they had been circumcised. My brother, who feared ELAS would find out that he was the nephew of the Admiral of the Fleet (later to become the Minister of the Marines) and a relative of Prime Minister Tsouderos, tore up his Greek identity card and swallowed the pieces.

Not long after Costaki had left Greece, in April 1944, units of the Greek armed forces and navy in Egypt who supported ELAS mutinied. They demanded the recognition of the ELAS government in the mountains and challenged the authority and political balance of the Greek government-in-exile in Cairo. This brought Britain's confused and divisive policy right out into the open. (The British government and the Foreign Office supported the government-in-exile and the King, while GHQ Cairo was supporting and supplying the guerrilla forces of ELAS and EDES.) But as a typical example of how events under the frenetic political climate in occupied Greece rarely turned out the way they were planned – my brother took the ride but had no intention of going to Egypt to join the mutiny. He stopped off in Turkey where he was bathed and de-loused, and joined a British undercover organization.

With my brother now away and not a glimmer of light at the end of the occupation tunnel – I began to look for a better-paid secretarial job. I first applied to the Swiss Red Cross. They, together with the Swedish mission, were in charge of the distribution of the US and Canadian gift food supplies which were now arriving regularly. I thought that I stood a good chance of being accepted by them and rather prematurely began looking forward to being able to use my French and German instead of struggling painfully in patchy Greek. But I was turned down. Later, I heard via the grapevine that the director thought my background was suspect. And with my father in England, although I was Greek, I was not exactly neutral. Undeterred, I thought I would try the Swedish mission, and to my surprise landed a job in the director Emile Sandström's office. There the atmosphere was calm, efficient and friendly. The reports were written in English; working on my new typewriter was like driving a Rolls Royce and my food package at the end of the month was as exciting as a Christmas hamper. It contained macaroni, flour, sugar and oil. Mother and I were now all right for food.

8

ATHENS 1944

The SS Knock on our Door

> 'His watch, which had been put in the prison safe deposit, would
> go on working until the spring was unwound; Then it would stop
> and no one else would wind it up again. The hands would remain
> fixed until either the owner died or all his possessions were
> confiscated. He wondered what time it would be showing . . .'
>
> Solzhenitzyn, *The First Circle*

Trying to jog my memory as to what the occupation was really like I recently asked a friend of mine who had been in the resistance in Belgium what she remembered most clearly. 'Walking and always looking back over one's shoulder – for that shadow' was her reply. Yes, I remember that too, but Gianni Georgakis, now a former Ambassador and Head of the Onassis Foundation, came nearer to what I felt when he said to a journalist, 'If you [in unoccupied countries] heard a knock at the door it was usually the postman or milkman. With us, we never knew . . .'.

Because of the electricity cuts – often caused by the leftwing labour unions' firm resistance to the Germans' many unsuccessful attempts to recruit a Greek labour force – neither our lift nor the bell in our apartment block functioned. So I vividly remember the knocking on our front door – I remember the gentle knocks and the loud, agitated knocks. I also remember trying to discern from the sound of footsteps coming up the stairs to our top-floor flat who the caller might be.

At night it might be black-marketeers offering 'meat' parcels. When these were carefully unwrapped on the kitchen table they usually turned out to be dead cat. Other nocturnal visitors were more welcome, but some were frightening too. There were those nameless, faceless men, with their collars up, their hats down, their jerky movements, who handed us tin cigarette boxes which contained rows of neatly packed gold sovereigns in brown paper. They were our only financial means of existence – but we never asked their names, nor where they came from. They left like bats at night – vanishing noiselessly – leaving an empty space in the hall as if they had never been. Were they a plant? Would they come again? We never knew, but we hoped they would come again before – the end.

One day, I answered the door to a brisk knock and saw before me a beribboned German sailor. He looked like something out of a nautical scene in a musical comedy – except for his flat, impassive face. His dark-blue sailors' uniform was starched and pressed to perfection – pointed creases down his trousers and a black ribbon dangling down from the back of his hat. Clicking his heels, he handed me an envelope and said he would wait for a reply. At least I knew that he was not going to arrest us! The note was addressed to my mother so I handed it to her and watched her face as she read it. She looked cross. She then came to the door and, sternly looking at the young sailor, snapped, *'nein danke'* (no thank you) and slammed the door in his face. The note was from Admiral Wilhelm Canaris who had been a friend of my uncle's* in what seemed then those long ago peacetime days. He offered whatever help we might need. 'How degrading', my mother said angrily, as she crumpled up the note and threw it in the wastepaper basket. What we did not know at the time was that Canaris was plotting against Hitler. He was executed on 9 April 1945.

Very early one morning – I think it was about four o'clock – I did not hear the knock on the door. Mother must have answered it. I was fast asleep – struggling with a dream that I had been arrested and was being taken to the interrogation centre in Merlin Street, the SS headquarters. Opening my eyes sleepily I suddenly saw a steel-eyed German soldier at my bedside. *'Raus!'* he barked. I had somehow known that this might happen – and it *was* happening – happening to me – *now*. Mother came into my room and, pointing to the bedroom door, ordered the soldier out. 'Get out while my daughter dresses,' she cried furiously. Strangely enough the man obeyed. 'Have you done anything for them to arrest you?' Mother then asked me. 'No! Of course not.' I assured her. I knew that the fewer people who knew about 'the milk run' (as my brother called it) the safer it was. I dressed quickly – funny, the dress that I picked out in such haste was an Austrian dirndl which Mother had bought me in Salzburg a few years ago. I remember it being rather expensive but I loved it – it was green and pink with silver buttons down the tight fitting bodice. As I did up the buttons that morning – there seemed so many of them – my hands moved automatically as

---

* My uncle had taken the Greek navy to Alexandria after the German breakthrough. During the ensuing battles, a third of the navy's strike force had been lost as a result of German air attacks. The Greek fleet that arrived in Alexandria to fight alongside the British fleet consisted of one armoured cruiser (the flagship *Averoff*), seven destroyers, three torpedo boats, five submarines and a number of auxiliary vessels. The British government provided six new destroyers and six corvettes to increase its strength.

if wound up by some hidden clockwork key. At one point I remember Mother coming back into my room as I was dressing; she was carrying a lumpy bath towel and opening my window she proceeded to throw it out onto the street muttering: 'I'd rather anyone get it than these men!' Turning to me she explained in a whisper that it was her jewellery she had just disposed of.

I was ready, and just before leaving my room – I looked round at my 'things' – my books on the shelf above my bed, my pictures, my icon and everything that had been part of my shell during those years in Greece. I grabbed three lipsticks and stuffed them into my pocket. What an inexplicable, meaningless, odd, last-minute action! Then I turned to kiss Mother good-bye but found her putting on her panama hat, tucking the elastic that held it in place carefully under her hair. She had picked up her little grey medicine case, which was always at her bedside and, turning to the soldiers (there were two of these ss men – the one who had arrested me and another who stood guard at the door) she said, 'If you are taking my daughter you'll have to take me too.' The soldiers looked confused, shrugged their shoulders and pushed the two of us down the stairs and into their jeep.

At the ss headquarters, just down the hill, Mother and I were separated. I was locked in a dark, dank cell in the basement – there were messages, last messages perhaps, names of loved ones and holy crosses scratched on the wall. I must have stayed there for two or three hours when the door was unlocked and a prison guard, in that grey-green ss uniform, frogmarched me upstairs and ordered me to get into the truck that was standing outside in the street. It was sunny, I remember that. As I sat on the dusty floor of the truck some young soldiers arrived carrying a very old lady in a dirty sheet – they held it at either end as if it were a hammock. She was all skin and bone, her greasy, yellowish-white hair fell in strands across her emaciated, dark-skinned face. She was still in her crumpled nightdress. 'One ... two ...' the soldiers chuckled, and on 'three' they swung the sheet up into the truck. I just had time to catch the old lady's head as she hit the truck. A soldier, pointing his machine-gun at me shouted, 'Are you a Jewess?' 'No,' I replied, wondering what was going to happen. (I did not know at the time about the holocaust; I did not know that out of ninety thousand Jews in Greece, mainly in Salonica, barely nine thousand had been able to escape.) 'Well, leave that old Jewess alone or else we'll shoot you.' After more prisoners had been roughly piled into the truck, and the sunburnt young soldiers giggled and enjoyed pushing the last ones in with the butts of their guns, we moved off. I remember how the truck made its way through the streets I knew so well; passing the pepper trees, the orange trees and bumping along as it reached the outskirts of the town past those barren hills covered with clumps of wild cistus and thyme – the hills I had passed so often on my way to my uncle's naval headquarters. I soon realized that I was being taken to Haidari, the dreaded SS camp I had heard of so often. But was it me they were taking? Or who was I? I tried to ask myself what I felt – but I felt nothing.

Haidari was a cluster of buildings, formerly an army barracks which had never been quite completed. It stood above the Eleusis road past the Byzantine church of Daphni. That morning the church domes, forming a cross, glistened in the sunshine, and the sombre ring of tall, dark-green cypress trees which protected the chapel pointed upwards – to heaven. As we turned off the main high road and entered the camp, the soldier perching at the front of the truck lifted his gun and pointed to the skull-and-cross-bones over the gate, 'See that?' he shouted to me with a broad, elastic grin. 'No-one comes out of here alive.' I looked up at the fathomless blue sky. How strange, the random words from prayers I had heard in Nell's church now came to mind, 'God be with me and give me strength ... the Lord is my shepherd'. The truck came to a halt at a barbed-wire enclosure and we were all ordered out smartly by a group of young officers who led us into a large hall. There we stood in line, wondering what would happen to us. Then the officers removed all jewellery, rings, crosses, and chains and any small possessions we had with us – they took my lipsticks. After that we were ordered to strip – men on one side of the hall, women on the other – and a doctor went round, taking notes. What was he looking for? Perhaps singling out those strong enough to be deported as a labour force or was it just part of German bureaucracy? I felt dizzy and sick. When I had dressed again an Austrian officer grabbed me by the arm and, roughly pushing me in front of him, told me that I was to be put in solitary confinement. I did not know what this actually meant but I remember him locking me up in a small, square room. It was dark, there was an army blanket on the floor. I do not know how long I spent there or how many hours I spent looking at the shaft of sunlight that came through the large keyhole and under the door. My watch had been taken from me. But I remember how daily an officer – with coarse grey hair and a cruel face, carrying a whip and accompanied by a fierce German Shepherd dog – would unlock the door, shout at me, and go away again. I believe he was Hungarian; the Gestapo employed hand-picked men. Food – I do not remember eating any food. But in my mind's eye I can still see the chipped tin plates and mugs that were left on the floor. There was a hole in my stomach.

Then one morning a new officer came – he too held a whip and had a dog at his heel. He ordered me out – 'for interrogation' he said with a smirk. As I stepped outside and clambered up into the truck the sunlight blinded me. But by the time I reached Merlin Street my eyes had once again got used to the bright light and the building – number 9 – was familiar. This time I was immediately marched up to the first floor. There I was led through a long, airless, narrow passage. On either side there was a row of men standing dejectedly. They were no longer human beings – they were something else – there was no life left in their drained frames. They stood – faces to the wall – swaying, sweating – about to fall. How long had they been there? I had reached the interrogation room. A blond, suntanned officer sat at a desk looking through a pile of photographs. He took no notice of me as I came in. Glancing over his shoulder I saw that the pictures he had taken were of the Acropolis. My grandfather had made the museum there ... had replaced some of the marbles that Elgin had stolen, with casts ... Greeks could no longer go there as young resistance heroes continuously tore down the German flag ... my mind wandered. I was not afraid. I felt that I was an onlooker viewing a scene I had so often been told about. I knew it all.

Finally, swinging round and facing me, the officer asked:

'Where is your father?' I noted a touch of irony in his voice.
'In London,' I replied.
'And your mother?'
'In Haidari. I believe.'
'Do you have any contact with your father?'

'No,' I replied. But at that moment I caught sight of a torn piece of paper in front of him. The writing was my father's – Mother must have forgotten to destroy it. 'This is not the information we have,' he said dryly. Then looking at me coldly he added: 'I want you to tell me where the following people are, and if you do not tell the truth,' – at this point he waved his arms towards the ropes hanging from the ceiling – 'we have methods of getting you to tell. Incidentally , a friend of yours is next door – a pianist. I doubt if he will ever play the piano again.'

I realized that George, who had continued to be a runner from the mountains, had been tortured. Would he ever be able to play that wonderful jazz music again? Did he know about Costaki? But I had to concentrate. No, the first three of the names he gave me I genuinely did not know, but there were four I did. I knew only too well that they were on their way to Cairo. Moving at night through friendly mountain villages they would be meeting the caique in a few days' time – then Turkey – then freedom.

'They are in Egypt,' I replied. 'They left some time ago.'
'What is this?' The officer shouted as he banged on his desk. 'A honey-moon? How do they get there?'
I was silent. I just stared in front of me.
'Tie her up and we will see if she knows.'

Two soldiers who were standing by the door tied my hands behind my back and then pulled the rope so that the whole weight of my body fell forward. As I hung from my hands an unbearable pain knifed my shoulders.

'Let her down,' the officer ordered after a while. 'Now tell us how they get away.'
'I don't know,' was my reply and at that moment I think I knew what hate was.

'Take her away!' the officer ordered sharply. And the two soldiers who appeared to enjoy the performance – trainees perhaps – led me down to the cell I had come from. As I came in, a man was washing the floor; I stood clutching my aching shoulders watching him. He came close to me, and without interrupting his task whispered, 'Don't worry, the Allies were bombing yesterday. The news is that they will soon land.' Finishing off his job, he walked away – dragging his wet mop behind him – swaying and whistling down the passage like a phantom dancer. The air smelt of his wet mop and disinfectant. Smells are something one remembers.

9

HAIDARI 1944

Camp Life

'Physical pain is not continuous or permanent. In an acute form it lasts a very short time.'

Epicurus, translated by R.W.Livingstone

It was difficult to climb back up into the truck after the interrogation. My arms would not function. But it was already full when I got there – the others pushed up, made a hole, and I slipped in on the floor. As I sat down I looked around at my fellow prisoners. They were, I thought, mountain villagers from areas where the resistance was operating. Several of them were slouched over their limp arms, their faces blue with pain. I knew why. On our journey back to the camp no one spoke; the guards perched on the corners of the truck, their guns pointed down on us, their fingers on the trigger. And anyway, what was there to say? As I gazed at the faces of my fellow countrymen – mostly uneducated peasants – my eyes like a chisel traced the curved outline of their rock-like features. Looking into their agonized eyes – deep pools of generations of sorrow – I was filled with admiration for these people who were part of me, and yet of whom I had known so little. I had reason to want to resist the Germans – to help the Allies – my home was in England, my father was there, but they, those proud sturdy peasant women who had hidden Allied airmen and shown them the mountain passes had no British ties. And yet they had saved 'those blond angels who fell from the skies' – as they called them – ignoring and defying the brutal occupying forces who burnt their villages and shot their menfolk as reprisals. They had been guided purely by their animal mother-love, and driven on by their longing for freedom. Uncomplicated, deep convictions – as natural to them as the caressing morning breeze on the mountains, as it shakes the almond blossom from the village trees. The echo of a song returned to me then, a gay peasant song that I had heard so often in Athens tavernas. 'They shook the blossoming almond tree' was its repetitive refrain ... I thought I could almost see those petals on the ground.

But by the time I had worked out in my mind who everyone was, where they came from, what they did in their villages, and why they were in the truck with me, we had reached the camp gates again. The truck bumped its way under the skull-and-crossbones, and on reaching the barbed wire enclosure we were ordered out. Two whip-carrying officers shouted their orders. Men were marched off first, then the women were pushed into line. Pointing at me, the officer commanded me to join them. To my surprise he led me to the main camp. My solitary confinement was over.

I think I can never forget the first glimpse I had of the large women's camp. As I walked through the barbed wire that segregated it from the men's camp I saw groups of women squatting in circles on the ground. In the centre of the largest group there was a small, neat figure sitting bolt upright on a broken, straw-seated chair which had lost its back. As I came nearer I saw it was – Mother – and she was wearing her panama hat against the sun! I fell into her arms. I cannot remember what we said to each other. I can only remember what I felt. I think we said nothing.

There must have been some two- or three-hundred women and a few small children in the camp. At night we all slept in the old barracks on the stone floor on single army blankets; in the daytime, we sat out in the dry, stoney yard. Beyond our barbed-wire fence, in the heat of the midday sun, the men prisoners were made to work, digging unneces-sary trenches. We just looked on, watched them fall from exhaustion or faint. Then their guards would whip them and set their Alsatian dogs on them. Like zombies we still looked on. One day a little boy in our compound recognized his father digging on the other side of the fence and he rushed towards him – arms outstretched – before his mother could hold him back. 'Papa! Papa!' he cried, 'Come to me...'. The camp guard aimed at his legs and fired. As he dragged the tiny, screaming body away he looked back at us as we stood in silent horror and said, 'A lesson'.

Every morning we lined up for roll-call, but as some of the prisoners were too ill to stand we carried them out into the yard and left them lying in a line; their balloon-like limbs were covered with festering sores and were grotesquely swollen from lack of food. I wondered why they had not died – perhaps they would soon. The camp commandant called out names at random from a list. Those he called out always knew why – they were the day's hostages and would be shot in reprisal for bridges or railways blown up by sabotage forces. But then, we were all hostages, all condemned to death. It was just a question of time. After the hostages had been shot, just to make sure that 'the lessons had been learnt', their blood-stained clothes were distributed among us. Some of the poorer prisoners in tatters were glad even of these.

Another camp routine was the handing-out of Red Cross parcels. This was done with the usual German precision. We were lined up; our names called out and our parcels handed to us. But the boxes were empty, the contents had been removed. Somehow I was never really hungry and I found it difficult to eat much of the camp food which was mainly hunks of bread and chick-pea soup or bean soup with what we called 'meat'. (This was little black bugs that floated up to the rim of the bowl.) The bread, I remember, we left out to dry in the sun so that it would last longer. I did not need my bread and gave most of it to the hungry peasant girls who missed their fresh-smelling home-baked loaves, and the Jews who were given only half rations, or on some days – no bread at all.

The Germans kept a network of spies and informers amongst us in the camp; they would report conversations they had heard or invented, as well as details of petty thefts and quarrels. I found it hard to understand how fellow prisoners could report on each other in order to settle a personal, trivial quarrel, knowing full well that it would result in harsh German punitive action. Reports on squalid little matters such as the disappearance of a slither of soap, a hairgrip or a broken comb, added to some incautious remark on the Allied cause could result in cruel punishment – and yet in this tense, cooped-up atmosphere, this was a common occurrence. (I learnt later that this short of thing did not happen in the men's camp; on the contrary, there they supported one another. No-one sneaked.)

Sometimes at night the strains of 'Lily Marlene' came from the camp commandant's house when he was having a party (how shocked I was when I heard the tune again when I was back in England!). Squatting on the camp floor some of the peasant women used to carefully comb out the lice from their children's or friends' hair; while others neatly folded their pretty pleated peasant skirts and laid them under their blankets to keep the pleats neatly pressed. Mother always put her hair up in pins to set her curls in place. I just looked on. But I admired these seemingly senseless procedures because they were really an exercise in strength. There were times, too, when in the middle of the night a wail or a stifled cry would be heard. But then we all knew that it only came from a newcomer to the camp; we had all been through it. And we knew that after a day or two a detached, mechanical mood would take over. It could not be called bravery, it was as if one were somewhere else and someone else. And there were no more tears, just a glazed look into space – that was the mask.

We none of us knew the time of day – for no-one had a watch. We none of us knew – or strangely enough – cared about how many days were left for us to live. When the guards came into the compound with their dogs and whips and ordered us from one place to another we never knew where we were being taken or if we would return. I remember the first time we were taken into another building to wash. I was delighted and could hardly wait to undress. But looking round I saw that the peasant women were terrified; they stood in front of the taps in horror and refused to take off their layers of heavy woollen clothes. I had heard that Greek peasant women never stripped to wash. Their washing was done in privacy, usually just face and hands; on rare occasions they would go further – washing bit by bit and covering up each bit as they went along. But as they stared at me, I was relieved in the end when I heard them mumble as I undressed, 'The English girl is not afraid – it can't be bad'. And they dipped their hands in the cold water and splashed their worn faces.

When we moved anywhere in the camp we were ordered to do so on the run with our guards following close behind; often older women would stumble or trip up on the sharp stones of the yard. The whip-carrying guards would then set their dogs on them to get them up quickly. It was all part of the degradation of camp life, every cruel detail, every humiliation was thought out and was there. Yet as I look back I feel no hatred now, nor do the Greek peasants who suffered most. They welcome German tourists today with their traditional warm hospitality – a new generation it is true – proudly using the one or two German words that they picked up at that time!

One day our guards ordered us to line up and called a few of us out. Rumour had gone round the camp – probably set off by the 'informers' – that some of the stronger women were being taken to work in Germany. I was relieved – even excited – as just sitting, waiting and doing nothing all day was torture. Little did I or the other women know what treatment awaited us in Dachau or Auschwitz. But along with a few others I clambered happily into the truck which took us to the railway station. There we were ordered into a waiting goods train. I do not know how long we sat in it, but during that time I remember trying to cheer up my fellow prisoners by describing Germany to them. Stupidly, I described the Germany I had known in pre-war days when it had been fashionable to be 'finished' or to spend holidays near Munich – staying with some *Gräfin* or in a finishing school. I did not, however, mention that on one occasion, when stepping off the train with Mother at Munich, I had bumped into Unity Mitford who had been a senior girl at Queen's before being asked to leave for plucking her eyebrows in the library during prep. I remember how we juniors had been enthralled by her glamorous looks and arrogance – the way she just propped up her mirror and started her beauty treatment. In Munich though, she was carrying a swastika flag.*

But my graphic description was cut short when two irate guards opened the train doors and herded us back into the truck which drove us once again to the camp. Later we learnt that Allied resistance fighters had blown up a bridge on the main railway line and that the ss scheme, dubbed 'Strength Through Work' had been abandoned. So back it was to camp life – but now the Allied raids were becoming more frequent, especially on moonlit nights. I remember lying awake and looking at the bright, white shafts of light that cut through the prison windows. I remember praying – almost as if I were praying to the moon, which I was convinced God had made larger in Greece than anywhere else in the world. On this last point my fellow prisoners were adamant too – since they like me saw the moon as God's torch lighting the path for the Allied planes. The hum above always came by moonlight.

On one balmy September morning – a day I shall never forget – I looked up at the sky just before roll-call; it was a cloudless blue. As usual in the courtyard there were two rows of prisoners. There were those of us who could still stand and those we had carried out and who were lying down because they could no longer stand. Our camp commandant, a tall, sunburnt blond Austrian officer accompanied, as customary, by his German shepherd dog, walked between our lines holding his list. That day he called out Mother's name and mine. We were marched off briskly and ordered into the Athens truck. As I clambered up and helped Mother, I wondered: was this it – was this the way they did it? Others had been taken away and had not returned. We had seen their clothes though. The truck followed the now familiar route into Athens and stopped outside No. 9 Merlin Street. There I was parted from Mother and taken upstairs – where I had previously been for that painful interrogation. This time the long passage was empty and I was shown into a different room. As I entered, a beribboned German officer who was sitting at his desk looked up – his cold steel eyes looked through me. He asked my name, my father's name, my address in Greece and my address in England. I gave it all – but I had given it before. I could not understand why these details were being taken down so meticulously – for a gravestone? Most unlikely. When the officer had finished filling

---

* One of five remarkable daughters of Baron Redesdale, Unity Mitford, who died in 1948, was notorious for her admiration of Adolf Hitler. Her sister Diana married Sir Oswald Moseley, leader of the British Union of Fascists, while another sister, Deborah, became the wife of the 11th Duke of Devonshire. A fourth sister was a member of the US Communist Party in the 1940s and 1950s, and a fifth, Nancy Mitford, was a brilliant writer of witty novels on English upper-class life.

in a form he stood up, clicked his heels and barked, 'London is a ball of fire, your father is dead, your brother who was a spy has been shot. You and your mother are now free'.

I cannot remember how I left the room or how I joined Mother and told her we were free. But I know that I did not tell her that my brother had been shot. We walked silently up the hill to our flat. Mother stopped on the way to buy fresh bread, 'for breakfast!' she said smiling triumphantly as she emerged with a paper bag full of warm, fresh rolls – as if this was just another ordinary day. So like her! But I kept on looking back over my shoulder – I kept on thinking that they would shoot us in the back. Was that their method?*

That night the British forces headed by George Jellicoe and officers of his crack commando unit the SBS (Special Boat Service) had landed outside Athens. But I did not know this. Nor did I know that Frank Macaskie – the legendary 'Scarlet Pimpernel', Chris Woodhouse and other British officers were already in Athens. Desperately weak and tired, when we reached the flat I fell into bed. I wanted to cry for hours but no tears came. I wanted to know if the German officer was right – were my father and brother dead? Just as I was falling asleep I heard a rap on the front door. I was too frightened to open it but stood inside and shouted out, 'who is it?' The familiar voice of Costa, the old porter, answered from behind the door; 'Miss, I have a parcel for you!' he said. I opened the door and Costa handed me the sponge bag which Mother had wrapped in a towel and which contained the jewellery she had thrown out of the window when we had been arrested. 'Welcome back, happy hour!' he gave me that traditional Greek greeting. I saw he had lost weight, his movements were slower and his face deeply lined. 'Yes,' he explained, noticing the way I was looking at him. 'We had trouble getting food but it will be better now the Russians are coming.' I could not believe the strength, honesty and devotion of this poor man who could so easily have sold our jewellery to keep his family – but had not done so. But why did he think that the Russians would be coming? I remembered then that his son was said to be fighting in the mountains with the left-wing guerrillas, ELAS, so perhaps he knew, or perhaps he had got it wrong.

I opened the bag and took out and looked at Mother's eighteenth-century French diamond brooch. It had been my grandmother's, but somehow now it looked so out of place. What was the use of such a

---

* I learned later that the Germans had shot all their camp 'informers' before their retreat.

delicate, sparkling cluster of diamond flowers tied up with a blue enamel bow? I did not know then that one day I would wear it with deep affection – as I do today. There are several stones missing, cracked as they hit the pavement. But I will never replace them.

PART IV

Liberation

10

Liberation

'. . . As the result of these revolutions, there was general deterioration of character throughout the Greek world. The simple way of looking at things, which is so much the mark of a noble nature, was regarded as a ridiculous quality and soon ceased to exist. Society had become divided into two ideologically hostile camps, and each side viewed the other with suspicion . . .'

Thucydides, *History of the Peloponnesian War*, Book III

When I woke at dawn the next morning I did not know what time it was. Was it still night or was it daytime? I had slept so deeply, but at intervals throughout the night – almost every hour – I had been woken with a start as hideous threats boomed out from loudspeakers which at first seemed to be coming from the foot of mount Hymettus and then advancing – clawing their way – nearer and nearer. 'Death to you fascist collaborators! We will liberate the down-trodden working masses from the reactionary forces of the monarcho-fascist oppressors. Long live the democratic army of EAM – ELAS. EAM – ELAS EAM – ELAS – EAM – ELAS . . .' was their repetitive, angry cry followed by the piercing crack of bullets. I was dazed. What was this? We had been set free – we were alive – the only group to come out of Haidari alive. Now we were being threatened with death – by whom? By shadows? By fellow Greeks and for what? I felt something terrible was going to happen. I felt I was groping for something – reaching for something to hold on to – but there was only darkness. The threats of death, recrimination and violence, opened up old wounds. Now it seemed to me that fighting the Germans was easy. They were there and they were the enemy. But fighting this new, invisible hatred of my own people, these voices behind stones, these shadows behind walls and trees, was shattering.

What did they want? I did not know at that time that civil war had broken out earlier in the mountains between ELAS and the non-Communist resistance bands. I had no idea of the Communist plan to take over Greece when the Germans left. I did not know of the political juggling which had preceded the delicate formation of the Greek government of National Unity which now included members of ELAS and of the Communist Party. And although I had heard that Greek politicians and guerrilla leaders had flown in and out of Greece from time to time – from a hidden mountain runway or rendezvoused with caiques by night – I knew nothing of the Caserta Agreement which outlined what action was to be taken on the liberation of Greece and spelt out the orders to be issued to the armed forces.* But like the majority of Greeks – no, thinking back I would have said like *all* Greeks – Mother and I had just been waiting and praying for this day – the day when we would be liberated by the British. Somehow it had not begun the way we had pictured.

Later in the morning and throughout that day friends of Mother's called to see us and other friends and relations telephoned. They were all amazed and relieved to find us alive. We were hugged and kissed and there were squeals of delight as we were given the latest news, which was that the Germans appeared to be leaving Athens. They were apparently piling into the battered, old, yellow town buses (which, I remembered had by strange coincidence, been bought by the Greek government many years ago from Germany) having first paid homage to the Unkown Warrior and with pomp and ceremony laid a wreath on the tomb at the foot of the 'Old Palace', the Parliament building. Remembering camp days, I thought how typical it was of German discipline, of the German mind, to have found time in their retreat for this final act of reverence. And then yet another disturbing night followed. More vitriolic slogans echoed from the foothills across the Ilissus River – cutting through the black silence of the night – like the angry curses of the ancient gods. It was terrifying. I tried listening to the radio, but there was no solace there either – it only relaying garbled news. One item reported that the friendly Russian forces were coming to save us Greeks, another that the Germans were blowing up all bridges, all electrical and water installations. Both stories were inaccurate – but at that time there was no way of finding out what exactly was happening. Who could one turn to? Who would know the truth? Under the occupation so many people had spent so many years telling lies or half truths – now who could one believe? Mother and I sat up that night, tensely waiting, hardly talking to one another, yet knowing well what was going on in each other's mind.

* Signed in Italy on 26 September 1944 after unanimous agreement had been reached by the Greek government and the Greek guerrilla leaders – both ELAS and EDES – Generals Sarafis and Zervas at a conference presided over by the Supreme Allied Commander General Maitland Wilson (see Appendix III).

At dawn relief came. The telephone rang and a friend of Mother's shouted down the receiver the exciting news. This was that the British had actually landed and were marching towards Athens without meeting much German resistance. Mother's friend had a friend, who had been rung up by a friend (this was always the way in Greece), whose friend had actually seen some British soldiers with her very own eyes. I remember quickly snatching up my best dress from the wardrobe – red and white gingham – which I had proudly cut out of a tablecloth as materials were expensive and scarce during the occupation. With a group of friends who had been rustled up in no time, I hurried down the hill to Constitution Square – Athenians' favourite venue for political gatherings and it could be said the centre of the Athens world. On the way I pictured – in rather a silly manner I realized later – a fine military parade with gay columns of dragoon guards, brass bands and fanfare. Something resembling what I had seen when Nell had taken my brother and me to the Royal Tournament. But instead, after a long wait, I caught sight of a single thin line of British commandos in drab, dusty battledress and a small group of sun-tanned SBS (Special Boat Service) officers led by a young, slightly dishevelled-looking commander. On closer inspection I noted that the SBS rather self-consciously sported dashingly-cut uniforms, with rows and rows of medals pinned on them and at least one or two bars to their purple-and-white MCs.* That morning they looked like bronzed gods – or so their image is still imprinted on my mind. On arrival at the square their commander, who later I learnt was Lord Jellicoe, disappeared into the Grande Bretagne Hotel – so recently the German headquarters. When he reappeared on the balcony overlooking the square, after what had obviously been a wash, shave and brush-up, the crowd was ecstatic. George Jellicoe, I remember, was then a young man of medium height, square shoulders, curly brown hair, a quick, engaging smile and a determined walk. I watched his every movement; I was fascinated. But then I thought I saw – standing between two of his officers, behind my hero – yes, was it? Could it be? No, yes, it was – Sophia, a former Haidari inmate who had offered to 'serve' the camp commandant in his quarters in order to get better food and treatment. She was a buxom girl with a lustrous mop of chestnut hair, curved, new-moon eyebrows, a full and pouting mouth and large, innocent, blue eyes. She was obviously going to serve the British now.

'Yellicoe! Yellicoe!' the crowd shouted, looking up at the young brigadier and waving their paper flags which were suddenly and inexplicably on sale everywhere. Then the crowds yelled, '*Sti Poli, Sti Poli!*' ('To the

* Military Cross

city! To the city!')*. A cry that the weary, liberating forces had to have explained to them, as not unnaturally they were unaware of that eternal Greek ambition to regain their lost Byzantine empire – particularly at this point! Although I do remember being told that earlier, when British officials were drawing up their final plans for 'Operation Manna' – the code name for the landings in Greece, they had been made well aware of the deep-seated feelings and forebodings which had governed Greek life since the fall of Constantinople in 1453. Apparently, when General Wilson had fixed 15 October as D-Day for Greece, with the official entry into Athens by the Greek government to take place on 17 October, the Greek Prime Minister George Papandreou had immediately demanded that the plan be changed. He had remained adamant, arguing that ever since the fall of Constantinople – which had occurred on a *Tuesday* – no Greek and certainly no member of his government would make an important move or decision on a Tuesday. And 17 October was a Tuesday. But the British authorities refused to budge and stuck to the original timetable – ignoring what they believed to be a ridiculous Greek superstition. So the top British officials, Harold Macmillan, (Resident British Minister in Cairo), and General Scobie (British general commanding Allied forces for the liberation), had sailed from Naples on 14 October at 0001 hours exactly. (Incidentally, that was at one minute past midnight, so as not to sail on 13 October, which was a Friday – was this not an Anglo-Saxon superstition?) On 17 October the VIPs came into Athens incognito – but of course all Athens knew, and I had a good view of them from my balcony. Meanwhile the Greek government had sailed from Taranto on 15 October in a Canadian ship as originally planned and rendezvoused in the Peloponnese in the Bay of Poros with the old, prestigious Greek battleship, the *Averoff*, which had sailed from Alexandria. But at Poros the schedule went awry. There was some delay in transferring to the *Averoff*, or as Reginald Leeper, HM Ambassador to the Greek government put it to me later – there was 'no hurry'.† The members of the government landed, shook hands, hugged and exchanged kisses with the joyful islanders who then led them up the hill to the blue-domed Church of St George. There the bearded priest chanted a moving thanksgiving liturgy. Candles were lit beneath the flaking icons, and the officials kissed the jewelled cross. Afterwards there were emotional tears as members of the government and officials and the Greek sailors – many of whom had not stepped on Greek soil for some four years – crossed themselves as they embarked on the *Averoff* and sailed towards

---

* I.e. Constantinople (the 'city', in Greek *poli*), founded as the colony of Byzantium by the Greeks and rebuilt by Constantine the Great.

† See also Reginald Leeper, *When Greek meets Greek*, p. 75 (Chatto & Windus).

Piraeus. Progress was slow in the old – only just seaworthy – ship which crawled through the network of minefields laid by the Germans, and it was dark before the lights of Athens came into view. (The Athens power station had been saved by a group of ELAS men and a British officer – Frank Macaskie – but the real hero of the operation was an old man who, when stopped by the German sabotage squad and asked the way to the power station, had pointed them in the opposite direction. (After a while the Germans had returned, asked him the way once again; when he repeated his directions they shot him.)

There was no question of trying to dock that night – and perhaps there had never been any question of it either. For it was on the following morning, in brilliant sunlight, that the *Averoff* – puffing out clouds of smoke and flying a giant Greek flag – anchored off the port of Piraeus. The Greek government – worthy of the wiles of Odysseus – then made their triumphal entrance into Athens. By then it was *Wednesday*, 18 October.

But for me, looking back on those days, whether it was 11, 12, 13, 17, or 18 October – it did not matter. And I cannot remember exactly what happened or on which day. All those days are now telescoped in my mind into a jumble of happy, unexpected, moving, amazing pictures which seemed to appear, turn up, click and go away again like lantern slides. In the streets I recall how British soldiers were swept off their feet, kissed, carried shoulder-high and crowned with flowers. At the *Te Deum* in the cathedral Archbishop Damaskinos showered rose petals on those British heroes who had been the first to re-enter Athens – George Jellicoe and Frank Macaskie and others. American, British and Russian flags were everywhere – who had produced them and where they had been hiding all these years, no one knew or cared. '*Zito Ellas! Zito Anglia! Zito Ameriki!*' ('Long live Greece! Long live Britain! Long live America!') were the cries of joy that mingled with the strident repetitive shouts from the EAM/ELAS* processions of young boys and girls who hurled out their ochlocratic slogans without understanding them but firmly and precisely – like a lesson they had learnt at school. Fierce-looking, bearded and bandoleered guerrillas were about too – although officially they should not have entered the capital with their arms. In the poorer districts of the city, below Mount Hymettus, below the Acropolis and round the port of Piraeus all the walls were splattered with blood-red Communist slogans. Looking down on all this one could have expected to find the ambivalent, smiling gods of Greek mythology, but it was their temple,

---

* The Communist guerrillas had cleverly chosen the initials ELAS resembling Ellas when spoken and also Greek for Helas – or Greece. The ambiguity was intentional.

the Acropolis, floodlit – in spite of the fact that the Germans had not yet left Greece – shining serenely, white against the velvet black sky that I will always remember. Also that garish sign on the Acropolis rock facing the city lit by harsh electric bulbs which read 'EAM'. This jarring picture was a taste of what was to come.

There were parties – I remember – and suddenly I felt like Alice – walking through to another world. People were talking openly, laughing and joking. I also remember being teased by Shan Sedgwick (*New York Times* correspondent and Marina Sulzberger's uncle) who was now back with us in his flat in Athens. He had come into Athens with George Jellicoe's SBS men and when he saw me excitedly looking out towards Piraeus, at the ships which were bringing in the desperately needed food supplies he said, with a wicked twinkle in his eye, 'It will be some time my dear before you see any of it. It has to be wrapped in plastic first to keep the germs out'. Of course, at that time we had neither seen nor known about plastic wrapping. And actually, the delay in unloading was due to the port being damaged by the Germans, and to the dockworkers insisting on being paid in kind or in gold sovereigns rather than in 'paper money' (i.e. British military currency notes).

But naturally my first thoughts had been to find out whether my father and brother were alive. And it was from Ian Patterson,* the son of a doctor, a neighbour of ours in Wimpole Street and a friend of my brother's, that I heard the glad news. They were both safe and well. Ian was a towering, strong, wide-shouldered young officer with a wisp of sunbleached hair that always fell over his forehead. He was utterly fearless, and had parachuted into Greece on 4 September while the Germans were still there. At Corinth his SBS squadron had been attacked by the retreating Germans, but hiding by day he had been able to continue his progress towards Athens. On his final lap he had joined George Jellicoe on a caique which had skirted the coast until they arrived at Scaramanga some nine miles from Athens on 12 October. It was dark when they landed and there appeared to be no means of transport to get them into Athens although they were under urgent orders to reach the capital as soon as possible. Scouting around, they luckily stumbled across two abandoned bicycles that the Germans had left behind. And although historians may well forget to relate this detail, it was very early the following morning, on 13 October, that the two first British officers of the liberating forces – Ian and George – reached the capital, entering Athens – or rather riding into Athens in a somewhat unexpected fashion.

At the continuous chain of parties – one seemed to go from one cele-

---

* Tragically killed in December 1944 in an air crash near Brindisi.

bration to the next, gathering up groups of new friends as one went – I saw and talked to people I had only heard of by their code names. I learnt the details of their daring exploits which up to now had only been whispered, suggested and passed on by word of mouth – often incorrectly. But that day they were all there – real people – not just names. The Greeks were happy to describe their experiences but often their drawn faces were masked by sadness as they remembered those who had not lived to see this day, friends who had been caught and shot. And then many of them, I noticed, were still convalescing from the noose – the tight German stanglehold that had gripped them for so many years. The British officers, on the other hand were lively, gay, relaxed and happy. Their's had been a clean war in comparison. As one Greek put it, 'You were able to fight, blow up installations and get away. We, our families and our homes were left behind'. There was no bitterness – it was just another kind of war.

Unexpectedly many of the British officers I met spoke Greek and several of them were classics scholars. They all talked of their love of Greece and of their admiration and affection for the peasants and the fishermen who had so often saved them, hidden them and helped them. But I think they were unconsciously looking on Greece as part of the classical world they had studied, loved and revered – confusing or seeking the ancient Greece they thought they knew in the modern war-torn Greece that they had found.

New names, new faces, as I look back, so many come to mind; not in the order I met them but just as if I were picking out pictures at random from a jumbled-up pile of photographs. George Jellicoe, Frank Macaskie, Xan Fielding, Nigel Clive, Paddy Leigh Fermor, Billy Moss, Derek Dodson, Andy Lassen are but the few I see before me. Yet Greek history books should record their names and their exploits for posterity, for they and others too, harassed the Germans, delayed their reinforcements, upset their military timetables and plans and played such an important part in the liberation of Greece. Far from their own country, far from their military base and often without adequate instructions, they had to take their own quick decisions on how best to fight the Germans. Inevitably, some became entangled in politics. In the same deep-rooted Greek political factions that today try to obliterate the love, daring and bravery of the British and Americans who operated clandestinely throughout the occupation – and even attempt to wipe out the memory of the frenzied joy with which the Greeks greeted their liberators in October 1944 – a picture and an emotion I can never forget, because I was there.

Paddy Leigh Fermor was perhaps one of Britain's most colourful and dashing heroes; though today he would be the first to say he was not.

He had lived in Greece before the war – at one time in a mill surrounded by lemon groves – and during the occupation he was dropped into Crete where his exploits have become legendary. He now lives in the Mani and is a writer of repute. Although I must have met him quite late after liberation, I still recall that his Cretan noises and gestures – picked up when he was in the Cretan mountains – surpassed any I had ever met. His *'Ya sou'* ('hail', or 'to your health!') was much louder than any Cretan's, his slap so much harder and his embrace a danger to one's ribs. This was youthful exuberance rather than heartiness. But it was his ebullient torrent of words, in almost any language, interlaced with classical quotations and his lively mind that are most vivid in my memory. It was Paddy who, with the help of Cretan guerrillas, had kidnapped the German commander of the 22nd *Panzergrenadier* Division in Crete, General Kreipe. The tale has been told* but for those who do not know it I must briefly give an outline of this brave and memorable escapade, as told to me by Paddy. And it was typical of Paddy that when he referred to the operation he always dismissed the personal risk and danger he had run, emphasizing the role of the Cretans, the guerrillas, peasants, shepherds and runners who became his friends.

During the Greco-Albanian war Paddy, at that time a young lieutenant, was first posted as liaison officer with the Greek army and then evacuated from Crete when the island fell in 1941. A year later, dressed as a shepherd, he infiltrated into Crete by sea to report on German positions, military strength and defences and to help organize the resistance. For over a year he carried out his mission hiding in caves with his wireless, often depending on snails and dandelion leaves for his diet or sharing the meagre supplies of friendly Cretans. After eighteen months in the mountains he came out of Crete by motor torpedo boat sent from Mersa Matruh together with the Italian general commanding the Siena Division in east Crete and some of his staff. (This was after the Italian surrender in September 1943.) But before Paddy left the island, a force of Cretan partisans, thinking an Allied invasion was impending, attacked a German outpost. The outraged Germans retaliated by ordering a large-scale sweep through the mountains, and a major battle ensued, villages were burnt and many Cretans rounded up and shot in reprisal. The German general responsible for the punitive operation was General Müller.†

Meditating in his mountain hideout, Paddy had for some time had the notion of waylaying a German general and taking him off the island – Müller's action stiffened his resolve and indicated the general as his

---

* W. (Bill) Stanley Moss's account is to be found in *Ill Met by Moonlight* (Harrap Ltd).
† General Müller was sentenced to death at a war-crimes trial in Athens in 1945.

target. In Paddy's words, he was 'to be captured without bloodshed and removed (with the help of Cretan forces) without, in German eyes, seeming to involve the Cretans, so as to avoid the excuse for reprisals'. Paddy saw this as an act that would raise Cretan morale after the horrors inflicted by the Germans on their villages; he also thought that the Germans could well interpret the action as a prelude to an Allied landing on the island, and that this might tie down more German troops.

Returning to Cairo, Paddy suggested the scheme to the headquarters of SOE, the Special Operations Executive, who were responsible for the execution of operations in Greece. They were immediately in favour as they too believed that it would give the impression of an impending invasion of the island, a threat that Allied forces might after all, land, and so force the Germans to increase their manpower on Crete at a time when it was badly needed elsewhere. Paddy was put in charge of the operation and, with his Cretan guide and friend Manoli Paterakis, and a seasoned campaigner, George Tirakis as a nucleus, he was left to find a British second-in-command. The first two men he chose somehow did not work out and finally he found Bill Stanley Moss – an enthusiastic, daring and debonair Coldstream Guardsman who was as keen as Paddy on the plan. And they became great friends.

The two Cretans and Paddy then went off to Palestine for instruction and training, returning later to join Bill in a house named Tara on the banks of the Nile which became famous for the sanctuary it offered those who came in and out from dare-devil operations in the Balkans. Other occupants of the house included a Polish Princess Tarnowska, who had escaped through the Balkans and sought refuge in Cairo, Billy MacLean of the Scots Greys, David Smiley of the Horse Guards and Xan Fielding.

Endless frustrating delays and setbacks followed and it was not until 4 February 1944 that the plane carrying Paddy's party and their supplies took off for Crete from Brindisi. As only one person at a time could be dropped, the plane dropped Paddy off first and he landed safely on a small plateau. But then the weather closed in and after several attempts to find an opening in the clouds the plane lost its way and was forced to return to Brindisi with the other three members of the party. Two months later, on 4 April, and after several abortive efforts to drop by parachute, the remainder of the party landed in a dinghy from a motor launch on the southern coast where Paddy met them on the beach. Many forced night marches followed until a hideout was reached in the mountains south-east of Heraklion, near the general's headquarters. Paddy then gathered the rest of his party, all tough and tried Cretan friends from the last two years, and left them with the others in the mountain hideout while he, with his 'man in Heraklion', Miki Akoumianakis who knew the area well, made their way to Knossos. Their objective was to spy out the land around the general's villa, the Ariadne, which had been the home of the archaeologist, Sir Arthur Evans, and to take careful note of the general's car, its colour, headlights and travelling schedule. Armed with these and other details, the plan was now formed, and Paddy rejoined his party in the mountains. Then, unexpectedly, General Müller was sent to the Russian front and replaced by General Kreipe. Paddy reported this to GHQ Cairo who replied: 'Proceed with operation!'

It was Eastertime when Paddy and the party left the mountains and force marched for two nights, stopping near Knossos in their chosen hideout – a house in a vineyard. From there they checked on Kreipe's routine – noted that he liked a game of bridge in the evenings and travelled twice daily from his villa to his headquarters at Ano Arkhanes sitting in front with his driver in his brand-new Opel. Paddy knew that the vineyard hide-out, in the heart of the German garrison, was dangerous – there were Germans everywhere, so he decided to move fast and set 24 April for the date of the operation. Final preparations were made and positions taken up. But on that day the general's schedule changed – he arrived late in the afternoon at his headquarters and left early to return to his villa – and as the ambush could only be carried out safely after dark the plan was shelved for two days. On 26 April the party went into action. The group, which now included a Cretan policeman Stratis Saviolakis, who was to direct them on their route through Heraklion, divided up in ditches on either side of the road the general took every night. At a given signal from those who had first spotted the general's car, Paddy and Bill, who had changed into German police uniforms (somehow obtained by Miki for them) stood in the middle of the road. They flashed their red torches, shouted 'Halt!' in their best gutteral German, and stopped the general's car pretending it was a traffic check. Paddy then asked for the general's papers, and while he was explaining and protesting, Paddy opened the door and seized him, while Manoli and the others tied him up. Meanwhile Bill knocked out the driver with his life preserver, took the wheel – and the driver's hat. The general was then bundled into the back and held down by Manoli, George and Stratis. 'All took under a minute' – or so Paddy recalled! They drove on to Heraklion, the largest town in Crete, and therefore the most unexpected place. The general's guards, seeing the pennants flying, presented arms as they passed the Villa Ariadne, and this smart military procedure was repeated at the twenty-two roadblocks they passed. On the journey the general started searching for his hat – but that was now on Paddy's head. He also searched for his decorations which had fallen off during the tussle – but Bill assured him he could easily arrange for replicas.

When they drove through Heraklion, as it was Saturday night the town was full of troops meandering in the streets and progress was slow as they honked their way through the crowds. As they reached the west gate a platoon tried to stop them but Paddy barked: *'General's Wagen'* and was immediately given a brisk salute. They drove on to the foothills of Mount Ida where the general, Bill, Manoli and Stratis left the car to begin their march towards Anoyia. Paddy and George drove on another five kilometres or so and ditched the car near the coast, at a point which the Germans knew was used by pick-up submarines. This was meant to give the impression that the party had already left for the Middle East. Inside the car they left the following note:

TO THE GERMAN AUTHORITIES IN CRETE

Gentlemen,
Your Divisional Commander, General KREIPE was captured a short time ago by a BRITISH raiding force under our command. By the time you read this both he and we will be on our way to CAIRO.

We would like to point out most emphatically that this operation has been carried out without the help of CRETANS or CRETAN partisans, and the only guides used were serving soldiers of HIS HELLENIC MAJESTY'S FORCES in the Middle East, who came with us.

Your General is an honourable prisoner of war, and will be treated with all the consideration owing to his rank.

Any reprisals against the local population will be wholly unwarranted and unjust.

Auf baldiges Wiedersehen! [See you soon!]
PS We are very sorry to have to leave this beautiful car behind.

Paddy also left two 'clues' in the back of the car – a commando beret and a greatcoat. He then joined up with the others and the long trek began. At times they had to march through snow and ice and blizzards as they climbed up Mount Ida to reach the British wireless post. But they were always helped by local guerrillas and shepherds who showed them the way and led them to safe caves and shepherds' huts where they would hide in the day time, moving on at night.

After Paddy had relayed a message to Cairo giving their progress and arranging for a boat to pick them up, they continued their march and, because the general's progress was slow – either on purpose or as a result of a leg injury he had suffered when he was dragged out of his car – he was given a mule. The journey was long, tedious and tricky. They had to avoid the German troops now on the alert, searching every-where, and their planes which flew low, dropping leaflets. But an army of friendly runners from the guerrillas, and shepherds and peasants were

their faithful guides, rushing them from one cave to another and mis-
directing the Germans. Local villagers also brought them food. Many
of these were Paddy's old friends and companions in the mountains and
they would often arrive with generous baskets of bread, cheese and wine
or *Raki* (the equivalent of French Marc). There were times though, Paddy
remembered, when dandelion leaves were their only fare. The general,
as it happened, turned out to be a classics scholar and Paddy and he
would often cap each other's quotations. Once, during a lull in the pursuit
... just as a brilliant dawn was breaking over the crest of Mount Ida
the general murmured to himself:

> *Vides ut alta stet nive*
> *Soracte....*

And being one of the quotations from Horace that Paddy knew, he continued from where the general had broken off:

> *nec jam sustineant onus*
> *Silvae laborantes, geluque*
> *Flumina constiterint acuto*

At that moment Paddy said, 'The general's blue eyes had swivelled away
from the mountain top to mine ... things were different between us
for the rest of our time together.'† Although there were of course days
when the general complained bitterly about the cold and the pain in
his shoulder, which he had hurt when he slipped off his mule, he was
well looked after. His arm was put in a sling, Bill shared his blanket
with him – and found that the general spent most of the time pulling
it over to his side – and Bill also lent him his greatcoat to keep him
warm.

After several false alerts, many garbled messages and many narrow
escapes from the German garrison who had now spread out and occupied
every beach on the southern coast, the party was forced to move west-
wards. Eventually reconnoitring Cretan guerrillas spied a beach free of
Germans at Rhodakino, and the party dropped down to meet their boat.
On 14 May, as the small craft sailed away, farewells and shouts of '*Kali
Niki!*' (good victory!') came from the stern and were echoed back by
the fifty or so guerrillas, shepherds and friends who had gathered in
the caves until the little boat was swallowed up by the night.

Much later Bill learnt from an Austrian prisoner that the escapade
had been a favourite joke in the Vienna cafés – particularly as the general
had just been promoted to lieutenant-general the day of his abduction.

* Horace, *Ode*, I.ix 'Ad Thaliarchum'.
† Patrick Leigh Fermor, *A Time of Gifts* (John Murray Publishers Ltd).

I have other pictures too that now spring to mind. There is one of Xan Fielding, an officer who, like Paddy Leigh Fermor, had lived in hiding in Crete. When I first met Xan in Athens he had been operating in Crete for long periods on and off since 1942. He was a slim, dark, handsome young man – like a polished bronze statue; he had inviting dark-brown eyes and gathered ladies round him like a maypole. He was a brilliant classics scholar who spoke fluent Greek and French. On the two occasions when he was infiltrated into Crete he had landed in a howling gale. His first 'drop' was made from the British submarine, the *Torbay*, his second, from the Greek submarine, the *Papanicolis*. On his second trip, as he paddled ashore in a dinghy with Arthur Reade* the sea was so rough that he lost all his carefully collected gear and was left to find his bearings 'blind' – with a wrapped-up torch and an unintelligible map, proudly provided by GHQ Cairo, which was printed on fabric and too small to decipher. Soaking wet and freezing when he landed, Xan remembered lighting a fire to dry out, using damp twigs boosted by his ether pads which, although supplied for knocking out German sentries 'quietly', acted as excellent firelighters.†

During the occupation there were several British officers operating in Crete – coming in and out – and among those who were there with Xan, were Paddy and Monty Woodhouse. When hiding in the mountains they were usually disguised as mustachioed Cretan shepherds: Xan wore a shepherd's cloak, black boots and a knotted black turban; Paddy's Cretan guise had been especially tailored and he sported a dashing waistcoat, while Monty dispensed with the moustache and looked every inch a handsome fair-haired Englishman in Cretan dress. Xan lived in mountain hideouts with his guides throughout his stay on the island and organized resistance bands – trekking for miles across the mountains; he also evacuated Cretan agents when the Germans were on their trail, and collected and arranged the evacuation of Australian and New Zealand troops.‡ There were a number of these valiant stragglers – former members of the British Expeditionary Force – who had been in hiding since the evacuation in 1941. Xan one day came across a dangerously noisy drunken party of theirs in a village café where they had been waiting for a boat which had never surfaced. Drowning their sorrow in wine, they were singing 'Waltzing Matilda' – which they repeated over and over again at the tops of their voices – oblivious of the fact that there were Germans around.

* Captain (later Major) A.E.E. Reade was a barrister and a member of the prosecution at the Nuremberg trials.
† Xan Fielding, *Hide and Seek*, p. 113 (Secker and Warburg Ltd).
‡ See Appendix I.

Xan's instructions from GHQ included the collection and transmission of intelligence reports over a hidden wireless. This was not always easy as the equipment often had to be moved in haste – hidden and then moved again, and Xan remembered the agony of struggling across the mountains weighed down by the leaden batteries. But unfortunately the whereabouts of the set became known only too frequently 'to everyone between heaven and Charing Cross' as Monty once remarked. This was not due to spies but rather to the gallant Cretans' vociferous enthusiasm which at times was difficult to contain before the echoes reached the enemy's ears. And such was Cretan unbounded friendship and warmth that Xan often found his hideout cave packed with enthusiastic villagers who cared little for their safety as they brought him and his party generous gifts of fresh baked bread and wine which they could ill afford.

Towards the end of his stay on the island Xan had several narrow escapes from the Germans but somehow he was saved in the nick of time by his intrepid Cretan guides, by his village friends and by sheer luck. Both Xan and Paddy often had to take the risk of visiting their agents in their village homes and, although coming out of hiding was dangerous, they were delighted to be able to sit on a chair rather than be crouching in a cave and their presence always boosted their agent's morale. There were occasions when they would come across Germans who were being entertained by their Cretan hosts and the scruffy British pair would be unabashedly introduced as 'our poor village cousins'.* It was useful and important for their agents to have friendly contacts with the Germans as they could pick up valuable information without being suspected. But there was one night which Xan remembers and described in detail† when he and Paddy joined a party at the mayor's house in the village of Prines. There they found two German sergeants rather the worse for drink who, after they had welcomed the new arrivals over-effusively, insisted on linking arms and singing *Brüderschaft*. As they were going through the tedious ritual, Xan felt his cloak slipping off and a moment later he noticed one of the Germans staring at the bulge in his jacket where he had hidden his Colt. The sergeant then lurched towards him and putting his hand on the bulge looked straight into Xan's eyes and muttered, 'Good night *cousin*' – emphasizing the *cousin* as he reeled out of the house. Xan never knew if and what the German knew or meant, but he could see that the strain on the Germans was beginning to tell.

Like many young officers in SOE Xan resented the amateurishness of

---

* For Cretans Xan's cover name was 'Aleko', Paddy's 'Michali' or 'Phileden'.
† Also in Xan Fielding, *Hide and Seek*, p. 154 (Secker and Warburg Ltd).

the outfit and its frequently pointless sabotage schemes which too often risked lives unnecessarily. There was for instance their plan to sink HMS *York* which was lying in Souda harbour and which the Germans were preparing to man themselves – an indignity the British navy could not allow. SOE believed the ship could easily be blown up by its agents diving under the ship, and Xan spent some time practising swimming (and often sinking) with dummy explosives tied round his body. This mock rehearsal for an impossible operation took place at the Haifa 'sabotage school' which Xan attended before returning to Crete. But on arriving back on the island he saw that the harbour was surrounded by Germans, and signalled Cairo that the best plan would be to bomb the ship from the air. And this was done successfully.

One of the most ridiculous schemes though, which was thought up by SOE, was a propaganda exercise which entailed dropping off on the Germans – at great personal risk – pornographic material such as a picture of a blond German wife lying in the arms of her Italian lover – both in a state of some excitement. The object of the scheme no doubt was to make a jealous husband immediately fly back home. None could or would. Finally for Xan there was GHQ's ill-timed plan to send him off to France for what he recalled as being 'a brief and inglorious drop' on the eve of the Allied landings where his presence was an embarrassment to hard-pressed resistance agents, and no help. In fact just two days after landing he was captured by the Gestapo and as he was in civilian clothes he was condemned to death. A few hours before his execution, his release was engineered, at the risk of her life, by the Polish resistance heroine Cristine Granville.* She warned the French *milicien* in charge of the prisoners that although the Germans would be considered as prisoners-of-war by the Allied troops who were landing, he as a Frenchman would be held responsible for the death of important agents, and would be shot. With this in mind the *milicien* drove Xan and the other agents out of the prison and delivered them safely into Cristine's hands. But why had he been dropped at that time? And why should GHQ have thought up a scheme that put the resistance agents at risk?

On his way back from France Xan stopped off at Bari, now SOE's HQ for operations in the Mediterranean. There he learnt that there were no plans for an Allied landing on Crete – something he realized would be a great blow to his Cretan friends who had for so long prepared for a British landing and a glorious internal uprising. But with Greece still in mind he managed to get himself attached to a commando unit which was stationed on the island of Poros and from there sailed towards

* Murdered in London in 1952, victim of a *crime passionnel*.

Athens. He was hoping to be among the first to enter the city, but in his own words 'I was pipped at the post by George Jellicoe'. He can't have been very late as I remember him so well at those first memorable liberation parties.

Then there is Nigel Clive, another British officer I recall. He was tall, ash-blond, with oversized blue eyes and a serious baby face which lit up when he spoke perfect, carefully articulated Greek to the accompaniment of very Greek hand gestures. When I first met him, Nigel had been living for some time in the mountains with the EDES Zervas guerrillas. He had been sent out by one undercover organisation – SIS* which was at loggerheads in Greece with another – SOE.† SIS believed that SOE was too busy on the political front – trying to unite the rival guerrilla and political groups, instead of concentrating on the 'main' enemy – the Germans. So Nigel's SIS orders from the Greek Office in Cairo were to keep out of politics; to report on the German order of battle that might face an Allied landing and to keep his reports separate from SOE but remain on good terms with them. When he asked about his predecessor, a Greek American called Costa Lawrence, who turned out not to be a Greek American and who was shot by SOE – the information he received was scrappy. There was talk of his being a double agent, of his signalling British positions in the mountains and of his open dislike for Zervas's EDES – to whom he was attached – and loud admiration for the Communist-led ELAS.

Nigel, under his new code name, Captain Jim Russell, was dropped in Epirus on 19 December 1943. Within a few months he had got himself into training for the unexpectedly tough, long, weary treks over the scraggy Greek mountains. And he had also adapted himself to Greek mountain village life so well that he found it easy to send Cairo the information the office wanted on General Hubert Lanz's battle orders. These he obtained in a manner SIS might well have disapproved of, as it was not, to say the least, a classic covert operation. Instead, Nigel very soon found out that every villager in the area knew what he was up to and was over-eager to help – to give him information or to collect it for him. And as every villager knew or invented everything about everybody and loved to tell his tale, very soon all names of German agents, spies, or suspected spies, as well as double agents and reliable

---

* SIS was the Secret Intelligence Service which collected intelligence and reported to the Foreign Office. It was headed by Sir Stewart Menzies whose office was in Broadway and who had Churchill's ready ear.

† The more powerful SOE, Special Operations Executive, came under the Ministry of Economic Warfare. It was headed by Lord Selborne with offices in Baker Street. Its agents carried out undercover operations, such as sabotage and the general harassment of the enemy.

sources were being passed on to Nigel. He also found that illiterate peasants and shepherds standing above the main roads and passes were able to give him the important and accurate details of the troop movements he needed. All this intelligence, once carefully sifted and with the embroidery cut out, was passed on to Cairo, who were duly impressed. The wireless used for this purpose had been mended by SOE's technicians, who were always extremely helpful to him. His own set had been put out of action when damaged on his parachute drop.

During the many months he spent living with the Greek villagers, Nigel shared their lives, their food – always so generously given – and their fears. Fears of German reprisals, fears from the threats of rival Communist guerrilla bands, fears from counterthreats from the puppet government's security battalions. He reported this state of affairs to Cairo, who appeared to be beginning to take an interest. He also drew their attention to the dangerous political rivalries among the guerrilla bands and the imminent danger of civil war which was being carefully fanned by the German support for the security battalions and their attempted contacts with Zervas. But no notice was taken of his warnings. His political reports were never passed on to London or to the Foreign Office. And alas! his military reports, as he later learnt, had been regularly intercepted by Lanz who had broken the code and knew all, but strangely enough had not acted.*

Derek Dodson† is another young officer I remember; he was known among our group of friends as the 'Scottish Baby'. Barely twenty-three when he first came to Greece, he looked much younger. He was an elegant, long-limbed, pencil-slim, round-faced young man with a snub nose, gay flashing eyes and a ready, engaging laugh. His close-fitting Royal Fusilier tartan trews were, I recall, the toast of the Athens maidens and later of the Salonica waterfront tavernas. But by the time I had met him in Athens he had been in and out of Greece three times – small wonder that my SS interrogator had referred to the Cairo 'run' as a honeymoon. The first experience Derek had of Greece was in September 1943 when he landed with the somewhat disgruntled EAM/ELAS delegation who had previously flown out to Cairo to pressurize the Allies – unsuccessfully as it turned out. (They had insisted that the King should not return before a plebiscite had been held and that the EAM/ELAS guerrillas should be officially recognized by the Greek government-in-exile. On liberation they demanded that EAM/ELAS become an integral part of the Greek national army and the civil administration.)

---

* Nigel Clive, *A Greek Experience* (Michael Russell).
† Now Sir Derek Dodson, KCMG, MC.

Derek's plane landed on an isolated strip near Kardhitsa in Thessaly, so well hidden that the plane nearly took a few grazing cows along with it as it taxied to a halt. Seconded to Force 133, which was part of SOE, Derek had orders to report back, among other things, on German positions and strength. I remember him saying that the officer who briefed him in Cairo evidently thought he was wasting his time. But it so happened, that just before Derek landed in Greece, the Italian General Infante, commander of the *Pinerolo* Division, had surrendered with the majority of his troops* and Derek was able to obtain from him the complete order-of-battle of the Axis forces in the Balkans. This he telegraphed back to Cairo. After continuing north on foot as far as Pendalophon, contacting the allied Mission on the way, Derek eventually returned by air to Cairo on 21 October.

Before his second trip to Greece in January 1944, he was briefed in Cairo by Brigadier Barker-Benfield who rounded off his instructions by warning Derek – just as my brother had been told too – not to 'carry on like the Greeks' and be sure to dig a latrine! Derek of course had no intention of digging a latrine on the stony mountain side and anyhow did not have the time when he parachuted into Epirus to meet EDES's General Zervas who was being harassed by ELAS. A month later, in February, he witnessed the signing of the Plaka agreement – Chris Woodhouse's attempt to bring together the warring factions of the resistance movements under Allied command.† On 15 March he returned once again to Cairo. This time he took a caique from Pelion to Turkey. On landing in Turkey he was nearly arrested as his agent had somehow missed him and he was found crossing the main square of Izmir in full British military uniform. He then travelled on to Aleppo where he was immediately fumigated by zealous British de-lousing medical orderlies before being allowed to proceed to Cairo via Damascus and Jerusalem.

Derek went back to Greece for the third time in August 1944, having parachuted into Thessaly with orders to try to obtain a German surrender. He met Frank Macaskie – now under the pseudonym of Major Parkes – and Gianni Georgakis near Athens, but after several unsuccessful meetings nothing was accomplished, and the Germans gradually pulled out,

---

* Although the Italian armistice, which was to turn the Division into co-belligerents, was signed on 11 September 1943 by 'Chris' Woodhouse, AMM, the General Infante and representatives of the Greek guerrillas – those Italians who did fall into ELAS hands often had their boots and uniforms removed. After seeking shelter in the woods some died of hunger and cold.

† The Plaka Agreement was signed by all the main resistance bands, EAM/ELAS, EKKA, EDES, together with 'Chris' Woodhouse for the Greek High Command and AMM and G.K. Wines representing the US component with AMM. It was signed at the Plaka bridge in Epirus on 29 February 1944 to end the civil war between ELAS and EDES.

blowing up bridges and supplies as they went with little harassment from the ELAS guerrillas. Derek and Frank Macaskie eventually reached Megara where they met George Jellicoe and Ian Patterson who had driven from Patras heading a detachment of the SBS. After some parachute troops had been dropped on the Megara airfield Derek set off for Athens in a motor launch.

He arrived in Scaramanga some time after George Jellicoe and Ian Patterson had landed and, like them, he too found no transport available to bring him into Athens. But luckily, just when he was starting off on foot, he caught sight of a fire engine on the main Athens road and scrambled on board. As he entered the centre of the city on this original vehicle he was carried shoulder high by the cheering, flag-waving crowds who deposited him in a somewhat dishevelled state in the hall of the Grande Bretagne Hotel.

A few weeks later he was off again to chase the Germans out of Salonica and was the first man to enter the city on 30 October. Here he was lucky once again, as on arrival he was informed that there was an important Austrian officer in hiding who wanted to join the Free Austrian movement. To his surprise he was taken to George von Schenk, ADC to General Loehr, who was seeking British protection as a prisoner-of-war, fearing the treatment he might suffer at ELAS's hands. As Derek had nowhere to keep a prisoner-of-war, he took von Schenk back to his headquarters, dressed him in British battledress to prevent him being arrested by ELAS, and kept him there for several days until the authorities in Athens were able to send a plane to collect him. He remembered the incongruity of having to take von Schenk out to meals at the local taverna but, incidentally, in return von Schenk gave him the latest German battle order.

Perhaps my favourite picture, and one I look at often as it hangs on the wall in my bedroom in London, is of Frank Macaskie, George Jellicoe and Shan Sedgwick with Archbishop Damaskinos on liberation day. They are lined up as in a school photograph – Frank and George's trousers are baggy and unpressed – but it is a record of that historic day and I treasure it.

When I first met Frank Macaskie* I thought that if Nell had been with me she would have warned me not to fall in love with the first British officer I met. She had after all rightly warned me about falling in love with the first Greek. But all those who knew Frank loved him and he was deeply in love with Greece and Greeks. He was sometimes

---

* Lt. Col. Frank Macaskie DSO, MC Bar. Became *The Times* correspondent in Athens in March 1947. Died in 1952 at the age of thirty-nine.

called the 'Scarlet Pimpernel of Greece', a title earned from his determination and ability to slip through the noose of his Italian and German
jailers. Throughout the occupation Frank had been arrested, broken out
of Greek prisons, hidden in so many Greek houses (often in Gianni Georgakis's home) and made so many Greek friends, that on liberation day
he was hailed and fêted by all Greeks – rich and poor alike – embraced
and welcomed by them as a cherished son, a friend or a loved one.

Born in Yorkshire, Frank had served in the Western Desert and in
Crete with the second battalion of the Leicester Regiment – a regiment
he was, I remember, very proud of. Tall, with a halo of fine golden
hair, almost too handsome, very gentle, with a quiet, caressing voice,
he spoke a little halting Greek and never learnt very much. He had deep-set
blue eyes, a shy stutter and a slight limp – the result of his war wound.
But behind this saintly, romantic façade Frank was strong-willed, firm,
self-sacrificing and heroically courageous. He always disregarded his
safety to help or save others. In October 1944 he reached Athens just
in time to accompany Archbishop Damaskinos (in whose house he had
twice sought refuge) to watch the Germans lay their wreath on the tomb
of the Unknown Warrior on their way out of the capital. That day,
as the crowds gathered round the archbishop's car, they caught their
first glimpse of a young Byronic figure in British uniform – an Englishman
who knew them well and loved them and who was once again risking
his life – hoping that by his early arrival in Athens he could negotiate
some form of political settlement with the aid of Archbishop Damaskinos
which would pre-empt the civil strife he had witnessed in the mountains.
But this was not to be – not then. Only later, after the December
bloodshed.

Frank's experiences from 1941 to 1944, which I picked up in snatches
from Alexis Ladas,* Gianni Georgakis and others who were near him,
might appear Hollywoodesque today. But if this is the picture they give
then it is not in focus. For it must be remembered that all the people
involved were real people – alive one day and perhaps dead the next.
Escaping from the punishment or death cell did not entail just agilely
scaling the prison wall – and Frank, a boxing blue, could do this with
relative ease – but it meant taking the hard decision as to whether, by
flaunting death for himself, he might not be condemning those who
had helped him and were left behind to face the firing squad.

---

* Alexis Ladas, Marina Sulzberger's brother, was a British agent during the occupation. In
  1948 he joined the UN Secretariat and later became Overseas Director of the International
  Services of the *Encyclopaedia Britannica*. He is now Director of the Hellenic Heritage Foundation in New York. He had described his prison experiences in detail in a series of articles
  in *Harpers Magazine* in 1961–4.

Back in 1941 Frank was wounded during the Cretan campaign and taken prisoner by the Germans. After several weeks in a German hospital he was moved to a prison camp and from there he made his first escape – a pattern which was to continue over three years. On this occasion it was Lela Karayanni, one of the most courageous Greek agents, who had saved the lives of a number of British officers and men, who organized his escape together with three other officers. She put them on the road from Athens across the mountains to the Peloponnese where a boat would meet them in a hidden cove. But on the journey one of the officers fell ill and urgent help was needed. At that point they were still dangerously close to the capital but Frank decided to take the risk and, leaving the others behind, he came down alone from the mountains to seek assistance. When he reached the first village, much to his surprise, the villagers were delighted to see and help a British officer, and not in the least afraid. Furthermore, they insisted that he bring down the whole party and arranged to hide them all in village houses. The procedure from then on was in true Greek form – one of the peasants knew a man ... who knew a man ... who put Frank in touch with George Tripanis, a Greek who had studied at Cambridge and who was living in Athens. George hid the party in his Athens home until Frank could contact Cairo on a clandestine radio and arrange for a boat to meet them at the coast. Then once again they all set out for their rendezvous across the mountains, but this time they met the boat without a hitch. It dropped them off in Turkey; from there they took a train to Aleppo, a car to Damascus and finally a train to Jerusalem and Cairo. Those were the stages along the main escape route at that time.

On reaching Cairo Frank decided something must be done to evacuate the large number of British and Commonwealth officers and men who were still hiding in Greece. He knew the danger they faced – he had just experienced it. Using an undercover organization which also ran caiques and sailing boats to and fro from the Greek islands and the Mediterranean coast called IS 9 and later 'A' Force, he began his own caique run. (Incidentally, 'A' Force was the organization my brother had joined when he escaped, and he and Frank met up in Cairo.) But in February 1942 Frank's caique was caught in a storm and was so badly damaged that the skipper had to pull in to the nearest island harbour. This was on the island of Kythnos. While the repairs were being carried out officers of the Italian garrison spotted this strange party – which included Alexis Ladas and one British and one New Zealand soldier – the latter both in uniform and on their way to Cairo – and arrested them. A few days later, as they were being transferred from their jail to the interrogation centre, Frank, Alexis and Ilias the skipper slipped their guards and fled into the mountains. There, friendly shepherds hid them in their huts and fed them until Frank reckoned that enough time had elapsed for the Italians to have given up their search.

Coming down from the mountains they took a small rowing boat which had been found for them by the shepherds and in which they were to row to a neighbouring island where they hoped to pick up a caique. It was a small, old boat which did not attract any attention, but once again a fierce storm blew up, the boat capsized and the party was forced to swim ashore. When they landed in their soaking, tattered clothes they were immediately arrested by the Italians and thrown into jail, bound hand and foot and given hardly any food. Eventually, when the Italians learned the true purpose of their intelligence mission, they were transferred to the Island of Samos to await trial by a military court.

Over the following months which they spent in the cells of the island jail along with other convicts they made several unsuccessful attempts to escape. Once they used piled-up prison benches and another time they constructed a ladder with the wooden side-planks of their prison bunks. But each time – having dropped over the prison wall – they were caught and thrown back into prison; beaten and locked up in an underground punishment cell with rats as their companions and slime on the dank floor.

Their camp commandant, whom they nicknamed 'the Dog', was an Italian bully of a man who, with the avidity of a butterfly collector, prized the rare and beautiful specimen he had in his net – that English captain – while he disregarded the two 'moths', those Greeks who belonged to a conquered nation. Frank's serenity and dignity impressed the brutish man; so did his impeccable appearance – Frank slept on his trousers at night to keep their crease in, always removed any stains or mud from his trousers and shoes and washed his white shirt daily. It was obvious to the commandant that the English captain was a prize not to be lost. Under no circumstances must he be allowed to escape. So one day he announced that a special prison was to be built for them, 'a drawing room', he said with a satisfied smirk. And as the British liked exercise they would now be allowed to walk up and down the yard. But the 'drawing room' turned out to be a thick-walled concrete box with hardly enough room to move in and a slit of a window high up near the ceiling behind bars. Frank was angry when shown into this 'drawing room' and although Alexis and Ilias had hoped for a rest after their unsuccessful attempts to escape, Frank immediately began to work on a plan to get out.

Alexis remembers how between keeping up their spirits singing songs like 'Carry me back to Old Virginny' at the top of their voices, teaching

Ilias English poetry and Frank reciting the ancient Greek epitaph to the three hundred Spartans fallen at Thermopylae, a plot was hatched. There could be no tunnel – the walls were too solid but the bars over the window could be cut if a hacksaw file could somehow be smuggled in. Just at that time the commandant had allowed a young girl, a welfare worker on the Bishop's staff, to bring them food. Her name was Danai, and although Alexis has envisaged meeting a beautiful Greek nymph she was plain, wore a simple black dress and black 'kerchief over her hair. But she was dedicated and one day when the guards were not looking she whispered to Alexis that she wanted to help them. Alexis thought at once of the blade they needed – but how could she smuggle it in as all the food Danai brought was carefully scrutinized – even the bread was cut up into small chunks. Then one night as Alexis lay awake, he hit on an idea – this was that if Frank discarded his shoes, the commandant would have to ask Danai to produce new ones and she could sew a blade into them. The next morning he whispered this message to Danai as she passed him her basket of food. But when he excitedly told Frank about the plan he showed little enthusiasm and was in fact reluctant to part with his carefully kept shoes. In the end, after quite a bit of persuasion, he did agree and joined Alexis and Ilias as they ripped his shoes to pieces. Then to the amazement of the guards at exercise time, Frank marched out into the muddy courtyard – upright but barefooted. This matter was soon reported to the commandant who was livid. He summoned Alexis and demanded an explanation for what had happened, and vented his wrath. Although Alexis was convinced that he was in for another beating he coolly told 'the Dog' that Frank's shoes had worn out and that it was his duty to provide a new pair and not allow a British captain to walk barefoot. He also mentioned something about the Geneva Convention and suggested that Danai might be asked to provide the shoes from her charities. Unexpectedly the commandant agreed, Danai was asked by him to supply new shoes for the English captain and she was able to sew a hacksaw blade in them. The plan had worked. On Christmas Day the delighted commandant produced the boots with pomp and ceremony; they were, it is true, unlike Frank's shoes – they were high boots – black and shiny – and had probably been destined for the bishop. After the presentation Frank asked the commandant if he might see the girl who had provided them to thank her – Danai had only been allowed to contact Alexis, but she longed to meet the heroic British captain – with whom, in her dreams, she was deeply in love. The meeting took place in the presence of the guards. Danai looked into the blue eyes of her hero, trembled and left.

Now with the blade in their hands they could saw through the bars, hoping to mask the noise by singing loudly as they worked. They would then signal with a lighted match to the house next-door and squeeze out of the window one at a time to make their getaway. While all this was being carefully worked out, and freedom was at last within reach, Frank suddenly asked where they were going to pick up Danai? Alexis replied firmly that they were not – she was not going with them; she had a crippled mother. 'Then it is off', Frank announced, and Ilias and Alexis looked at the British captain with amazed horror. But they knew he would not leave Danai to face her fate alone, they knew they could not persuade him to change his mind, and Alexis realized that now he and Frank would soon be taken to Athens to face the firing squad after the military trial. Time was up; it was over a year since they had been captured. Alexis remembered visualizing what his blood-spattered shirt would look like.

The military trial in Athens was purposely built up into a theatrical affair. It was open to the public and Alexis caught sight of his mother's anguished face as he came into the dock. After thirty minutes or so the verdict was pronounced. Captain Macaskie was condemned to death '*fucilazione al petto*' – to be shot in the chest. Alexis was to be treated as a spy and '*fucilazione alla schiena*' – shot in the back. The two prisoners were then led to the death cells of the Averoff prison.

In the meantime although Frank and Alexis did not know it, negotiations had begun to try and have their death sentences commuted and among those I remember who were involved at the time were the Pope, the Rumanian Minister in Athens and the Swiss Consul, as well as Archbishop Damaskinos. One day before the sentences were due to be carried out, Frank and Alexis were told that their execution was postponed – but not commuted. This happened to coincide with the Italian collapse and Frank rightly feared that when the Germans took over the prison they would carry out the sentence and they would immediately be shot. With the Italian guards in some disarray – jittery about their position in Greece at the time – Frank managed to bribe the jailers to let them out. I believe that part of the deal was paid in gold sovereigns that Frank had received clandestinely. Frank also promised to arrange the safe conduct to Cairo of three Italian officers in return for his and Alexis' freedom if they wished to escape from the Germans.

On leaving the prison Alexis and Frank parted. For Alexis, being Greek, his escape which ended safely in Cairo was perhaps easier (he was able to hide in his aunt's garden while arrangements were made for his escape) but for Frank, now well known and sought by the Germans, his route was complicated. His first stop was at the house of the Swiss Consul, Monsieur de Bavier, where he remembered a memorable, delicious dinner, served with champagne. But in the middle of the night a telephone call warned him to get out at once and realizing that the Germans were after him, he left hastily for Archbishop Damaskinos's villa. There he was greeted by the Archbishop and Gianni Georgakis like an old friend and hidden at once. It was just in time too, because very soon after Frank's arrival the Gestapo jeeps pulled up outside and heavy-booted ss officers stamped their way in, demanding to search the house. They ransacked the villa, but they did not find Frank who, I believe, had slipped away to Gianni Georgakis' house. Meanwhile the irate Archbishop and Gianni strongly protested to the German authorities about this behaviour and demanded an apology and the assurance that an outrage of this kind would not be repeated.

After the Germans had left, and with an apology too, Gianni planned Frank's escape. The problem was how to get Frank out of Athens and through the German road blocks. But Gianni had an ingenious plan and this he arranged with the chief of the Athens Police, Colonel Evert. Gianni, Frank and the Chief of Police – the latter in full dress uniform – drove out of Athens in the official police car with pennants flying to the coast where they were to meet up with an agent in a bus who would then take Frank to the hidden inlet where a caique would be waiting for him. The signal the agent would give from the bus would be a chicken which he would hang out of the window. (Though this may sound fanciful – villagers often travelled this way with their hens!) All went according to plan until the police car reached the rendezvous. One bus after another passed by – but no hen appeared out of the window. To avoid likely suspicion as to why the car had stopped at the bus station, Evert told his driver to get under the car and start fiddling with the engine. And this he did. But as time passed Evert and Gianni thought that they should return to Athens so as to avoid awkward questions and offers of help from passers-by; Gianni recalls to this day the sight of Frank's 'black moustache' beginning to run down his chin as he left the car and they drove off. But happily Frank did not have to wait long; his contact did turn up – there had been trouble finding a hen, and he directed him safety to the caique.

From Cairo Frank went home on leave but he was soon back again and insisted on returning to Greece. On 1 January 1944 under a new name, Major Parkes – as the Germans were still after him – he parachuted into Greece in the Carpenissi area and joined the Allied mission there. From the mission headquarters he was able to organize the safe escape of a number of British and American pilots who were in hiding after their planes had been brought down during operations over Greece. (The route out to Cairo now was easier as the planes could now take off from a hidden mountain air strip.) He was also able to follow the danger-ous political climate and clashes between rival Greek guerrilla bands in the mountains and rightly, as it turned out, feared that Cairo had not assessed the situation seriously.

But Frank was so reticent, so shy about describing his experiences. He only liked to talk about those who helped him – and always with such love and gratitude. When I first met him, it was at a party at our flat on liberation night. He was, I remember, carrying a mountain of army rations – tins of bully-beef, which to us was like caviar, butter, marmalade, jam, biscuits, Lee & Perrins sauce – all the things we had forgotten. On top of this pile of gifts there were two long-stemmed, sweet-smelling tuberroses.

It was at this party that I first met George Jellicoe, and I remember him interrupting a conversation I was having with one of his SBS officers – Anders Lassen – better known as 'Andy the Terror Viking of the SBS'. Although initially a Commando officer, Andy had later joined the SBS at Jellicoe's request and under his command carried out the most daring raids on the German and Italian occupied Aegean islands. (He was killed in April 1945 at Comacchio in Northern Italy and was awarded the VC posthumously.*) That night Andy had come into Athens by sea, dodg-ing the mines, after reconnoitring the Greek islands he knew so well in search of a suitable British naval base near Athens. He was a handsome, statuesque, towering, straw-blond, cold grey eyed Dane with a deep, deep, cavernous voice. He was asking me about collaborators and at the same time carefully taking down the details I mentioned in a note book, when George came up to us and with a knowing chuckle said: 'I think I would not go on with those names and addresses, my friend here might look them up and . . .' Then he added: 'We are moving off to liberate Thebes tomorrow. Would you like to come with us? But I warn you – you will have to get up at dawn and do a bit of interpreting.' Of course, I immediately accepted – I was thrilled. Then suddenly I came out of my dream world and realized that although we Athenians were free – and were celebrating our liberation – the war was not over for the British. And tomorrow George and his men were moving on to capture the retreating Germans – the enemy.

Gay chatter I remember went on till late that night, and before the

---

* Although three Danes received the VC in World War I, Andy Lassen's VC was the only VC to be awarded to a foreigner in World War II. In April 1987 a bronze bust of Anders Lassen was unveiled outside the Freedom Museum in Copenhagen, which was the centre of the Danish resistance. Since Andy trained in Scotland a copy will stand outside Lassen House, Dundee, the HQ of D Squadron of the 23 SAS regiment. The bust shows the Viking hero in uniform, wearing the SAS beret and sporting his VC and MC with two bars.

party was over I had learnt and was beginning to be able to follow the plethora of confusing initials which peppered everybody's conversation and which I at first found hard to follow. In the end I learned that ML stood for motor launch, HDL for a harbour defence launch, MTB for a motor torpedo boat, LCI for landing craft infantry – all used by the raiding forces. And I also began to try to differentiate between the various military and paramilitary groups which had operated in Greece during the occupation. There was MO4's undercover Secret Intelligence Service, the SIS, then the SAS, David Stirling's Special Air Service and its later offshoot, George Jellicoe's SBS, the Special Boat Service, as well as the LRDG, the Long-Range Desert Group who joined the raiding forces after fighting in the desert, the AHO or Anglo-Hellenic Caiques, and the BMM, the British Military Mission who operated mainly in the mountains and which included Brigadier Barker-Benfield's Force 133, another name for the Special Operations Executive SOE. I also learnt more about George Jellicoe – my host on the morrow's exciting liberation drive as both he and his officers were talking in a throw-away, breezy fashion about their courageous operations. And from George's account of his experiences I very soon realized that he was a very romantic young man but at the same time a firm, decisive leader of men. I remember one of his SBS officers – I think it was Ian Patterson – saying to me that night, 'We'd follow him anywhere – if he told us to walk across the sea – we would'.

George's first glimpse of Greece, he told me, was in June 1942 when he peered through the Greek submarine *Triton*'s periscope and snatched a view of the dramatic, rocky north eastern point of Crete – lashed by its dancing, sun-speckled waves that bounced up and down and in and out of his picture. He was at the time technically second-in-command to David Stirling's SAS, 'Though David, its creator,' he remarked with a smile, remembering how little rank mattered on such missions, 'never took much account of that sort of thing'. Accompanied by a group of four Free Frenchmen as 'their guide to British habits – naval and military – counsellor and friend' with their commander, Georges Bergé* – 'a marvellous, remarkable man' – George's task was to blow up German bombers on the Heraklion airfield in Crete. The operation was timed to coincide with two SBS raids on other Cretan airfields and the passage of a convoy from Alexandria to Malta. It was hoped, George explained, that their sabotage raid would dent the force of the German attack on the convoy.

After a long and arduous paddle ashore the party landed at night on Crete and George remembered the difficulties they encountered making

* Now a retired general.

their way inland up the precipitous and rocky Cretan hills. Identifying the right ridge which would lead them to the Heraklion airfield was also difficult, and three times they took the wrong route and had to turn back. 'All the ridges looked the same' George said shrugging his shoulders, 'you know what it's like.' Finally, a day late, they reached the airfield where the team blew up 'twenty plus' German bombers and then walked across the island for the next three or four days making for the point where he and the French party were to be taken off by a caique commanded by Lieutenant-Commander Campbell RNVR. (I remember George's modest description of this exploit, making out – in his characteristically dismissive way – that blowing up twenty German bombers was as easy as letting off a handful of fireworks.) As the party were resting one morning in a quiet, secluded valley, George and the Cretan guide went ahead to make contact at the rendezvous and lead the French party to it. However, in his absence the French party had been betrayed by a quisling, 'The rarest of breeds, especially in Crete,' George angrily remarked. 'He had offered us all bread and wine and then when my party had moved off he went back to inform the nearby German garrison.' As a result the Germans had encircled the French party, who succeeded in fighting their way out but lost two men, one killed and one captured. Three days later, when George finally left the island in a rubber dinghy to board his caique, he passed another dinghy going the opposite way; in it was none other than Paddy Leigh Fermor.

George was back in Greece for the second time on the night of the Italian armistice in September 1943. He had parachuted into Rhodes with an interpreter, Major (Count) Dobrski, and a wireless operator, Sergeant Chesterton. The drop was a day late since on the previous night, as George explained with some hilarity, 'The pilot had lost his way and spent the night flying all over Turkey looking for Rhodes'. George's mission was to carry out instructions from General 'Jumbo' Wilson to try to persuade the Italian commander-in-chief of the Aegean, Admiral Campioni, to come over to the Allied side with his 35,000 men. But when George and his party landed, the nervous Italian garrison opened fire on them and since George had orders not to let Wilson's instructions fall into enemy hands under any circumstances, he hid behind a rock, tore up the instructions and ate them. 'The embossed paper', he remembered, 'was damned hard to swallow.' Eventually, after George had shouted 'amici, amici', the firing ceased and the party was led by the Italians to Campioni's headquarters. Although the hard bargaining continued for some twenty-four hours, and in spite of George's powers of rhetoric, his charm and his diplomatic and persuasive skills, he failed to persuade Campioni to fight the Germans. 'It was an impossible deci-

Phanariot grandparents (*back left and centre front*) with their children (*left to right*) Zoe, Helene (the Byzantine), Aleko, Mother, Julia and George. Grandmother was in a very bad mood that day Aleko remembered.

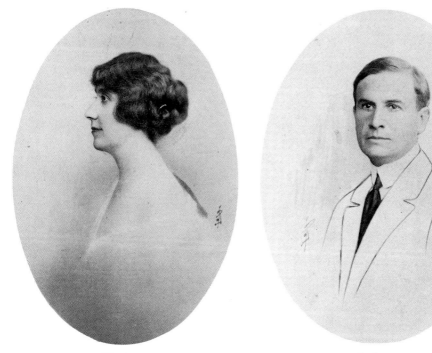

Mother.

Father.

Father's Heidelberg fencing friends.

Uncle 'Nonda', Epaminondas Cawadias, Admiral of the Fleet.

In Greek Red Cross nurse's uniform.

Brother Constantine, 'Costaki', after he had escaped from Greece.

Mother in Alexandria in Bedouin costume.

Athens, 12 October 1944. Frank Macaskie and Archbishop Damaskinos, having watched the retreating Germans, lay a wreath on the tomb of the Unknown Warrior.

Liberation Day, 13 October 1944. George Jellicoe, Archbishop Damaskinos, Frank Macaskie and Shan Sedgwick.

The abduction gang. *Standing, left to right*: Stratis, Manoli, 'Wallace Beery', George and 'Nikko'. *Seated, left to right*: Grigori, Patrick Leigh Fermor and W. Stanley Moss.

German Victory Parade in Athens at the tomb of the Unknown Warrior, May 1941. Field-Marshal List reviews the German troops.

Sitting with Aunt Helene in her Byzantine salon.

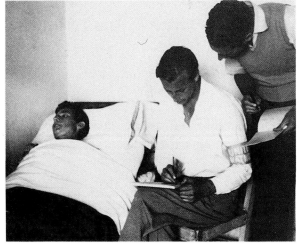

Born in Asia Minor, Marcos Vaphiadis was the Communist military commander-in-chief of the Democratic Army, the ELAS forces, 1946–49. (Photograph taken by the Russian UN delegate.)

US officer briefs the press.

Setting out with the Greek army from Komotini for a night patrol.

UN officials in Florina talk to Nicolas Sinos, a fourteen-year-old peasant boy abducted from his village by ELAS and shot as he tried to escape.

Random pictures of the Civil War. ELAS guerrillas; gun-toting peasant girls (*simoritises*); a camp guard ready to shoot or smile; young ELAS prisoners, sullen and shorn in National Army jail; old women left behind in empty villages as guerrillas flee before the National Army's final assault.

sion', George admitted. 'The Italian forces on the island were more numerous than the Germans, but they lacked transport and they were scattered around the island.' When the talks broke up, Campioni,* in a most gentlemanly fashion lent George an Italian motor torpedo-boat together with his chief-of-staff. As they were sailing out of Rhodes a storm gathered and they were caught in a howling gale. As the waves lashed the boat the Italian chief-of-staff shouted to George, '*c'est mauvais!*' (it's bad) and a few minutes later, '*c'est pire*' (it's worse) – but they disembarked safely at Castelorizo which had previously been occupied by a squadron of SBS men. After a couple of days George took this squadron on to the islands of Cos and Leros. There he had more success, and the small Italian garrison at Cos agreed to go over to the Allies and the more substantial one at Leros did likewise. The following week George flew in an Italian seaplane on to two more islands – Samos and Astapata – where both garrisons came over to the Allies. But the Germans very soon hit back, and recaptured all the islands. George was taken prisoner on Leros but managed to escape via Samos to the Turkish coast. Then early in 1944 he was operating again in the Aegean, this time to direct several perilous raiding operations against the German reoccupied islands of the eastern Aegean. His forces now included men from the Greek Sacred Squadron as well as his own SBS units; they sallied forth from bases in rocky hideouts along the crenellated Turkish coast.

George's last contact with occupied Greece was in September 1944 when his SBS unit had been transferred to Italy. There he received a directive from Brigadier Davy (commander of Land Forces Adriatic) to take a small force to the north-west Peloponnese, to occupy the airfield at Araxos and then, using true military jargon, to 'exploit' with his small force which some unkind authority had labelled the 'Bucket Force' towards Patras.

The mixed force George had collected included a squadron of his SBS under Ian Patterson, a detachment of RAF light armoured cars and a troop of the Long Range Desert Group. Ian parachuted into Araxos with his men and occupied the airfield. George flew in later in a Dakota with another group of men, and the main detachment came in by sea. When the force had been assembled, George moved on to Patras and occupied the area. It had been held by a considerable German garrison, but when they saw that the Greek Security Battalions, who had been persuaded by Ian to surrender, had done so, they hastily left by sea followed by punishing British gun and mortar fire.

---

* Campioni was later handed over by the Germans to the Graziani government and executed.

As he moved on to Corinth and harassed the German withdrawal, George was named 'Military Governor of the north-west Peloponnese' – but he admitted that it was 'a title that was a good deal less grand than it sounded as the man who actually wielded force in that area was the bloodthirsty ELAS guerrilla leader, Aris Veloukhiotis. And I must admit it was with some relief that I greeted the arrival of the Greek commissioner for the Peloponnese, Panayiotis Kanellopoulos (who had been sent back from Cairo in advance by George Papandreou's government-in-exile), and BMM's able commander "Chris" Woodhouse'. But George now had orders to press on to Athens as soon as possible as the situation there was unclear – the Germans were moving out and General Scobie's forces had been held up from landing on time by German minefields.

George and Ian pushed on, and by 2 October they had reached Corinth – alas! too late to prevent the Germans from destroying the canal. They continued on to Megara where they were held up by the large German flank which was protecting the withdrawal from Attica. At Megara George had to take the hard decision to flash down the drop of the 4th British Independent Parachute Brigade in spite of bad weather and the casualties on landing were heavy. But reinforcements were vital and George – now promoted to the rank of brigadier – had orders to proceed urgently to Athens with as many troops as he could collect. As there was no way to break through the German lines and time was running out, George with Ian, Shan Sedgwick and two others went ahead and left Megara in a caique which they had commandeered. They skirted the shores of Salamis and landed at Scaramanga. Before George and Ian had found the two bicycles with which they entered Athens they had taken cover behind rocks and watched the final German withdrawal – there was nothing else they could do.

On arrival in Athens George recalled how he was met by Frank Macaskie who took him to meet General Spiliotopoulos. The latter had just been named military commander of Attica. And George remembered with some hilarity how, being so proud of his new rank, he had introduced himself in French – not knowing any Greek – to the general as '*je suis le Brigadier Jellicoe*' only to notice that Spiliotopoulos was cool and unimpressed. It was only later that he remembered that *brigadier* in French stands for 'corporal'. Thus ending the tale of his Greek exploits in his characteristic, rollicking, debunking manner – George left the party to prepare to press on to Thebes the following day.

I slept tight that night. The agonizing fear I had experienced before had somehow evaporated. I fell asleep with happy recollections of home – of England, somewhat embroidered no doubt. But once again I felt safe and once again I felt British and proud to be so. (I was however still a Greek subject. But my father had become a British citizen.)

The next morning, as I was rather awkwardly climbing into the back seat of the leading jeep, I remember George Jellicoe insisting that I should sit in the front. 'After all, you are the heroine,' he said, or over-flattering words to that effect. And although I protested that I was not a heroine, I did however, change into the front seat, only to realize later that my host had not been quite as gallant as I had imagined. George had had previous experience of these 'liberation drives' on his way to Athens and knew what to expect; I of course was a novice. As we passed through villages the peasants, lining the roads, frenzied with delight, threw anything and everything they had at our jeeps – flowers, vegetables or fruit (I particularly remember the sticky grapes). All these happy missiles hit the front seats only and often landed in my hair or slap on my face. But when I looked back at young Brigadier Jellicoe as he sat perched high up and immune on the back edge of the jeep – he looked neat – spick-and-span and smiling radiantly as he waved to the crowds.

I cannot claim to have battled my way into Thebes, for the town was liberated with ease, the Germans had just left and the population was jubilant to see the British arrive. But I must say that I felt very happy as I waved and laughed, and could not really believe that all this was really happening to me: that liberation had come at last and that I was taking part in it.

On our drive back to Athens we met up with a group of Greek guerrillas going the same way. They were bristling with criss-cross bandoliers and machine guns, their mules heavily weighed down with ammunition. Their leader, or *kapetanios*, as the Greek guerrilla leaders were called, was a romantic, bearded figure in a Russian-style fur hat riding a tall white stallion. On his chest, instead of medals he sported a sparkling round antique brooch set with semi-precious stones. Pulling up his horse he formally greeted our British party and then moved off to the next village. When our jeeps reached this village we found the guerrillas had stopped there and assembled in the main square where their *kapetanios* was addressing the inhabitants with a flowery speech heavily laden with heroic classical misquotations. Winding up his harangue he loudly proclaimed, 'We have fought victoriously against the Germans; now we will fight the reactionary forces who are keeping the Greek people in servitude and are hiding the collaborators. The collaborators will hang. Long live liberty! Long live Greece!' With that final rousing cry the guerrillas remounted and cantered off towards Athens.

George asked me to translate this speech and he and his officers seemed puzzled as to why the guerrillas were going the wrong way – why were they going to Athens rather than pursuing the Germans, and where had all this military equipment come from? I pointed out that the arms and ammunition, as they should well have known, had been dropped by the Allies! (Some could also have been captured by the guerrillas from the Italians after the Italian collapse.) The guerrillas, it is true, had been supplied by the Allies with arms so that they could harass and fight the Germans, but instead, as I had only recently learnt, the left-wing guerrilla forces had used these arms mainly to fight the right-wing resistance groups and to terrorize their supporters in the mountain villages. And as to the guerrillas motive that day as they moved towards Athens instead of chasing the Germans – that was to become clear later. But George lost no time and with his own detachment reinforced by a parachute battalion he pressed on to the Yugoslav frontier.

Liberation now changed my life completely. Friends in England had given my address to British officers and suddenly, after being shut off from the world, I found myself surrounded by handsome, amusing and admiring young men who came to our flat bearing such 'treasures' – and treasures they indeed were in Greece in those days – as parachute silk, spam, marmalade, tinned milk, Irish stew, bully beef and biscuits. Sometimes we dined and exchanged experiences in our flat, at other times we went to tavernas at the foot of the Acropolis or down by the sea. Here too the British army rations supplemented the meagre taverna food and brought loud exclamations of delight from the proprietors.

I remember now, and perhaps I will always remember, a trip I made at that time to the Peloponnese with Frank Macaskie and Shan Sedgwick, in order to look up and pay 'A-Force' agents who had helped and hidden Allied forces. Shan, the perfect companion on any journey, his dog-eared poetry books hanging out of his tattered sheepskin coat, recited his favourite lines of poetry intermittently throughout the drive between the wretched bumps on that stony road. Those loving sounds mingled with the evening air, with the sweet scent of the mountain cistus, and wild lavender and the heady, very Greek, sharp aroma from the sprawling tufts of thyme. When darkness fell a large moon smiled at us and lit up a countryside that I had not seen for so long and not smelt for so long. As I was dreaming and looking up at the starry sky, suddenly our jeep protested. It spluttered, spat, jerked and came to an abrupt halt. Frank tried to start it up again – I do not think he knew much about engines, but he did look at it – he lifted up the bonnet – and then closed it. Shan and I took no part in this operation and did not even pretend to understand what had gone wrong. But in spite of Frank's patient coaxing, pushing and pulling, the jeep would not budge and, since it was getting late, we decided to sleep in the fields and walk early the next morning to the nearest village garage. As I was the only woman in the party I moved off by myself and curled up under an olive tree a few yards away from the jeep. Just as I was closing my eyes I heard Frank's gentle voice. He was standing near me – the moon outlining his silhouette with a silver pencil line. 'Are you all right, darling?' he asked. 'I've brought you my coat.' I remember he wrapped it round me, kissed me gently – as if I were a child – then walked away. I was dog-tired and fell asleep immediately.

As the sun rose I woke with a start to find a peasant woman standing over me. She had brought a pitcher of spring water and a bowl of fresh fruit. Over her arm was a white, starched, heavily-embroidered linen towel, no doubt part of her wedding dowry. I could not believe the scene was real. It was too like one of the pictures in my school Bible. The woman said that she had seen the jeep on her way to the fields and with a seraphic smile added, '*Kori mou*' ('My daughter', a Greek term of endearment towards a young girl) 'I thought you might need a little help'. Her husband meanwhile was under the jeep unscrewing almost every screw and tying things up with string in true Greek manner. Miraculously the jeep did eventually start and we clambered in merrily, thanked our saviours, waved them goodbye, and drove off again. (We paid the peasants, I remember, in army rations and cigarettes for their help – much to their embarrassment and delight, as they expected nothing.)

One of the agents we visited on this trip, and who remains vividly in my memory, owned a village taverna with vines trailing over the balconies and bright-coloured plants and flowers sprouting out of large oil tins, saucepans and chamberpots. The Germans had shut it down during the occupation, so when our jeep arrived, Gianni, the owner, greeted us very emotionally. He hugged us, planted hefty kisses on both our cheeks, vigorously shook our hands and crossed himself over and over again, thanking the Holy Virgin for 'this happy day'. As we sipped cups of coffee (made from roasted chickpeas as there was no real coffee available at that time) accompanied by rather stale Turkish delight and glasses of fresh spring water, Gianni went over the horrors of the German occupation and the day an envious villager had denounced him to the Germans for hiding a British officer. 'I put the *kirios* (gentleman) in a barrel overnight. He smelt a bit of retsina', Gianni said, eyeing me and obviously enjoying the horror on my face, 'but I got him away safely the next day. The Germans never found him.' Rather uneasily and haltingly Frank then broached the subject of payment, 'I know that we cannot p-pay you enough for what you have done or for what it m-meant to my c-country but is there a small thing – something that we can give you?' The immediate reply came back like a bullet, 'Tomato ketchup! I *love* tomato ketchup – and, well, neon lights for my new taverna'. Ketchup was easy – there was a bottle in the jeep with the army rations, and more would be sent. Funds for the neon lights were handed over too, and quite a bit extra. But as I watched Frank seal the envelope with the money in it I realized that in a way this gift was a disaster and the atmosphere of this romantic peasant taverna would now be ruined for ever. But then Gianni would be happy and the garish new look would no doubt give him added status in the village. Getting up to go, and after more kisses and handshakes, we climbed into our jeep, waved good-bye and drove off in a cloud of dust. As I looked back I saw Gianni hugging the little red bottle. 'I will put ze bottle under my pillow tonight!' he shouted after us as he broke into a few steps of a rhythmic peasant dance – bottle in hand instead of the traditional handkerchief.

PART V

Revolution

11

The Second Round

'In a real revolution the best characters do not come to the front. A violent revolution falls into the hands of narrow-minded fanatics and tyrannical hypocrites at first. Afterwards comes the turn of all the pretentious intellectual failures of the time. Such are the chiefs and the leaders. You will notice that I have left out the mere rogues. The scrupulous and the just, the noble, humane and devoted natures; the unselfish and the intelligent may begin a movement – but it passes away from them. They are not the leaders of a revolution. They are the victims: the victims of disgust, of disenchantment – often of remorse. Hopes grotesquely betrayed, ideals caricatured – that is the definition of revolutionary success.'

Joseph Conrad, *Under Western Eyes*

I feel I have to call this period the second round because historians and scholars – so much brighter and better educated than I – have divided modern Greek history thus. (The Civil War in the mountains was the first round. The third round was the guerrilla war, 1946–9.) And, I must admit, it helps my untidy mind fall into the right grooves and concentrate on events in more or less the right order. But looking back – those years are really more like three acts in a Greek tragedy – so like those I have watched under the starry sky, sitting on the hard marble seats of the ancient theatre in Epidaurus where my grandfather had excavated* many years ago. All the elements are there – joy, ambition, murder, retribution, violence, guile, the thunderous warnings of the gods and even the dramatic, slow, rhythmic repetitive classical Greek chorus. For what could be more moving and more similar than those black-clothed Greek peasant women whom I watched through the 'three acts', bathed in sorrow and tears as they cried out in pain for their burnt homes, their murdered menfolk and their lost children.

But for me personally, after the hysterical happiness of liberation I gradually had that strange, uncertain, tingling feeling of beginning to live again – that feeling one has when a nurse tells you after an operation

* Professor Panayiotes Cawadias, 1881–1928, General Ephor of Antiquities and Fine Arts.

to hang your legs over the bed before taking your first steps – and then finding that you can walk – but not very steadily. I remember I saw quite a lot of Frank Macaskie at that time; he was a great friend of Shan's and often called at the flat. He always brought some precious – to us – tins of army rations and bunches of sweet-smelling flowers for me – hyacinths, violets or sometimes tuberroses. I still remember their dizzy scent. Then one evening we had a dinner date and he was late. I filled in the time leaning over the balcony watching the comings and goings in the British Embassy courtyard – there seemed to be preparations for VIP visitors* – but I was not interested in this and when Frank eventually arrived we went out to a taverna for dinner. But that night he seemed to me to be ill at ease, more silent and serious than usual. Over dinner he often stared at me with his penetrating blue eyes – I have a fixation about blue eyes, no doubt because mine are brown – but Frank's were of the palest blue, rimmed with darker blue, and had a pool-like depth. He seemed to be not so much looking at me as through me; I waited for his words. 'Darling,' he finally said. 'I don't want you to be hurt. I love you but I am not in l-love with you. P-perhaps we should stop seeing each other?'

I remember at the time this dissection of love was new to me – and I presumed it was very British. All I knew was that I loved Frank, warmly, totally – like a foreigner no doubt. And as I could not bear the thought of not seeing him again I tried to be very British and said something like 'Oh no! Let's go on meeting just as friends'. And from then on we only met in a crowd. The crowd included, I recall, Ian Patterson who told me he was in love with me and one day shyly asked me to marry him. And there were several other flirtatious, amusing new British friends who also talked of love. But by then I had once again retreated inwardly from day-to-day life – and none of them meant anything to me. At night I argued with myself about love and being in love and in the daytime I tried to keep that 'stiff upper lip' which I had been taught at Queen's. But although tightly wrapped up in myself, in my feelings – in my own warm blanket of love – I was becoming aware of the mounting tension and anxiety that gripped Athens at that time.

I remember endless discussions among my family and among my Greek and British friends; arguments which often took place over cups of Camp coffee – a British gift and for us a great luxury – and which often went on late into the night. What should or should not have been done in the past – and what should or should not be done now? Had the British

* Harold Macmillan, Sir David Waley (financial adviser) and General Sir Maitland Wilson were among the many visitors who came and went – in and out of the British Embassy.

caught the Greek disease of making and breaking governments? Should they have kept out of politics as the Americans had? Why did they arm the Communists and not realize what this meant? And now who but the British could save us from the threat of armed Communism or the backlash of right-wing vendettas? How and when could this be done? There were no real answers to these questions. The clarity and happiness of those early liberation days had gone. Fear – that feeling at the bottom of one's stomach and the sweat in the palm of one's hand – was back and I was afraid of something I did not understand.

Every night the silence of darkness was shattered by sporadic firing and by angry threats booming out of Communist Party megaphones. The voices came from the poorer districts and were beamed towards the more wealthy Kolonaki area. 'Traitors, Glucksburg lackeys, collaborators, you will die!' But who were these enemies who must die? Among the more wealthy Greeks were those who had hidden British officers, hidden secret radios, fed starving children, worked in hospitals and suffered in German concentration camps; now they were being accused of being enemies of the people? Was it not perhaps that anyone who was not in the ranks of EAM/ELAS was a traitor? Almost every day there were noisy processions, young boys and girls – more girls than boys I remember, and a few older people – bearing red flags and amateurishly daubed placards demanding food for the people, retribution, revenge and ochlocratic freedom. More and more blood-red slogans were splattered on walls, coming nearer and nearer – further up Kolonaki hill – even reaching across a British Embassy wall.

There was one procession which I remember vividly because it was so different. It was the proud march past of the Greek Sacred Squadron and the Rimini Brigade as they made their way to the Goudi barracks on the outskirts of Athens. Girls in the street showered them with flowers and crowns of laurel, friends and relatives along the route shrieked with joy when they recognized and kissed their menfolk. It was a heroic, happy and spontaneous event with no slogans, no placards, no megaphones – though there was evidence of right-wing blue daubs on some walls. The Brigade had fought valiantly in the desert and in Italy alongside the British but little did they know that they would soon become one of the main Communist targets because there were no EAM/ELAS sympathizers among them. (After the mutiny in the Middle East on the eve of the Italian campaign, the EAM/ELAS leaders had been interned.)

I remember meeting one of their most daring and courageous leaders – General Tsigantes. He was a friend of George Jellicoe and a companion in battle. (Today in the small country churchyard at Tidcombe in Wiltshire, facing George Jellicoe's Manor home there is a tomb stone with

Greek letters on one side and English on the other. It marks the temporary resting place of Tsigantes' ashes. When he died in Britain he asked that his ashes be transported to Greece only after the dictatorship of the Colonels had been overthrown. This was done and a guard of honour accompanied them.) At one of the Athenian parties I recall how he laughed off the tales of his daring exploits, swiftly moving on to his favourite story about the time when he applied to join the parachute training course and was turned down because of his age. Looking round the room to be sure that he had his audience with him, his face puckered up with impish delight and his large hands gesticulating to emphasize the important points of his tale, he described how, after some insistence and a good deal of help from friends, he was accepted. Recalling the memorable night of his first drop, he explained that when the moment came for his jump his young companions on the plane looked round and found him fast asleep. However, with no time to lose, they then tapped him on the shoulder – he woke, stepped out, landed with ease, and earned his wings – now sewn over his uniform pocket. And he was so proud of them – as he caressed them affectionately – showing them off to the enthralled guests, who together with their hero downed several glasses of brandy and wine to his health.

But the political atmosphere, I remember, at that time was becoming menacing – more and more so. And while every day the crowds in the streets were shouting – and sometimes now including in their repertoire 'Death to Papandreou! (the Prime Minister) Death to *Scobie** the Glucksburg Lackey! Death to *Leeper*!' – Greek politicians met, discussed, disagreed and resigned from the delicate government of National Unity which had been pasted together with such care by the British. General Scobie, Harold Macmillan and others attempted to heal the breach and to unite the un-unitable – no longer left and right or Royalists and Republicans but armed Communists and non-Communists. I tried to learn from British friends what was happening, what had become of that original British plan which seemed so clear and was to bring in food supplies, to stabilize the economy and restore law and order so that the Greek people could choose a government without external pressures. It had, it was clear, obviously failed. Food supplies were insufficient and not distributed quickly enough, inflation had gone wild, useless drachma notes floated into the gutters. A loaf of bread which had cost three billion drachmas two weeks ago now cost eighty billion. We were lucky because we still had gold sovereigns, but even these Mother had to spend carefully

---

* Lt. Gen. Sir Ronald Scobie was the commander of the British forces in Greece and under the terms of the Caserta Agreement (see Appendix III), the guerrilla forces were also placed under his command, since the Greeks could not agree on a Greek commander-in-chief.

as they had jumped from 700,000 million drachma to 1,300,000 in a day. The Communist ELAS were being pressed to disarm, but with so much power in their hands they had no intentions of giving up the guns which had brought them their strength. British economic experts came and went, but to little avail. Confidence was the only cure and with the knife poised over the divided political scene there was no confidence. Those with gold hoarded it, those without shouted for food and revenge. Those who had arms kept them. A general strike was announced. The shops closed their shutters as they had sold out of candles and food. People filled their baths if they had them, put out their candles and matches – and waited. We did the same.

I was not there when it happened. But the international press corps were. From their Grande Bretagne Hotel bedroom balconies, or moving away from the bar to the front entrance hall they had an uninterrupted view of the central police station across the road next to the Athenians' favourite cafe – Giannakis. They watched the nervous policemen with their guns pointing down towards the street. Were all their cartridges blanks? They watched the procession of demonstrators, with their flags, placards and ochlocratic cries. Were any of them armed? They saw the shooting. Begun by whom? Anyhow did such details matter at that point? Death looked so unreal on that sunny Attic morning. The scene could well have been just the last act of a play – a death scene when the leading actors are 'dead', lie flat on the stage as the curtain drops catching the tops of their feet before they rise, take their bow and collect their bouquets. But the audience on Sunday 3 December – pressmen and passers-by – suddenly saw before them hundreds of bodies lying flat on the pavements and in the street in front of the monument to the Unknown Warrior and the Houses of Parliament. Hundreds of terror stricken young girls and boys, men and women praying to be spared the punishing police bullets. Those who were hit oozed blood – I only saw the dried up pools surrounded by leaves, pathetic flowers and crosses hastily made out of twigs when I walked down to the centre of the city late that afternoon. But each reporter saw and reported the scene through eyes that matched his or her political beliefs. One US press man saw British tanks moving in on the crowd – no British tanks were involved. One British reporter said he heard the police give the order in Greek to shoot. He knew no Greek. Some said the 'Fascist' police fired – others said the 'nervous' police who had been attacked fired. And others said the crowd was armed and fired first. Some said the firing lasted an hour – others that it was thirty minutes and others remembered it was fifteen minutes. The number of dead and wounded rose and dropped according to whose side the witness was on. EAM/ELAS claimed twenty-two dead and hundreds wounded; other estimates gave the figure of eleven dead and sixty wounded.

Mother and I had just experienced yet another night of mounting tension. I had woken early to the sound of church bells ringing – I can still almost hear their angry, unholy sound – short, sharp peals that came from the poor shack area beyond the Ilissus River. These were followed by the wail of air raid sirens – but there were no enemy planes that morning in the red dawn sky. And then came the familiar venom against Scobie, Leeper and Papandreou and a rallying cry to all EAM/ELAS patriots to assemble for a demonstration in Syndagma Square. In the background came the usual crackle of small-arms fire.

Late that morning, it must have been some time before midday, as I stood on the balcony I caught sight of a large procession making its way down the main street – Kifissia Street – towards Syndagma (or Constitution Square). I could only see a few yards of the demonstration through the street gap between the houses, but their sharp, angry cries were carried in the air for some time. The protestors were mainly young girls, a few young men and older men and women – about ten abreast. They carried Greek, Russian and American flags – very few if any, British flags (a point quickly picked up by US correspondents). Their placards and their threats condemned Scobie's intervention (referring to the dis-arming of all guerrilla bands) and attacked 'Leeper and hireling Papan-dreou' for their support for 'collaborators' (i.e. the Security Battalions), and the 'Fascists' (the Sacred Squadron and the Rimini Brigade). I won-dered as I looked down on the British Embassy's pink building how Mr Reginald Leeper felt as he viewed the scene from his sunny garden window that gave on to the main street. There were, I noticed, friendly British tommies guarding the gate on to the side street and it was open as usual.

Though wild threats and processions had been a daily event, somehow after that uneasy night I felt there was a pall of gloom and foreboding over the city. I had heard rumours of EAM/ELAS forces massing outside Athens, I had read the Communist press calling for gunpowder action, I had heard that the somewhat jittery Greek government had been uncer-tain how best to act and had first permitted this mass demonstration and then forbidden it. Now it was taking place. How was one to know? The general strike had already begun a day early and that morning we had no light, water, transport or radio bulletins. We depended on candles and rumours. Mother, whose heart condition needed rest and no worry was over-anxious and sick, but pretended not to be so and busied herself teaching our new cook how to make *keftedes* (Greek meatballs) with bully-beef and Spam, and how to make mayonnaise out of white sauce diluted with vinegar.

Just as I was coming back into the house that sunny morning to describe the procession to Mother and to calm her down as the protestors did not seem to me to be more vociferous than usual – I heard two loud explosions. Those who could differentiate between the various battle sounds told me later that the explosions came from hand grenades which had been thrown into the Prime Minister's house. (This turned out to be true, one civilian passer-by was killed and the policeguard was wounded.) A moment's silence was then shattered by a sudden, continuous splatter of rifle fire – or was it Sten guns? I am no expert. And then the haunting echo of a huge, loud wail filled the air – or was I imagining it? It was impossible to know what was happening at the time and it was only later that evening that we heard from friends who knew friends who knew others who had been there and from relations who had gathered 'reliable' information from witnesses. Everyone had a different tale but everyone was shattered. I remember Shan with his head buried in his two hands, his hair on end – rocking backwards and forwards and moaning in misery and despair.

Again early that afternoon the sound of wailing voices and the clatter of hundreds of feet brought me out on to the balcony. They were near. Looking down the side street that flanked the British Embassy I saw a large crowd pouring into it; they were packed in tightly between the houses, right up the hill. Outside the Embassy the chanting began – 'Death to Scobie! Death to Scobie! Revenge for the new victims! Revenge for the blood of our sons!' Women clothed in black held placards demanding justice, retribution and revenge, others carried banners dipped in the morning's blood. I watched the iron Embassy gates close and the guards take up their position outside, facing the crowd. A delegation was admitted through the side gate. I believe they handed in a note or had a word with the Ambassador. I then saw them return to their ranks and the crowd move off in a sad, slow, sullen shuffle. It was an orderly exit.

I cannot remember what happened on which day but the next two days are just short flashes in my mind – recollections of my disorientated feelings – my fear, my terror as I tried to avoid accepting what was bound to come. I remember the curfew from dawn to dusk, I remember the British tanks and armoured cars patrolling the streets. I remember the firing at night and often now during the daytime too. There were rumours of Communist executions without trial of 'collaborators', there were rumours of right-wing executions and retaliation. EAM/ELAS forces were moving into the city in spite of the ban accepted by the Greek government. But the Prime Minister and his government had no power

– EAM/ELAS had, and they occupied the police stations in Athens and Piraeus, often cruelly massacring their occupants. And then there was the largest, blackest demonstration I had ever seen. A huge, black serpent making its way through the centre of the city. Again they were mainly young girls in black, a few young men and some older women who, with the families of those shot in the square wore black mourning veils and tearfully wailed and shrieked out their pain as they followed twenty-two ill-fitting, half-open coffins which were carried shoulder-high. Dirges and the death march were played by a band; flags were dipped in blood and the cries of 'death to the murderers! revenge for the victims!' were angry and sharp, but orderly. I was told that the procession had come from the cathedral and as it reached Syndagma Square the crowd knelt in prayer.

That night some friends, British officers who could circulate during the curfew, came to see us. They said – what I dreaded most – that General Scobie had received orders from Churchill to use force if necessary to re-establish law and order, and that he had given ELAS until dawn to evacuate the city. Happily it was only very much later that I learnt the actual wording of Churchill's telegram:* 'Treat Athens as a conquered city' or I would have been shattered at the time. I had not yet adjusted to the fact – or perhaps I did not want to face it – that Greeks were to fight the British – our liberators – and that the British were to fight the Greeks. When our guests left that evening I heard a loud spatter of bullets hitting the pavement outside. I looked out of the window and saw our friends duck and then walk away safely. The sniper on our roof was our new cook. We never saw her again. But early the following morning the battle for Athens began. There were no longer just threats hurled through megaphones, but bullets coming through the windows (probably aimed at the British Embassy), the continuous crackle of Sten gun and machine-gun fire and the thud of distant guns – ELAS's 75 mm guns. Later that morning I received a message from one of the guests who had dined with us the night before – I think it was Frank. It gave the latest news – ELAS forces were cutting off the airport and the road to Piraeus, they had attacked the British forces and there had been many casualties. Nurses were needed at the temporary paratroop dressing station at GHQ. Could I go there as quickly as possible? The note ended, 'Please take care darling'. I remembered this as I ran down the hill in my nurse's uniform. I was not being brave, for as long as shots do not hit you – you cannot believe they are real.

---

* John Colville *The Fringes of Power, Downing Street Diaries 1938–1955*, p. 533 (Hodder and Stoughton).

As I crossed the main street – Academy Street – to reach the British Military Headquarters, machine-gun bullets like a thousand marbles splattered across the pavement and I passed British soldiers setting up sand bag barricades. In the centre of the main street there was a large, gaping hole – not the usual drainage trouble – but the mark of a communist mortar bomb. The temporary dressing station was, if I remember right, on the same side of the street as the Grande Bretagne Hotel – just round the corner. When I arrived there the RAMC (Royal Army Medical Corps) doctor was too busy to look up. I stood for a while pinned in horror in the doorway. The scene before me was so different to the Greek hospital I had known and so different to what I had expected. There were British tommies lying on stretchers with hideous open wounds that reminded one more of the coloured pictures in medical textbooks than real, sliced, torn-away flesh, veins and bones. Broken limbs hung limply, grotesquely away from bodies over the side of stretchers; blood, blood, everywhere. A medical orderly was going round with mugs of hot tea and blankets, and much to my surprise, I noticed that his 'medicine' worked wonders as the wounded waited patiently for the doctor's round. A businesslike matron, seeing me standing at the door, beckoned me in and took me under her wing. I worked with her and handed her instruments and bandages moving like a zombie – I could not believe it was true. A nightmare – surely – and I would wake up soon. But no, it was all very real.

Nursing methods were different to those I had known; there was now no eternal boiling of instruments, sterilizing and swabbing. Instead, there was penicillin and packets of sterilized swabs and bandages – something I had never seen before. And then the wounded were so much more silent and uncomplaining than my Greek patients had been. Or perhaps my Greek 'children' had less of that British self-control and just poured out their pain and agony to their 'sister'.

Today I have no clear picture of how many days or how many hours we worked while shells fell outside shattering windows. There was no time to think, no time to realize that the Grande Bretagne and the few streets beyond were the only part of the capital now 'held' against the Communist EAM/ELAS attack. And even that island could not be called safe as snipers in civilian clothes infiltrated the apartment buildings at night. But there are, as I look back, two of my patients that I will always remember. They were so brave, so totally unpolitical – as in fact all the British forces were in this confused situation. They were just bent on doing good, carrying out their duty and once again saving Greeks. But this time not from the Germans but from themselves. It was the red-haired British paratrooper – from the Sixth Parachute Battalion, I believe – who is still so vivid in my mind. I held his hand to ease his pain. His grip was tight. 'She was lovely,' he said looking up at the ceiling as if to picture her once again. 'Black eyes, long, black, shining wavy hair, down to her waist. She cried for help from her window. I had to go. I just *had* to go. I climbed up to her window. I was almost there. She vanished – must have bent down – I could no longer see her. As I reached the sill she reappeared. She had a gun. She aimed it at me. She fired.' His arm, a pincushion of bullets, was later amputated.

The other casualty I remember had long, beautiful hands and wore a crested gold signet ring. It was hands one held for comfort – and it is hands I still remember. He was a handsome, romantic-looking British officer with a faraway gaze in his pale blue eyes – no, blue eye. Just one eye, the other was bandaged. Apologetically he asked me for his blood-matted jacket I had just cut off. I handed it to him and watched him fumble for a while in the top pocket, then he brought out a photograph. It was of his young, fair-haired wife. She had one arm round a beaming, curly-haired baby girl in a smocked dress and the other round a smiling, silky retriever. He tucked the photograph under his pillow. He had lost one eye.

On one of the mornings when we were particularly busy (EAM/ELAS had, just the night before, attacked the Air Force headquarters outside Athens. They had taken several British prisoners and those who had managed to escape were badly wounded), I heard Doctor tell Matron that 'Some "sissies" from the Embassy would be coming for injections'. With so many dead bodies lying unburied – not enough wood for coffins and no nails – there was now a real danger of a typhoid epidemic. I recall how our doctor that day rapidly jabbed a row of five or six young men who looked so awkward in civilian clothes as they stood in line with their shirt-sleeves rolled up. One of them struck me as being different – he somehow did not look like an official. He sported a huge, tufty handlebar moustache, was broad-shouldered and quite short and sturdy. He was dapperly dressed in a suit – Prince-of-Wales check, I think, and wore a jaunty bow tie. As the needle went into his arm his eyes rolled upwards and then closed. He was just about to faint when I caught him and dragged him on to one of the couches. Our doctor did not help; he just looked on scathingly. But I stayed with him, bent over him and held his hand until he came round. Then, looking up at me, he gave me a grateful, impish smile. His name was Osbert Lancaster, and for years I teased Osbert about him fainting in my arms, but at that time he was the Information Officer at the British Embassy; he must have brought a light touch to the grim news he had to give out. He was an excellent mimic and a nimble Greek folkdancer. His sense of humour was a wonderful antidote to the black sadness which enveloped us all, though I believe that correspondents often found his vocabulary original and sometimes hard to interpret – it could have been an act put on on purpose, perhaps.

Late in the evenings at the casualty station one could take a break, and I remember one evening as I was sitting down in a corner, totally exhausted – mentally and physically – I watched the orderly complete his round of tea mugs; these were always filled brim-full with jet black tea, thick with tinned milk and sugar. (The orderly never understood why I could not drink mine.) He then pasted up the shattered windows once again and settled down with a pile of booklets which had been issued by the War Office to the British troops landing in Greece. Peeping over his shoulder I noticed that on the first page, the introduction read 'You are lucky to be coming to Greece ...' and then it went on to give a short history and a glowing description of the country. With pen in hand the orderly was neatly adding a 'p' to 'lucky' and correcting all the booklets in this manner which he thought more appropriate before distributing them. I hid my smile.

Matron came and joined me that evening and told me that the following day we were to undertake the medical supervision of the women's prison camp. 'Prison' and 'prisoners' were words that stirred something at the bottom of my stomach – a kind of deadened fear perhaps. But I tried to take the remark casually and made some ridiculous answer like, 'Oh! How interesting,' and it was not at all what I meant.

The women's prison camp I visited was housed in a basement nightclub, Maxime's. There were after all not many buildings to choose from in the small perimeter held by British troops. I can still, to this day, see those rows of sunken faces and the dejected gaze of rows of unkempt women squatting on the floor. A grisly contrast to the cabaret's back-ground of garish blue and silver mirrors. I accompanied our 'no-nonsense' army matron as she walked round in her firm, businesslike manner. I held her medicines and acted as her interpreter. The usual treatment meted out to most patients by her ran something like this: Matron, 'What's wrong my dear?' Translation by me to depressed, pallid girl who then gave minute details of her head, ears, stomach, etc. Half way through my translation of these symptoms Matron interrupts with, 'Yes, yes, my dear – Oh! dearie me – take two of these now and two at night if you are no better'. And she would then turn round and delve into the huge bottle of Codeine which I carried. The effect was electric, as at that time we Greeks had no foreign medicines and these tablets were snapped up with alacrity as if they had been toffees. More gentle care was taken, I remember, of a little tearful peasant girl – Ekaterini – who, after an incoherent explanation of her symptoms and how she did not want anyone to know – ran into the toilet and a few minutes later gave birth to a premature baby on the pink ladies' cloakroom floor. I recall how Matron wrapped up the baby boy in a shawl (lent by one of the prisoners) with such loving care. She could have been carrying out her duty at Queen Charlotte's Hospital in London, her movements were so gentle, so efficient. Handing the baby back to his terrified mother she said, 'There, there, my dear, it's a boy. He's a bit small but a lovely baby'. I translated the bit about 'lovely baby' only. A few minutes later the baby died. (Ekaterini had been caught hiding a gun under her skirt.)

Some of the faces I passed I recognized. They had been in Haidari with me and after peering at me – and finally recognizing me, in spite of my Red Cross nurse's uniform – they muttered sarcastically, 'It's all right for *you* now the British are here – but what about *us*?' Matron asked me what they were saying – but I did not interpret their remarks – it would have been too complicated to explain. Shrivelled up with inner pain I just said, 'Oh! Nothing much, they are only grumbling' – or something like that.

As we were leaving the camp a pretty little woman called Fotini – Greek for 'light' – grabbed my arm and begged for help. 'I am only here,' she blurted out, 'because my husband wanted to be rid of me. He wanted to be free to marry his mistress, *Vromokoritso* the dirty girl! – so he told the local police that I was a Communist. I am no Communist, just a broken-hearted woman. What should I do?' Her big, round, black eyes veiled with tears searched for mine – for help. 'How can I prove that I am not a Communist now that I am in prison?' Matron had moved on and was climbing into the jeep. I had to follow. As I looked back at Fotini's black, imploring eyes I longed to be able to help – but how? There were so many of these pathetic tales. So much injustice. So much personal hatred. But how could justice be done? Who was right? Who was wrong? Who had led these peasant women – fed them with false promises and now deserted them? The Civil War seemed to me to be a brutal, personal, mad vendetta. How could my fellow Greeks, I wondered – whose hearts seemed larger than anyone else's in the world and were so full of love – of love for their country, of love of beauty, of the sea, the sun, the moon, of love for their family and above all love of freedom – destroy everything with such inhuman hate, vengeance, and cruelty? And for what? For power?

At night sometimes, when there was not too much work, I used to go back to the flat for a rest and to see Mother. Shan sometimes fetched me as the Grande Bretagne next door was now filled with pressmen, Greek government officials and British military personnel. On the first night he took me home, Shan, whom I had adopted as my *'psychopatera'*

– I suppose this untranslatable title could be said to be my 'soul's father' – looked at me sternly and said, 'Now look here, my dear. Understand this – when I duck, you duck, or I look a fool'. I wanted to burst out laughing, but as shells fell around us – obediently I ducked when he did. Suddenly I felt very British – I don't know why – perhaps because it was all so funny – funny sad?

During the six-weeks' battle for Athens my nursing duties prevented me from following in detail the daily political events, the rumours and nuances – the Communist peace-feelers, General Scobie's terms for a ceasefire (reiterated several times in an attempt to end the fighting), and the negotiations which preceded the setting up of the Regency. (This last was to prove that the British had no wish to force the King on the Greek people, which was what the Communists claimed.) But what was quite clear to me was that ELAS had military superiority in those early days and at night their megaphones called on their followers to hold on for a while longer as the Russians and the Bulgarians were on their way to negotiate a settlement.* There was of course no truth in this. But since I had dismissed everything the Greek government and the Germans had put out during the occupation as propaganda, and since there had been very little opportunity during those years to follow the political scene, I had not really graduated much from the early dictums set out by Nell and Queen's College. The latter, I remember, had been clearly voiced by the Bishop of London on our speech day – when we were all dressed in virgin white, 'Serve your country, do good *every* day and help those in need' were his words. My political world was therefore somewhat restricted, to say the least – tightly corseted and still naïvely divided into 'goodies' and 'baddies'. The British and the Greeks were the 'goodies' and the Germans and now the Communists were the 'baddies'. But intermittently I picked up various aspects of this tragic period – gradually I was learning the political power game.

The American role during the battle was one of strict neutrality – to be honest – it was a hostile neutrality. And it was a gift to the Communists who hoped for support from the US and Moscow against Britain's stand. Indeed, initially, the US press and a number of UK journalists did paint ELAS in shining liberal colours and daubed the British with accusations of colonialism. I remember Shan angrily describing his fellow US correspondents who, in the thick of the fighting, complained that they were not given 'facilities' to report on 'the other side'. I remember the US jeeps covered in large stars-and-stripes, the US correspondents

---

* The Russians did not intervene in the battle; they stuck to the agreement reached in Moscow in October 1944 allowing Britain freedom of action in Greece.

with US armbands and some with stars-and-stripes on their backs. US directives were that US personnel should restrict their activities to welfare operation only – the distribution of food supplies etc., which the British incidentally carried out too, in spite of the fighting. But I could hardly believe it when I heard that the US Ambassador, Lincoln MacVeagh, had refused to allow the worn and thirsty British troops permission to drink from his garden well during the battle to safeguard the centre of the city. He had, however, accepted his delivery of army rations.

Perhaps it was typical of Greece, that in Athens at that time – while bullets whistled past one in the street and several became lodged in the walls of our flat – round candle-lit tables, huddled up in overcoats or blankets in the bitter December cold, the talk was of – politics. Often until late into the night Frank, Shan and British Embassy officials would discuss the urgent need to nominate Archbishop Damaskinos – a revered figure by all Greeks – as Regent. But it appeared that some Greek politicians and the King disagreed, so the move was held up. Similar discussions and meetings with Greeks took place in the British Embassy round the corner where David Balfour – formerly the Orthodox priest who had officiated in the little Orthodox chapel of the Evangelismos hospital where we had taken communion as children and who was now second secretary at the Embassy – was the official translator.

Meanwhile, ELAS were gaining ground. They had attacked the Averoff prison and a bloodbath had only just been averted by the brave defence of a small British and Greek force. ELAS then overran the British RAF headquarters in Kifissia and the casualties were high – something in the region of eleven British killed and some 585 prisoners taken. The Communists now had infiltrators dressed in British battledress with red parachute berets, and they employed a ruthless 'police' strike force – on Gestapo pattern – the OPLA (Units for the Protection of the People's Struggle). These carried out summary executions on so-called 'collaborators and informers'. They took prisoners and shot them and refused the Red Cross access. All these actions were under the smokescreen of 'fighting for freedom and fighting the British Fascists and the Greek collaborators to avert a Monarcho-Fascist coup'. I suppose the British at that time could have replied that they were fighting for Greek freedom and the prevention of a Communist coup – but both officials and the military in Athens were too busy trying to stop the carnage to have time to issue such statements. The words were however spoken by the Greek Prime Minister, George Papandreou, and by Winston Churchill in the House of Commons, but neither had much effect on the fighting in Athens. And always keen to whip up hatred among Greeks against the British, ELAS had lately claimed that the British had thrown in blacks, *arapades*, and Ugandan dwarfs to fight the Greeks. They were perhaps referring to that brave Indian contingent who had suffered severe casualties in Piraeus when ELAS had advanced on them from behind a row of small children.

It must have been harrowing for the British tommies as ELAS dropped leaflets calling on them to 'stop fighting in a war waged by the Fascists Scobie and Leeper and the Greek government quislings'. Yet they had before them the evidence of ELAS's savage treatment of prisoners and their butchery of innocent mothers and children. Day after day as the fighting continued I began to be able to distinguish between the various battle sounds – the small-arms fire, rifles and Sten guns, the hand grenades, the 75 mm guns and the 25-pounders. Then one morning we had news which brought a small ray of hope. I had noticed more activity than usual at the Embassy, and it was the lightning visit by Harold Macmillan and Field-Marshal Alexander, now Supreme Allied Commander Mediterranean, that changed the scene. We were told that they were surprised to have to make the journey from the airport in a tank – instead of a 'soft car' to use military jargon – since ELAS snipers were posted along the route. And seeing the danger with their own eyes – the small perimeter held against ELAS – they had wired for immediate reinforcements and air support to be sent under General Hawkesworth's command.

But Christmas was approaching and I must say that there was no spirit of comfort and joy and no Christmas trees either. General Scobie had issued a note to the effect that there would be no Christmas festivities and that Christmas would be celebrated 'when it was appropriate to do so'. I remember how grim those days were, without heating or light; I remember going to the corner of the street at a given time with buckets to collect our ration of water. The Grande Bretagne Hotel, now overcrowded with Greek government officials, British military personnel, international pressmen and some foreign representatives like the Russian Lieutenant-Colonel Popoff and his six Red Army colleagues, was no better off. There was no service, no water or electricity. A notice posted in the rooms read:

Water is now cut off in the Central Athens Area and will remain so until certain key points can be secured.

Until such time all units have to exist on their own reserves. To ensure that this reserve lasts water is RATIONED TO HALF A GALLON PER HEAD PER DAY.

Do not:

1. Use the lavatory.
2. Use water for personal washing except when absolutely necessary.

3. Use water for washing clothes.*

But there was of course the sweet Samos wine at the bar to fall back on!

On Christmas Day, however, Father Christmas did appear. Not in the traditional red, fur-trimmed costume, but in a warm, buttoned-up blue RAF greatcoat. Not down the chimney but out of the sky in a c54 – a Skymaster. It was on Christmas Day in the evening that we first learnt that the British Prime Minister, Winston Churchill, had flown into Athens – unexpectedly and secretly. (Surely, the only well-kept secret in Athens – a capital of a thousand eyes and ears!) What a gift for the cold, hungry, terrorized and besieged inhabitants of the capital, and what comfort for the British forces – so maligned in the British and American press. When we heard the news Mother and I could hardly believe it. I do not know quite what we expected would happen, for the din of battle continued unabated – but suddenly there was hope.

Because of the bitter cold and the lack of heating anywhere, Churchill, who had brought with him his Secretary of State, Anthony Eden, held his preliminary talks in his plane as it sat on the runway. To his greeting party – Harold Macmillan, the British Ambassador Reginald Leeper and the Chief-of-Staff Field-Marshal Alexander – he outlined his objective: to immediately convene a conference of all parties representing all shades of Greek politics under the chairmanship of Archbishop Damaskinos if he would accept the task. He also discussed the possibility of setting up a Regency and nominating Archbishop Damaskinos as Regent. In London there appeared to be differences of view about the Archbishop – some feared he was too pro-ELAS, others that he would use the position to become a dictator.† I think it was at this point that Churchill's words, repeated to me later, were: 'Is he a cunning scheming, medieval prelate more interested in temporal power than celestial glory?' and on receiving no immediate reply, continued, 'Good, then we can use him.'

Because of the need for strict security, the *Ajax*, the British light cruiser lying off the bay of Piraeus, was to be Churchill's 'home' for the duration of the visit, and he and his party travelled there from Kalamaki airport in armoured cars. His Private Secretary at the time, Jock Colville,‡ remembers how he was dryly greeted by his driver on clambering up into his seat with; 'The last man who sat where you are sitting died

---

* Though I knew the gist of the note, the full text comes from W. Byford Jones *The Greek Trilogy*, (Hutchinson & Co. Ltd).

† Winston Churchill; *The Second World War*, vol VI. (Cassell Ltd.)

‡ Now Sir John Colville.

yesterday morning'. But the party arrived on board safely.

Later that evening the Greek Prime Minister Papandreou and Arch-bishop Damaskinos joined the *Ajax* to confer with Churchill. It was dark when they arrived and while Winston was talking to Papandreou – outlining the details of his scheme which he hoped would end the fighting – Archbishop Damaskinos, who was on deck, somehow became embroiled in the crew's Christmas fancy dress festivities. As the band struck up 'The First Noel', the Archbishop, a towering, bearded figure in his black robes, tall, draped, coal-scuttle hat and jewelled staff, was greeted with side-splitting applause. He had been mistaken for one of the sailors in disguise. Happily, I was told, the Archbishop was not aware of the error. (Other versions of this episode which were going round Athens at the time went even further to add that one of the crew had tugged at the Prelate's beard to see how well it was stuck on. But I think this was a stitch of Greek embroidery. Churchill, however, adds that the sailors danced round the Archbishop, who thought it was a 'premeditated insult'.)*

Churchill got on well with the Archbishop. The two men understood and admired each other. And after discussing the arrangements for the conference Churchill put forward his plan for a Regency and his proposal to nominate Damaskinos as Regent. His words, worthy of Byzantine wile, were repeated to me as being; 'It would distress me to think that any task Your Beatitude would assume as Regent might in any way inter-fere with your spiritual functions'.† I do not know what Damaskinos' reply was, but I am convinced it must have been reassuring.

That night there was an attempt to blow up the Grande Bretagne. A group of sappers checking the sewers discovered a large quantity of wired-up German dynamite – only just in time. And in the bay of Piraeus where the *Ajax* had released depth charges against under-water attack, ELAS mortar bombs splashed round the vessel at dawn, forcing it to move further out to sea. On Boxing Day which was the following day, Churchill drove to the Embassy where he had further talks with Damaskinos and British officials. Much against his will he was asked to sit in a back room which was on the only safe place, beyond the reach of ELAS bullets. Churchill, I was told later, kept his coat on and he and Damaskinos wrapped blankets round their knees though there was a little heat from some evil-smelling paraffin stoves which had been lent for the occasion by the military. It must have been a wonderful sight. After thanking the staff and Mrs Leeper for their fortitude during the siege, Churchill

---

* Winston Churchill, *The Second World War*, vol. VI.
† See Reginald Leeper, *When Greek Meets Greek* (Chatto & Windus Ltd.).

left for the Ministry of Foreign Affairs – the venue for the All-Party conference.

In the grim, cold Ministry building, hurricane lamps dimly lit the oval conference table, casting eerie shadows on the ill-assorted gathering. Apart from Churchill, Eden, Macmillan and Alexander, there were representatives from France, America and Russia, the Greek Prime Minister, General Plastiras – the titular head of EDES who had recently arrived from France,* Greek officials and the Communist representatives of ELAS – these last in British battle dress. Archbishop Damaskinos headed the table with Churchill on his right and Alexander on his left. Churchill's opening address was repeated twice since ELAS representatives had been late in arriving and the conference had already got under way without them. Their delay could well have been caused by the formalities at the various checkpoints round the city and also because the ELAS delegation arrived bristling with weapons which they did not wish to give up. After some discussion and in order not to be seen as 'giving up' their arms, these were left in an adjoining room under lock and key. When both the Greek and British formal speeches were over (General Alexander made the point that the Greek troops should be fighting in Italy alongside the British instead of fighting the British in Greece; and the three Communist leaders, Partsalides, Siantos and Mandakas, spoke courteously of peace and thanked Churchill for his initiative) the British and foreign delegates withdrew. In Churchill's words, 'We British, and other representatives of the great, united, victorious Powers, will leave you Greeks to your own discussions under the most eminent and most venerable citizen ... For all eyes are turned upon this table at this moment, and we British trust that whatever had happened in the heat of fighting, whatever misunderstandings there may have been, we shall preserve that old friendship between Greece and Great Britain which played so notable a part in the establishment of Greek independence.'†

I was not at the conference, but news at that time sped as fast as bullets and we had news from British officers, Greek friends, foreign news correspondents and from members of the Embassy.‡ I also remember Randolph Churchill coming to dinner one night. I am not quite sure exactly when it was, but he gave a graphic description of

* General Plastiras was a Republican who led the army coup against King Constantine in 1922. He had returned from France where he had been living in exile.

† Churchill, *The Second World War*, vol. VI.

‡ I learnt about the conference at the time and later, but there are detailed descriptions of it in Harold Macmillan's and John Colville's *Diaries* and in Churchill's *Second World War*, vol. VI.

his father weighing up the pros and cons of the various Greek politicians as he was lying in the bath just before flying out to Athens (or was he perhaps polishing up his pronunciation of Greek names?) Randolph had peeped into the bathroom and caught sight of his illustrious father throwing up a huge sponge and catching it, as he muttered, 'Can Ellopoulos *can't Ellopoulos Papa dread oh*! – Papa *dread oh! Plastir arse ... plastir arse*' (Kannelopoulos, Papandreou and Plastiras). For some reason – I do not know why – Randolph also talked vehemently about that '*Unspeakable* Mr Leeper'. I think that at that time it was wrongly thought that Leeper supported the King. And then finally I remember his memorable description of the Greek language – as it sounded to a foreigner. 'Your language my dear,' he said to me, his large, childish face bursting with fun, 'sounds like a pile of plates crashing down the stairs.' He was a great life enhancer – just what we needed at that time.

With the All-Party conference underway, Churchill returned to the Embassy where he held a press conference* to a background of gun-and-mortar-fire and the splatter of British Beaufighter rockets as they swooped down over ELAS positions. In the street outside the flat – and outside the Embassy – there was the usual crackle of small-arms fire. As Churchill left the Embassy that evening, I leant over the balcony, hoping to catch a glimpse of my hero whose voice had been muffled so often on my little radio set as it lay hidden in the wastepaper basket during the occupation. I noticed that Embassy officials were hurrying him into the waiting armoured car and then to my delight, he appeared to be refusing to be hurried – instead, he stepped out towards the street, beyond the gate, he eyed the surprised passers-by, smiled, and gave his 'v' sign. As he walked back into the car a sniper's bullet bounded off the wall across the road. 'Cheek', I am told he muttered. I cannot vouch for the accuracy of this remark – but it is that beaming round face, that chubby hand and the 'v' sign that I can never forget.

In the Ministry of Foreign Affairs the conference broke up several times as the Communists only wanted peace on their terms. In the end though, unanimous decision was reached that Archbishop Damaskinos was to be nominated regent. This news was immediately relayed to Churchill in London who was left with the difficult task of trying to obtain the King's approval, and meanwhile the battle in Athens continued. But British reinforcements had now arrived and with air support and the gradual clearing, street by street, of the capital, of Piraeus and Patras, and with the mounting evidence of Communist atrocities, the tide turned.

* A detailed description is to be found in W.Byford-Jones, *The Greek Trilogy* (Hutchinson & Co. Ltd.).

As ELAS withdrew they took hundreds of hostages with them – rich, poor, even the sick from hospital beds. It was never known exactly how many they were, but official estimates give a figure of around fifteen to twenty thousand.

I cannot remember how we heard, or when the battle actually ended since the clatter of gunfire continued in scattered pockets around the city – erupting here and there until the truce was announced – and even after that. The date of the cease-fire was finally to be 11 January and was to take effect at midnight on 14 January – such was the chaos in ELAS ranks that it took that long for orders to reach their commanders. Few Greeks, and Mother and I were among them, believed that this was the end; and all Greeks were horrified to learn that although the truce had taken into account the exchange of prisoners – no mention had been made of the hostages. But visiting British trade unionists and members of the foreign press, who had at first believed that Communist atrocities were trumped-up stories, now had evidence before them of ELAS's brutal executions when mass graves were uncovered. They also heard the horrific tales from the few ELAS hostages who had managed to escape their captors. They spoke of being forced to march for days barefoot across the snow-covered mountains (ELAS sorely needed shoes and boots for their comrades), of being beaten with rifle butts when they lagged behind, and of the fate of those who had fallen out of line from exhaustion and had been shot on the spot, their clothes ripped off them and their twisted dead bodies left lying on the rocky mountain-side. What do figures mean to those who have lost sons, or daughters, fathers or mothers? Or to the parents of those British tommies who came to liberate Greece? But for what they are worth – in giving a picture of Greece's tragic second round – the figures issued by the Greek Ministry of Information in 1945 were: fifty thousand Greeks killed, and the number of British casualties was said to be around two thousand. (And this at a time when Britain was still fighting the Germans on two fronts.) Among the mangled corpses found in Athens's mass graves – their hands tied with wire, shot at close range in the back of the neck or hacked to death with an axe – was the body of that pretty Greek actress Helene Papadaki whose crime had been that she had once been a friend of the quisling premier John Rallis.* Her body was found – skinned.

* Rallis, arrested by representatives of the Greek government in exile, was imprisoned on 11 October 1944. This was before the Germans had evacuated Greece. He was tried with other collaborators on the 21 February 1945 during the 'hundred days trials' and sentenced on 31 May to life imprisonment. He died of cancer on 26 October 1946. Though still a prisoner, for humanitarian reasons he was allowed home two days before his death.

As time passed we learnt that the king had finally accepted Archbishop Damaskinos as regent. A new government under the Republican General Plastiras was sworn in and promises were made to do what others had failed to do. After the truce ELAS had withdrawn from Attica but negotiations for a final agreement were long and devious. On 12 February the Varkiza Agreement* was finally signed. It had obvious loopholes for both sides. ELAS withdrew to its headquarters in Trikala but they still wielded power over almost three-quarters of Greece.

On their way back from Yalta, Churchill and Eden visited Athens. It was just a few days after the peace agreement. I remember it was a sunny day – a day of blinding, dazzling Attic light as the sun rebounded off the marble temples above the city. That day, like the thousands of Greeks who had gathered in Sindagma Square, I stood on a balcony overlooking the scene. A large black car with two white-skirted Evzones on the dashboard drew up in front of the old palace building at the foot of the Unknown Warrior's tomb. Archbishop Damaskinos, Churchill and Eden alighted and stood in the centre of the terrace flanked by the Evzone guard. The band struck up the British national anthem and we all stood in silence and at attention – some had tears in their eyes. Then the band played the Greek national anthem and, to my surprise, Churchill who perhaps did not recognize the tune, walked up and down beaming and offering up his 'v' sign while we all stood at attention. Damaskinos said a few words and then Churchill spoke looking towards the Acropolis, the cerulean sky and the sea of expectant faces in front of him. First he spoke of his pride at the role the British Army had taken 'in protecting this immortal city from violence and anarchy'. Then he added, 'Let right prevail. Let party hatreds die. Let there be unity. Let there be resolute comradeship. Greece for ever, Greece for all!'† His voice thundered across the square; it was obvious that he felt he had saved the cradle of democracy. For a brief moment it looked as if he had.

But party hatreds die slowly if at all after a civil war. Getting back to normality was an impossible task even with the rules of amnesty spelt out on paper. Prisons bulged with those awaiting trial and daily we learnt of arrests and revenge in the countryside while in Athens political juggling (which resulted in the rise and fall of four Prime Ministers) continued unabated. It was time now to try to control the economy, yet in spite of British experts our gold sovereigns bought almost double one day than they had done the day before. Relief supplies which had been held up by the fighting were now pouring in through UNRRA

* See Appendix III.
† Reginald Leeper, *When Greek Meets Greek* (Chatto and Windus).

(United Nations Relief and Rehabilitation Agency)* but a good selection of these were being sold on black market stalls at the foot of the Acropolis. So it was a wonderful surprise and relief when just after VE Day we heard that through one of Father's 'important patients' arrangements had been made for us to take the first troopship which was calling in at Piraeus on its way back from the Middle East. (I believe this was arranged by Lady Churchill.) And suddenly – just like falling through a trap door – Greece and what it had meant to me dropped into the background – I was going – home.

---

* After the initial relief and rehabilitation operation by the Anglo-American Military organization (ML), the United Nations Relief and Rehabilitation Agency (UNRRA), took over the
task and signed an agreement with the Greek government in 1945.

12

Home-coming? Which Home?

'Sail away, sail away,
When in trouble sail away.'

Noel Coward

It was an unusual way, to say the least, and a special privilege for Mother and me to travel home on a troopship; we were just two women among several hundred men, with a guard at our cabin door. As the ship glided out of Piraeus harbour, I felt no pangs. I did not even bother to look out of the porthole for a last glimpse of my other country. No, I wanted to get away, right away, to somewhere safe. I wanted to go home and home to me at that time was England. Not much of the actual journey remains in my mind with the exception of the incongruity of boat drill. Our life jackets were called 'Mae Wests' by the crew and I think Mother and I only joined in the exercise once, and half-heartedly then. For we reckoned that if we did strike a mine and were ordered to take to the life boats, Nanny Nell's rule of 'women and children first', would stand us a good chance of survival.

As I think back I can still see in my mind's eye my first glimpse of Scotland as the ship sailed up the Clyde to Greenock. The ice-cool blue sky was clear and clean, it seemed to sponge out the ugly past. The fresh dewy grass looked greener than ever before and the blond, apple-cheeked children running alongside the ship were like a band of frolicking cherubs – laughing, singing and waving to the ship as it docked. (So unlike the bare-footed, sunken-cheeked ruffians who now sold black market cigarettes on Athens street corners.) I had not seen such beauty nor felt such pure freshness for many years and as Mother and I disembarked I found I could not stop tears streaming down my face. But why? I was home at last.

We took the train to Euston where Father was on the platform to greet us. He looked a small, shrivelled, grey figure, bent and tired, not how I remembered him. But when he caught sight of us leaning out of the train window suddenly his whole expression changed – happiness, in one second, had transformed him – he was the Father I knew. 'How are you? You – you look fine', were some of the silly, obvious words which I uttered as I fell into his arms. But there was so much more I wanted to say. All those thoughts that I had rehearsed and spoken in my mind on the journey back just stuck in my throat. They never reached my mouth. When we had collected the little luggage we had, we took a taxi and I heard Father give a strange address, 'To the Mirabelle, near Shepherd's Market', he said; then he squeezed in on the back seat between us and explained, 'You see, I could not tell you before, but our Wimpole Street house was bombed. Luckily I was at the Clinic (this was the London Clinic) at the time but your little Whiskey (my Scotch terrier) was killed. And you will never believe it, but all that was salvaged from the rubble on the ground floor was the contents of Mother's glass cupboard which was locked. For some unknown reason the whole set of French crystal glass goblets was intact. I don't know quite what we will do with them now!' Turning to me he then added with a touch of fun, 'On the nursery floor there were packets of photographs and cards of the Prince of Wales strewn all over the place – yours I presume?' I think I laughed rather flatly as I recalled my early crush on the Prince when I was at Queen's. So Whiskey was dead.

On our way to our temporary home, as I looked out of the taxi window, London appeared so odd to me, unreal, not what I had pictured. There were now huge gaps between the rows of offices and houses where bombs had fallen and some of the bomb-sites were mysteriously beautiful. Wild flowers, weeds and grass covered the shattered walls – like a stage set for *Sleeping Beauty*. But then I remembered how at the Gestapo Head-quarters in Athens I had refused to believe the German officer's propa-ganda and yet now I saw that he had been right. London must have been what he had described to me as 'a ball of fire'.

It was thanks to George, the Greek porter at the Ritz, who was a patient of Father's, that we were given extra coupons to buy much-needed new clothes. George would often receive coupons as part of his tips and he generously gave these to us. But shopping, which I had so looked forward to, was so very different from what it had been before I left England. There was little choice, and what was there was drab. Shop-assistants exhuded a self-righteous, stand-offish, take-it-or-leave-it atti-tude, there was no attempt to help or please; they took up a school-mistressy pose, looking down on us in a crushing, disapproving manner, and indicating that we were extremely lucky to be offered what was on display. In the end I bought some furnishing fabric and had a dress made by a little Greek dressmaker who had survived the blitz in her poky Bayswater basement flat. (Shops in Athens were well stocked at the time but at inflationary prices. I had never gone near them.)

Buying food was also different in the same sort of way; shopkeepers were not helpful unless they knew you. They expected tips, compliments and cajolling and they hid items which were scarce, offering these – already wrapped up – to their chosen customers. This sly, under-the-counter, money-grubbing attitude, was again not how I had remembered Nanny Nell's Britain. But then I realized that with so much destruction, suffering and loss of life, people had changed and attitudes had changed too. Also at that time, although I did not know it, I was searching unconsciously for the paradise that I had built up in my mind during the occupation – and that did not exist – had never existed. It could not exist anywhere.

I looked up several friends I had met in Greece but often, seeing them now in civilian clothes, they appeared not only less glamorous but strangers too. My picture and knowledge of Britain had, I suppose, stopped with the British evacuation in 1941 except for the brief period during the liberation and that period had now been overtaken by the tragic civil war in Athens. But one night Michael Forrester* a young British officer I had last seen when the British were evacuated in 1941, asked me out to dinner. When I said that I would rather have dinner at the flat he arrived with tins of delicious delicacies from Fortnum & Mason – unrationed I presumed. And we heated these up in the tiny kitchen cupboard – or kitchenette as this box was described in our service flat brochure. It was fun, perhaps because Michael's genuine love for Greece was a link with my past. I remember squatting on the floor in front of the electric fire and listening to him describing his narrow escape from the German Stukas as they dive-bombed the British forces on Crete. And I recalled how I had watched those planes from our balcony in Athens – and how helpless, angry and desperate I had felt. Michael had also fought with the 8th Army in the desert – a battle I had not been able to follow in Greece during the German occupation. And he described the fighting that had preceded the British victory at El Alamein and how it had united all those who had taken part in an unforgettable bond of friendship. To my surprise, I also remember him praising the Germans. He said he greatly admired Rommel and his men and so did other British officers and soldiers. Yet, as he was talking, and as I looked back at my own experience, I could not believe that Greeks would ever admire the Germans who had treated them so brutally – reserving their prison etiquette for their British prisoners only. The Germans – I knew from my Gestapo prison days – had a love-hate relationship with the British. And they admired them. But I remember Michael – so incredibly handsome – his soft, pale blue eyes, his serious face, his gentle voice describing

* Later Major-General Michael Forrester, CB, CBE, DSO and Bar, MC and Bar.

what a battle was like and what it actually meant – that superhuman force – almost a guiding hand from above – that united and drove men forward. Michael did not, however, mention a miraculous feat of his in Crete in 1941 when he had saved a whole village, but I had heard of this. Supported only by Cretan villagers, men, women and children, who hurled out their savage war cries as they brandished their conglomeration of weapons – antique pistols which had seen the War of Independence, knives, pickaxes and pitchforks – Michael had led an assault on a strong German garrison. When the Germans caught sight of this terrifying, frenzied mob, led on by a young English Captain waving his cap in the air – they withdrew.

As he got up to leave that night I remember Michael saying, 'I am glad you still sit on the floor, I have always remembered you that way.' Somehow these words and that evening brought back memories of those happy days in Greece, the early victories against the Italians and the joyous liberation, moments that the civil war in Athens had stamped out so cruelly – tearing away the bond I had with my other home. But it was only to be a temporary break.

I was not happy in London at that time. I remember that. Poor Mother and Father were always trying to find ways to amuse me – to cheer me up. They complained that I was permanently sad, pale and appeared to be thinking all the time. At one point I recall Mother in exasperation saying to me, 'What *is* it you are permanently turning over in your mind? What *are* you thinking of?' But I could not tell.

On my birthday Mother decided to give me a surprise; she secretly rang up all my old schoolfriends and invited them to a party. She hoped that this would amuse me and make me forget the past – the Greek past. I can still clearly see that long table in the Mirabelle dining room, laden with cakes made out of powdered eggs, margarine and swirls of non-cream. I remember feeling far away – I could not believe that it was I who was sitting there. Looking round at my old friends they seemed weird, evil caricatures of my past who were staring expectantly at me. 'Ooh! Do tell us about your war experiences, Xenia darling, we just can't wait ... were the Germans really beastly to you? Do give us the grisly details of their nasty tortures!' This was Jane speaking, she had been my best friend at school, that was how she came to be sitting next to me. But now as she smiled and waited for an answer I hated her – or was it England, or was it myself? I remember leaving the table, crossing the room which seemed a mile long and rushing up to our flat. I locked the door and cried myself to sleep. It was an unhappy birthday.

I was obviously disillusioned with Britain, so different from the country which I had so vividly pictured in my fantasy world during the war, and now I longed to return to Greece – my native land. The land I loved. I applied for a job in UNRRA and was delighted when, without much delay, I was accepted as the assistant to one of the directors. I travelled to Athens on an UNRRA military plane. It was a Dakota, with none of the comforts of civilian planes, and it had to stop over in Rome on the way to refuel. But when the two engines revved up on the runway and we took off into the sky – I was thrilled. I cannot say that I had a glorious career in UNRRA. I was unused to large organizations, to memos and meetings that rarely ended in action of any kind. And the economic and political situation in Greece was hampering UNRRA's work. I was working in a section dealing with reports on war devastation, but figures have never either interested me or been my strong point. And when my boss dictated his reports he happily did not notice that what I typed out for him carried only the gist of what he said but not the actual words he had spoken. I had completely forgotten my shorthand and was so nervous that I could not read back my longhand notes either. And anyhow, at that time I was unable to concentrate. A young, blue-eyed, correspondent, with childlike looks, Stephen Barber, was in love with me – I was not in love with him but admired his brave, dashing manner. I was in love with Greece. When he asked me to marry him I recalled Mother's old fashioned view of marriage – namely that one always falls in love with one's husband after marriage – and I accepted. Our marriage lasted a very short time. It was a mistake, we were not suited to each other. In the end I walked out. But years later when we were both in Washington, he, the brilliant *Daily Telegraph* correspondent and I, the British Ambassador's wife, he summed up our short marriage to the eager US press thus, 'Today we would just have had an affair – then, in Greece, it was different.'

I owe Stephen my journalistic career which shielded my feelings of failure, my sadness and loneliness after I had left him. And he often generously helped me during the guerrilla war in Greece. I went back to London briefly where my parents were good enough not to discuss my broken marriage. But a short while after my arrival I received a telegram from *Time-Life* in New York offering me the post of their correspondent in Greece. Robert Low, their correspondent there (I had interpreted for him when I was in Athens with Stephen) was returning to New York. They suggested I stay in the Grande Bretagne where the Foreign Editor would fly out and discuss arrangements. There was also mention of the *Time-Life* jeep which was being transferred to my name. Without further delay I took the first plane available to Athens.

The civilian plane I flew in this time was larger than the UNRRA Dakota but it was almost empty. Just as I was settling down in a window seat a large, square-built American moved in beside me. He sat down and spilled over his seat. I buried my head in my book and tried to read, but I was too excited. Presently my American neighbour inquired, 'Would you like to see my home?' I really did not want to do so, but it would have been rude to refuse so I said, 'I would love to.' He then extracted from his bulging wallet a photograph of a clapboard house; two-up and two-down and a tree on either side – a picture-postcard home. 'And', he proffered another photo, 'This is my horse ...' and another, 'these are my cows ... and this is my wife', a worn, grey-haired woman with a wan smile. 'Want to see the grandchildren?' he inquired. At this point I felt that this conversation might go on for ever, so I explained that I was sorry but I had to get down to my work. And went back to my book.

As we approached Athens I looked down on the coastline. The sun was setting on the barren, shaven islands, marking them out in the blue sea; each one stood ringed with an emerald-green border where the deep sea gave way to rocks and sand below the surface. I began – almost – to smell the orange blossom, to see the feathery pepper trees swaying in the breeze, to hear the little waves breaking on the pebbled shore ... all my very Greek romantic vision of half-truths came back to me.

Flying into the airport the plane passed over the Acropolis, and I remembered then how the Germans had forbidden the Greeks to visit this shrine after their flag had been torn down several times by daring EAM resistance agents. 'Was that the Acropolis?' my American fellow passenger asked as we disembarked, and when I said it was, he muttered, 'My goodness, the Greeks sure need our help – it looks in real bad shape'. I wanted to laugh and to explain that part of the beauty of the Acropolis today was that it was old and 'in bad shape'. Greece I knew was receiving generous US aid and needed it badly but the Acropolis – well, that was all right and had been for many years.

When I reached Athens I found that the Grande Bretagne Hotel was full, so I rang my favourite aunt, Helene Stathatos. I remember her clear voice over the phone – half in Greek and half in French, which was the usual way Greeks of her generation spoke – she said, 'My dear, not *today* it is a bad day, it is a *Tuesday*, but come tomorrow and I will get your room ready.' I had forgotten that *Tuesday** was the day Constantinople had fallen in 1453 ... so I stayed at a small hotel nearby and moved to my aunt's house on Herodotos Street the following day. Aunt

---

* Even today Greeks will refrain from taking any major decisions on a Tuesday. The loss of Constantinople to the Turks on a Tuesday in 1453 is still fresh in their minds.

Helene was better known among her friends and admirers as 'The Byzantine', for she had an important collection of Byzantine jewellery and icons. These were displayed, dimly lit in her blue-domed and magnificently carved panelled salon, where the scent of fragrant wood mixed with burning incense filled the air. She was the *grande dame* of Athens, receiving royalty, museum directors and archaeologists robed in her flowing, gold-braided, velvet teagowns. She had an impish sense of humour, a mocking smile, very heavy, lidded eyes – like those in her icons – and a trailing voice. Self-taught – her only education had been, like my mother's, from an English governess. But she had became an expert collector whose advice was sought by all those interested in Byzantine art. I remember how later, wanting to make sure that her collection would be well displayed, in the Athens museums after her death, she donated it to them in her lifetime and set it up herself, pinning the objects on velvet stands with the help of her lady's maid's needle and thread.*

While I was in Aunt Helene's house I was able to arrange for her former chauffeur – now a taxi driver – to teach me how to drive. This was vital for me as my *Time* Inc. editor Manfred Gottfried was arriving any moment now, and when I had accepted the *Time* jeep I had not admitted that I could not drive as I was ashamed of this. When Gottfried arrived some days later I remembered how nervous I was when I drove to the airport to fetch him. On our way back the jeep stalled and stopped dead. I got out, opened the bonnet, looked inside (although I knew I could do nothing about anything) and then slammed the bonnet down again. When I got back to my seat the engine started up immediately and, turning to my editor, I saw that he was impressed. (Much later in New York we laughed over this episode.) At the Grande Bretagne Hotel we discussed what I was to be paid. And I remember my naïve request that my salary should simply cover the cost of the hotel – adding that, as I had never stayed at a hotel in Athens before, I did not know how much this was. I think my editor was amused and perhaps glad that his new correspondent was ignorant of the usual antics and mathematics of expense accounts. He named a generous salary and after we had discussed the confused political situation in Greece, he returned to New York.

At first I felt very unsure of myself in that tough journalistic world. I could not spell but then I thought that New York might well think that my cables were garbled. Nor did I know any journalistic jargon, and I remember spending several hours once trying to work out what

---

* There is now a Helene Stathatos room in the National Museum in Athens. The Benaki Museum and the Gennadion Library house parts of the collection too.

a 'peg' was that New York had asked for. In the end, in desperation I took the cable round to a friendly Associated Press correspondent, Socrates Chakles, who explained that a peg was an event of some kind which the editor would 'hang' a story on in order to up-date it and make it newsworthy. But my interviews and my work in general gave me – for the first time – a new insight into the intrigues and cunning and the various facets of Greek politics. I was also required to travel and this allowed me to get to know and see Greece – outside Athens – something I had never done before.

The political scene in Greece which I was to report on was at that time tense – to say the least. The elections, held under US, French and British supervision had been boycotted by the Communists and won by the right-wing Populists. After that governments and Prime Ministers popped up, came and went like a row of jack-in-the-boxes. The plebiscite which was to determine the return of the monarchy, and which followed the elections, was first on, then off and then on again. The return of King George II (for the third time in his royal career. The first had been in 1922, then in 1935, now in 1946) was welcomed by Royalists and by those non-Royalists who reckoned that a Monarchy was a better bet than the Communism which they had suffered – but it was no placebo. And the following year when the King died and was succeeded by his brother Prince Paul with his German wife Frederika, Royalists continued to fight Republicans, and both hurled abuse and accusations against each other in spite of the fact that the greater part of Greece was virtually under Communist guerrilla rule. In the North, ELAS guerrillas, helped by their 'friendly states' (Albania, Bulgaria and Yugoslavia) carried out daily punitive skirmishes and raids. These, and the mounting number of victims of their road mines, forced hundreds of peasants to flee from their villages and seek refuge in towns which had no adequate means of sheltering them. In the countryside atrocities and personal vendettas were continuously carried out by both left- and right-wing groups. There were shootings and summary executions of former Security Battalion* members or of loyalist gendarmes while in Athens and in the main towns prisons overflowed with both Communists and collaborators awaiting trial. This chaos heightened the bitterness and anger felt on all sides. When Mother and I had left Greece, the battle for Athens had, thanks to British support, been won, but now I realized that the battle for Greece with US support was only just beginning. The US had become deeply

* These had been formed during the occupation by the quisling government with German blessing and were considered collaborators. In some cases though, they had saved non-Communist villages from Communist raids or personal vendettas. On liberation loyalist gendarmes took their place.

involved in Greece after first sending observers to supervise the elections in 1946 and then, when the British were forced to pull out in 1947 owing to postwar economic difficulties, the US had stepped in with emergency funds to the tune of $400 million under the Marshall Plan. But now, hampered by politics, inefficiency and in some cases graft, the Plan was taking some time to get going and there was little doubt that the civil war was outrunning US aid.

As *Time* Inc.'s new and inexperienced correspondent I had to report on this tragic war – in a country I loved; a country ravaged by pain, politics, ideology and ambition which had already lost half a million dead.*

---

* Out of a population of some seven million. These losses were the highest sustained by any of the Allies with the exception of the Russians.

PART VI

Civil War

13

The Third Round

'...Our constitution is called a democracy because power is in the hands not of a minority but of the whole people...'

Thucydides, *History of the Peloponnesian War*, Book II

Looking through my old *Time* Inc. files of cables sent to New York during the guerrilla war, I see that there are regular, careful assessments – 'backgrounders' – on the political and military situation. A time-to-time line-up on some of the prima donna politicians in Athens and of the military forces in the field, from the early years when the Communist-led 'Democratic Army' of ELAS was clearly the strongest, to the later period after first British and then US advice, help and equipment had reorganized the National Army. But, as I look back on those years, it is not the politicians that I remember, although I can hardly forget the Minister of Public Order who locked the door behind me when I entered his office to interview him and then chased me round his gigantic desk in an attempt to kiss me. Neither is it the military briefings – the maps that showed the Communist and the National Army positions and equipment depots. Although there again, I recall the agony I felt at these complicated expositions – figures and directions meant little to me, and in an army jeep at night I was never quite sure where north or south were. No, finally my most vivid recollections and the ones I can never forget are of the Greek peasants – the toil, tears and heartrending tragedy they were living through day by day.

At that time I was young, and my heart, which felt as big as the bulging Greek moon, clearly belonged to Greece. And it overflowed with passion, anger and misery for what Greeks were suffering. My mind, though, had been formed in England and it inquired, reasoned and sought out the truth. To satisfy this union – or was it a split? – as a green journalist I wanted to actually see everything myself before reporting it. I wanted to be there and witness events instead of joining my fellow correspondents in the Grande Bretagne bar – or the 'snake pit' as it was called. It was from there that some of the more seasoned correspondents would send their cables date-lined 'outside' whatever town it was that was being attacked by the Communists. And I suppose there was nothing really inaccurate about that! But this urge I had to take part in events myself meant a great deal of travelling, something that was not easy during military operations, during the guerrilla war. But it did pay off at times with good copy for New York. To me, on the other hand, it gave a disturbing insight into a complex, ambiguous human tragedy. What *was* the truth? I saw so many innocent victims unwillingly caught up in the political net when they had no knowledge or desire to take sides. All they wanted was to live in peace, keep alive and save their children.

Travelling to cover the guerrilla war was, I remember, not easy – although I was often able to hitchhike on a US mission plane. But apart from anti-personnel mines on the mountain roads my main trouble was telegraphic communications. In spite of being armed with a handsome Cable & Wireless document, which was supposed to assure local post-offices that 'collect telegrams' should be paid for on acceptance by the bearer, getting them accepted at my end was another matter. It usually involved some lengthy discussion, during which time I had the opportunity to examine the telegraphic equipment to which I was entrusting my message. This was not always an encouraging spectacle. Looking back I remember an assignment from *Time* Inc. which was: 'To report on the day in the life of a US military adviser'. For this I flew to Kavalla where I joined Major Winston W. Ehrgott of USAGG (United States Army Group Greece), at the British army mess – which the US advisers shared – a villa overlooking the crescent-shaped harbour of Thrace's tobacco port. Ehrgott was a ramrod-tall, dyed-in-the-wool, forty-six-year-old cavalry man, whose family had served in Custer's 7th US cavalry and whose favourite song, which he sang at a drop of a spur, was 'Garry Owen'. (He also, I remember, argued so fiercely in support of Custer at the battle of Little Big Horn that Greek officers listening to his tale in the mess believed that this battle must have taken place in World War II.) During the German occupation, in the winter of 1943–44, he had led a squadron of ELAS cavalry and though he said that most ELAS did not fight the Germans – reserving their forces for their later pursuits – his squadron did and he was proud of them.

Ehrgott,* when I met him, was planning to join the Greek 7th Division cavalry at Komotini, some eighty miles from Kavalla, that night. He wanted to accompany a Greek patrol which would flush out guerrillas in the surrounding area near the Bulgarian frontier where they had been raiding isolated villages. It was quite evident to me that this enthusiastic

---

* Ehrgott was the first American officer to join BMM during the German occupation converting it into AMM in September 1943.

US cavalry officer was very much looking forward to the operation and without delay we set off in an army jeep flying the US flag. With Ehrgott at the wheel we covered the distance in half the normal driving time. (But on leaving the mess I had noted that the officer in charge of vehicles had been fairly unwilling to hand over his Signal Corps jeep, referring gloomily to the number Ehrgott had already smashed up.) And as he drove away at breakneck speed, Costa, his driver, held on for grim life shouting out, 'You do know that the road is mined!', and 'It is a good thing you are not married so that there will be no widow to mourn you!'. Eventually we did arrive safely that evening though I was pretty shaken up after the villainous ride. But by nine o'clock we were mounting our horses in spite of the Greek officers' reluctance to go out at night. 'Too dangerous,' they had argued, 'the horses could trip and fall, the patrol could be ambushed. Let's go *avrio* – tomorrow. Let's sing songs tonight and have a drink.' But Ehrgott downed several cups of coffee and glasses of brandy with the officers and then insisted on getting going.

When our cavalcade of fifty horsemen, armed with six Bren guns, eight Thompsons and rifles, trotted down Komotini's cobbled streets, the inhabitants hung out of their windows to see what was happening. A curfew was in force because the rebels had shelled the town with a 65 mm cannon a few nights before. As I am fairly blind at night I was glad to find a white horse in front of me, and once out in the country I followed the line of bobbing black shadows trekking through the muddy trail. The scent of almond blossom filled the damp air; overhead the sky was clear and the stars shone back from puddles of water and the shallow streams we crossed. Occasionally glow-worms, kicked up by horses' hooves, lit the path. Just as I was lost in thought – in wonder at the beauty of the night – Ehrgott who was in the lead, reined in beside me. 'A white horse in the advance guard,' he muttered, 'officers smoking cigarettes. Troops chatting. No security patrols out on the flanks. We're a sitting target if anyone cares to ambush us.'

Two hours out we reached the first of the five villages on our marshy route. As we approached, the sound of barking dogs echoed through the air. 'Never would have thought there were so many dogs,' I heard Ehrgott mutter, along with his repetitive 'no security', as he dismounted and led a search party on foot. Most of the village was empty, the peasants having left either to sleep outside in the fields or to join the guerrillas. One door we knocked at was answered by a woman: 'Is that you com-rade?' she shouted as she pushed out two loaves of bread through the door and then slammed it shut again. The accompanying Greek officer looked down at his feet and said uneasily: 'She thought we were bandits'. The next village we stopped at was a Turkish-minority village where, in keeping with tradition, a large dimly-lit, carpeted room was reserved for travellers to sleep overnight. As we entered this, we were greeted by the befezzed, baggy-trousered headman Mavromati (Greek for 'black eye') and the scene before us was a poor man's version of Aladdin's cave. Mavromati said that the guerrillas had been there the day before and had carried off forty men and boys. In a corner of the room I noticed a frightened woman, whose husband had been one of the forty men taken off by the guerrillas and, clinging to her crying children, she said, 'Don't cry, the man is an *American*, it is good to see an *American*.' 'It is good to have Americans here,' one of our troopers then muttered under his breath, and leaning on the butt of his gun added, 'to have peace would be even better.'

At the next village, which we reached at dawn, we spent some time trying to wake the innkeeper who, in reply to our first loud knock, leant out of the window and shouted, 'My wife is not here'. Later, reassured that we were not guerrillas, he opened his door and offered us glasses of raw cognac. The guerrillas had come the night before, he said, and rounded up women and girls. Those who were left slept out in the fields, coming into their cottages at daybreak. When we asked him if he had given food and clothing to the guerrillas he replied, 'I wouldn't be here if I hadn't'.

It was obvious and frustrating for Ehrgott that the grapevine had preceded us and we never met up with any guerrillas. But we saw villagers who had slept out at night, returning with their bundles at dawn and they were happy to see the Greek army and particularly pleased to see an American. They waved and smiled. Perhaps they hoped they would soon be able to sleep in their homes again.

I remember that our ride back went off smoothly until my horse got tired, sat down and rolled over in an icy stream. I felt a fool as I remounted, dripping wet, hoping that this indignity had not been noticed by too many of our patrol. And apart from the usual stiffness a thirty-mile ride – on a giant, ex-German cavalry horse – can bring on an amateur horse-women, I was amazed to find that I was not in too bad shape the next day. But then I made the perilous four-hour jeep journey back with Ehrgott to Kavalla – after which I could no longer walk, sit or breathe.

Having written my story, I wanted to file it from Kavalla, but the telegraph official had never seen a cable in English before and his apparatus seemed to date from pre-Edison days. I tried to get back to Salonica by rail, but the train blew up before I got in. I tried to go by bus, but the buses were not running because one of them had been smashed up by a mine the day before. A plane was the only solution, but although I went to the airfield daily I could not get a lift for two days. I recall

I was late in filing, but *Time* were generous.

One of my first tastes of military action in the field was at Konitsa, a northern town which lay close to the Albanian frontier in the lap of the two snow-capped mountain peaks of Prophet Elias and Niphi – Greek for 'bride'. It was here that ELAS planned to set up their 'free government' on Christmas Day, 1947, and their forces had launched a major attack, encircling the town. After heavy fighting the National Army eventually cut through the guerrilla lines and brought in reinforcements and food for Konitsa's garrison. As the first loads began secretly infiltrating along perilous goat tracks, I offered *Time* an 'eyewitness story' ending my cable 'If and when I get there unless you are already fed up with Greece'. I was conscious of the fact that they were not necessarily as interested in the Greek story as I was. The reply never caught up with me but they ran my story.

By the time I had reached the front the main road to Konitsa had just been opened and the bridges blown up by the guerrillas had been replaced by Baileys and flimsy, unsteady, wooden planks. Faced with the choice of either braving the remaining mines on this road or footslogging up the muddy goat track which was still under rebel fire, I chose the road. Approaching Konitsa that morning a few shells passed overhead as I bumped along in a Canadian-built truck which the makers would not have recognized there was so much wire and string holding it together. Dangling on the windscreen was a large blue bead against the evil eye and a painted tin picture of the Holy Virgin which the Greek Army driver pointed at every now and then crossing himself as he dodged the mine craters and disemboweled mules. With me was Patrick O'Donovan,* the *Observer*'s gifted correspondent. I remember him so well – his tweed cap right down over his face and his war-correspondent's uniform pockets bristling with pencils and pens and bulging with notebooks. He was working out in his mind – his lead – his description of Konitsa. And as we approached the town he muttered, 'Lies in the lap ... perched on the side ... sitting on the slopes...' and so on. But periodically this string of words would be interlarded with the chanting of snatches of Catholic prayers and hymns. I recall interrupting him at one point and asking him where – if he could choose – would he like to be that very minute? He replied without hesitation, 'In my best Sunday suit walking up the steps of Brompton Oratory'.

We were far from Knightsbridge that day, but it was on this hazardous road that, for the first time, I encountered the Greek peasant's customary

* A sketch of his work is to be found in Patrick O'Donovan, *A Journalist's Odyssey* (Edmonde Publishing Ltd).

mine-sweeping device – a peasant woman leading a donkey on a long
rope while behind her, her husband sat in safety and comfort on the
donkey. The reason for this division of labour – I was to learn later
– was that if the woman stepped on a mine, although she would be
blown up, the man and the donkey stood a good chance of survival
– both, in the eyes of the Greek family, much more valuable assets.

On our route I remember passing dazed peasants with pathetic bundles,
who begged a lift back to their villages. Their mules, their only form
of transport, had been taken by the rebels or requisitioned by the army.
(In theory the army paid for them but the peasants had no idea how
to collect this money.) We also had with us a bearded priest who periodically asked the driver to stop as he clambered out – hitching up his
black robes – to bless the groups of soldiers passing by. Our driver,
I recall, had been reluctant to take this cleric in his truck as there is
a deep-seated Greek superstition that to travel with a priest brings bad
luck, and he was nervous enough travelling over the recently mined road
without this added 'curse'.

On the outskirts of Konitsa we came across the rebels' artillery site
where thousands of empty 65 mm shells lay in the deep mud and slush
between the clumps of cypress trees. Then, just below the town the
truck stopped. As I walked up the steep cobbled alleyways I found it
hard to realize what was happening, hard to realize that this was the
front line – although I was challenged several times by army patrols
and armoured cars rolled past me up the narrow streets. There was too,
the occasional burst of shell-fire and the splutter of machine-gun fire
but the sturdy grey stone Turkish period houses with ivy and moss clinging to their damp walls showed only minor chips, and in traditional
fashion their balconies were hung with gay, brilliantly coloured fleece
rugs* laid out for airing. Only the bowed peasant women, silently carrying water from the wells looked benumbed as I passed them by. Dressed
in their traditional costume – long, dark, pleated skirts, tunic coats
trimmed with coloured embroidery, and a black handkerchief tied tightly
under the chin – they stared at me vacantly as if they were looking through
me – and beyond me.

In the evening, as I entered the military headquarters which, in the
eighteenth century, had been a Turkish Pasha's harem, in a small, dark
corner of a magnificently panelled hall where once Ali 'Tepelenlis' Pasha
of Yannina must have wooed his favourite wife, I caught sight of the
wounded garrison commander, Brigadier Dovas, lying in a sheetless cot.
Tiptoeing past him I entered the military operations room. There candles

---

* In villages these are used as blankets.

threw up strange, wild, flickering shadows on the finely carved pine ceiling and pilastered walls – and suddenly I remembered that Aunt Stathatos' carved, panelled room had been brought from a house in this area. But the scene before me was far from the traditional military picture I had expected and yet the Greek National Army officers pored over their maps as Communist loudspeakers blared from the outskirts of the town: 'Kill your commander! He has been bought with American dollars and has sold you out!' As far as I could see, there was little evidence of American aid except for army rations, and these I knew only too well were not what a Greek soldier likes to eat. (Later they were often bartered in the towns for beans and oil which were more to their taste.) I remember watching a muleteer opening a tin of US sweetcorn. 'This was alright during the siege, *chryso mou*,'* he said looking up at me, 'but, begging your pardon, it is not even the kind of corn my mule Nicola would like to eat'. I was soon made aware that the lack of US military aid was a very sore point indeed and I was highly embarrassed when one of the soldiers asked me to get a message to Mr Truman quickly – as if I had any means of doing so! 'Ask him if the Americans are going to help us or let us go under – we want a quick reply, please, Miss. My fiancée has fled from our village. The Communist guerrillas have beaten her ninety-year-old grandfather to death and seized her dowry. Now how can she hope to marry without her dowry?' The soldier turned away. He did not expect an answer. There was none.

On the other hand I saw ample evidence of the help the guerrillas were receiving from Communist sources. Among the weapons which had been captured by the National Army and which were piled up in a corner of the operations room, were German-type bazookas and Rumanian mines. One pathetic sixteen-year-old guerrilla prisoner who was squatting dejectedly on the stone floor wore a grey-green Rumanian military jacket and told me that he had been forcibly recruited. Three of his friends, he said, had tried to run away but they had been caught, and tied with ropes and kicked to death by old-timers in front of the new recruits 'by the light of the moon'. He himself had tried to escape and had been hung by the legs, head downwards over a brazier of coals. To prove his point he then pulled up his breeches to show me the marks. Like the other teenage prisoners the army had captured, he had been armed in Albania – he himself had been handed an old British Enfield rifle. 'The *kapetanios* told us,' he said, 'that Konitza would be an easy job and that our government would be set up there. Then we would move on to Yannina where we would find the Anglo-American Commis-

* Greek for 'my golden one', a common form of endearment.

sion. (This no doubt referred to the UNSCOB field team.) We were to take them prisoner, tie them up and take their clothes away', he added.

But as the shells fell around us the Greek officers told me they had little time for these sad stories. And they were cynical about the miserable, tattered, teenage prisoners. 'When you catch them they say they have been forcibly recruited, but when they fight they fight like hell,' Colonel Valadas, the commanding officer, remarked as he pushed towards me – across his desk – a red enamel star with a hammer and sickle on it which he had just removed from one of the prisoners' caps. 'And is this Greek?' he snapped.

When I left Konitsa rebel guns were firing and Greek National Army guns returned the fire on rebel positions. Spitfires flew overhead. Looking up at the sky Valadas muttered, 'We are not allowed to get closer than two kilometres from the Albanian border, but we have to take losses from shellfire from guns across the frontier. We have to wait for the UN people to come and look through their field glasses and scribble down a note. Our hands are tied. That's a hell of a way to fight a war.'

On my way down the hill I passed a Dutch UN observer in khaki jockey cap sitting silently on an upturned ammunitions case in a trench. He was noting down positions of the guerrilla guns in Albania. His notebook bore the neat marks, '272/498 263/495 245/467' – I did not know what the figures meant, but I understood what Valadas and six million Greeks felt.

Back in Athens I found that I was turning over in my mind – over and over again – what the Greek officer had said about young guerrillas being forcibly recruited and yet 'fighting like hell'. In the end I decided that I must see for myself what it was really like to live in a village occupied by ELAS. Stephen, whom I consulted, felt just the same and together we planned a trip to the Vitsi area where, because of its proximity to the Albanian and Yugoslav borders, most of the villages were in Communist hands. There was no demarcation line on the military map that we both studied as this was an untidy war where villages were lost one day and recaptured the next by one side or other. And the only way to reach a Communist-held village was to travel from village to village picking up information as one went along. Early one morning we drove off from Athens in my jeep, taking the main roads north. After spending a night in Kastoria in a hotel with no water, damp beds and the strong smell of the seized-up lavatory, we continued our journey, at first bumping over the stony mountain roads and later manoeuvring through the mud and slush. When we reached the snow-line the road suddenly gave up completely. Stephen, who was at the wheel, accelerated so as not to get stuck in the snow. Slipping and sliding from one side to the other we eventually managed to reach a cluster of houses hugging a stone church. There we stopped.

Within seconds of our arrival a ring of villagers closed round our jeep – little boys asked for chewing-gum by moving their jaws up and down, older boys for cigarettes as they puffed through their fingers. Then the older people who had been eyeing us from the *cafenion* – the coffee shop across the square – came forward. Pushing the kids to one side they shouted angrily, 'Shame on you – beggars! 'Aren't you ashamed, dirty boys? Mother of God, what have we come to?' Just then a middle-aged man appeared. He was led towards us by the crowd who pointed at him. Like most of the villagers he was wearing a variety of garments of different origin, thick tweed cap, old army jacket, baggy heavy woollen trousers and felt boots with slices of old car tyres tied round their soles with string. His black curly hair that protruded from under his cap was as shiny as his darting, intelligent eyes. 'My name Gianni,' he said with a strong Greco-American accent. 'I live in United States, I bring back good things', and he held up a huge orange alarm clock and pressed it to my ear for me to hear its loud tick. Then, adjusting the bell, he set off the alarm and the crowd shrieked with delight. When the laughter died down I asked Gianni if we could leave the jeep in the village as we planned to go further on foot. I explained that we were reporters and wanted to see as much of Greece as possible. 'Georgiou my cousin he look after your car, he put it with his goats. I walk with you, Sergio my donkey, he carry your bags. *Pame* – let's go!' Gianni was obviously proud to be with the foreigners and delighted at the thought that he would be able to replenish his stock of tales with which to regale the village *cafenion*.

At first Gianni carried on a running commentary on life in the United States. 'Good people ... good money ... not like us Greeks ... we fight ... steal and kill ... I love hamburgers ... now we have no meat.' Then, after a two-hour climb, we came to a village where a ring of houses on the outskirts had been burned to the ground. Here Gianni stopped. 'I go no further,' he said, and, pointing to the village above, he added, 'Up there they kill and they take Sergio from me. They may kill you – Mother of God, I don't know if I see you again.'

Unloading our bags and muttering to himself – Gianni left us and slowly made his descent. We looked up at the next village. Built on the edge of a cliff with tiny balconied houses spilling down a cruel crag, it seemed to be very much like any other Greek village. But, as we walked through the village where Gianni had left us, we were warned again. A group of villagers came towards us, blocking our path; they all seemed to be dressed in black – or that is the way I remember them. They surged forward like a huge black wave. They were silent and sullen. A black-robed priest who was among them pointed up to the next village and said, 'The devil he lives there – why do you go?' I pretended that I did not understand, the crowd parted, and we moved out of the village.

Now we were treading on virgin snow, crushing it down as we walked, and laughing as our feet sank deep, deep down, leaving behind us huge elephant-like foot marks. And now we were on our own. We could be ambushed and shot. The thought came into my mind. An American journalist, a friend of ours, George Polk, had recently been murdered. His body had been washed up near Salonica. He had been shot in the back of his neck – his hands and feet were tied. He too had wanted to see for himself ... But it was so beautiful, so sparkling, so bright; the blue sky above, the white, untouched snow, and not a sound – except for the clear echo of our voices – and no-one about.

After we had been climbing for some time, with the sun in our eyes, we stopped dead when a loud, threatening voice which seemed to come at us from nowhere, cut across the snow. 'Halt! Halt or I fire!' Looking up to the outskirts of the village we were approaching we caught sight of a soldier in unidentifiable uniform running towards us with a gun at the ready. He stopped a few yards from us and shouted angrily, 'Who are you? Do you know the password? This is Free Democratic Greece. Do not move or I shoot'. My heart was thumping – the proximity of the gun brought back memories, but this time it was a Greek, not a German gun. Quickly deciding to speak in broken Greek so that I would not be suspected of being a Greek spy – it would have taken too long to explain how and why I spoke Greek anyway – I replied in what I hoped was a matter of fact fashion, 'We are British journalists, we wish to meet your *kapetanios* and see your village'. I remember how relieved I was when the soldier lowered his gun and a broad, ugly grin lit up his face; as his cracked lips parted I saw there were gaps between his tobacco-stained teeth. He wore an ill-fitting khaki uniform of nondescript origin and a bandolier slung across his chest. 'Good hour!' he said, giving the familiar Greek welcome. 'I will take you to Kapetanios Pythagoras. I will show you the way – follow me.'

As we entered the village in the sunlight it seemed once again very like any other Greek mountain village I had seen. But then I noticed a difference – the villagers did not come forward to greet us or inquisitively to ask questions. Instead, they eyed us in silence from behind their slit-opened doors or from within their deep, snow-covered courtyards. Only the little boys, who were obviously fascinated by the guard's gun and bandolier and generally with what was going on, stood out on the street corners. Their large eyes – like shiny black olives – followed us intently.

When we reached the centre of the village we found the main square packed with young guerrilla boys and girls who had assembled there for military drill. A group of older men were there too. The girls looked odd and un-Greek, some with their traditional pigtails cut off and with baggy brown uniforms (which I learned later had been specially tailored in Yugoslavia) taking the place of those graceful, swinging dark woollen pleated skirts and embroidered overcoats. Their mothers still wore them but they were hard at work baking, cooking and washing for the guerrillas and chopping wood for their fires.

Our escort led us to the *cafenion* at the far end of the main square where a group of guerrilla officers were bent over a map. There he left us. As we approached the group, a frizzy, red-haired officer, sporting a dozen stars across his chest, stepped forward and introduced himself, 'I am Kapetanios Pythagoras, there are my comrades and this is my friend'. He pointed to his group of officers and to a dour-looking 'commissar' in a loose-fitting Russian-type uniform (it was in fact Rumanian), and invited us to sit with him, drawing up two more chairs. Clapping his hands, he summoned a little boy who was standing by in a daze, mesmerized by the *kapetanios*'s gun which was lying across the table – and longing to finger it.

'Quick, my boy,' the *kapetanios* shouted. 'Don't stand there doing nothing – go fetch the glasses and the *Tsipouro*.' As the boy turned to go he landed him a hefty slap on his bottom. The boy returned within minutes – a broad smile on his face – delighted to have been of service to his hero.

Filling our glasses and his own, the *kapetanios* stood up and drank a toast: 'Death to the Fascist beasts!' he cried. 'Long live freedom and democracy!' Tilting his head back he drained his glass, bringing it down with a crash on the table. Then, smacking his lips, he eyed us suspiciously. We of course could drink to this toast – giving it our own interpretation – and Stephen drank up. But I was worried. I had never drunk wine or spirits before and I knew their *Tsipouro* was strong, it was the local vodka. I also realized that if the *kapetanios* noticed that I had not emptied my glass, he might well query my allegiance. Happily though, the *kapetanios*, a flamboyant bully of a man, with eyes that darted from side to side seeking a victim for his black humour, was at that moment busy diving in his pockets. For several minutes he searched for something and this gave me the opportunity I needed to tip my glass of *Tsipouro* down behind my chair. Having found what he was looking for, the *kapetanios* triumphantly brought out a piece of lined paper which could have been torn out of a school exercise book. (And I was much relieved to see he had not noticed what I had done with my drink.) Like most Greek documents, the paper which the Kapetanios flattened out with his large clumsy hands had an impressive round stamp and several illegible signatures. The stamp read, 'Democratic Army Headquarters Vitsi'.

'I show you how big and strong democratic Greece is and soon it will be bigger as our friends' – and with that he waved towards the northern border – 'are generous. This list shows the villages *we* have armed and what ammunition they have. Below is a list of the villages the Fascist murderers have armed – they are not free – *yet*.' And turning to me as I was pretending to drink the last dregs from my glass, he gave a jocular laugh. Slapping his shins, he continued, 'We could all be free soon if it were not for the enemies of the people, Truman and Churchill,' and seeking out my eyes with a crafty look he added, 'I hope you both write *that*'. Pointing to the village girls who were lifting their heavy guns he said, 'We teach the girls rapid fire, booby-trap laying and ambushing. We teach them how to live – they are happy with us. In Greece a girl cannot sit at a table with a man, not even with her father – here they live and fight side by side. We also give them books to read,' and he pushed a small, badly-printed book towards me which he had picked off a pile on the Commissar's table. The text, printed on cheap paper, was written in Greek, French and Russian. The first paragraph read:

'The other countries of the world, former allies or enemies during the great anti-Fascist war, which has been over for some three years now, have dropped their guns and taken up their reconstruction spades, pitchforks and shovels. Greece's former allies, the British and the Americans, have forbidden the Greek people to do likewise – to engage in the reconstruction of their country ... Instead they have transformed the country into an arsenal against the new Democratic Balkan States and the Soviet Union ... For the Greek people there was no other choice – either to accept the chains of submission or to take up arms for honour and national dignity ....'

An ELAS song tailed the chapter: 'With my gun on my shoulder I open the road to freedom...' There were blurred pictures too, of marching guerrillas – boys and girls – of posed, moustachioed guerrilla *kapetanioi*, open-shirted politicians and leaders of the Greek Communist Party. I just wondered what the peasants would make of this book. I wondered if they might not prefer their traditional ballads and the tales and gifts that their menfolk, who had lived in the US, brought back to the village. And how long would it be before these young men and girls would be taken prisoner or killed in battle? Did they know what they were fighting for? This was not a toy war they were playing at, although, with that paintbox-blue sky above, the sparkling, snow-covered mountains, the fringes of icicles hanging from the village roofs and the sunshine playing on their guns – it almost looked that way. While I was going over these thoughts in my mind a priest passed by. 'Papa Nicolao,' the *kapetanios* shouted out to him, 'Are you going to sit on the village council? Ha, Ha! And what news from God, hey?' The *kapetanios*'s derisive words brought peals of laughter from his officers. 'Tomorrow we will attack the Fascists – did your Father tell you we would win?' The boys and girls in the square were standing at attention, watching their *kapetanios* in silence – a number of them clapped their hands over their mouths to stifle a giggle.

Getting up from the table the *kapetanios* asked us with a grin, 'Do you want to come with us? Tomorrow we start at dawn to attack Truman's lackeys'. I do not think he ever expected us to accept, and as it was late we explained that we had to get back in time to write our stories. 'You will write the truth – that Greeks are suffering through the Monarcho-Fascists – or else...' and fingering his gun he broke into hoarse laughter. I could not make him out – he looked jocular and then suddenly – grim. As we walked away through the village once again the women peeped at us from behind their doors. Outside the courthouse, formerly a school building, we passed a group of villagers standing in line. Their sunken faces were worn and resigned. They had seen it all before – with the Italians, the Germans, the Communist ELAS, the right-wing security battalions – now once again it was the Communists who were putting them on trial, perhaps for the help they had given the National Army when they were in the village – or because they had brothers or uncles fighting on the other side. And would the National Army come again? What sentence would the village council pass? Would Pythagoras be lenient? He was off tomorrow.

As we descended the slope outside the village I looked back. A soldier was standing guard, his gun at the ready – pointing it at us. I wondered if he would shoot. I recalled the feeling I had had when I left the German ss headquarters – why do thugs always shoot in the back? But he did not shoot, and by nightfall we had reached Gianni's house. The villagers were happy to see us again and quickly produced wine and cheese – the cheese I knew they could ill afford to offer – but Greek peasants are proud. No questions were asked and soon we drove away in the jeep they had kept safely for us. On the journey I tried to work out in my mind the true picture of the ELAS village we had visited. What did it feel like to live in that village? But as in all things in life – there was no clear black-and-white image. The little boys had obviously been keen to play the war game. It was thrilling and new. Some of the girls were excited to meet boys and be with them on an equal footing. But the following day these untrained youngsters would be thrown into battle – something they had not experienced. It was of course something their parents knew well. Some of them had already fled, or hidden their children – I had met them in other villages; others had been caught and found out: they were now perhaps among those we had seen standing in line outside the courtroom. Was this what the Cold War really meant? Who was fighting whom, for what, with what – in the name of freedom?

Later – in March of the following year – when that glistening, crackling, virgin snow had melted and after the guerrillas had fled before the advancing National Army, a National Army soldier told me what he had found in the village I had visited, 'the preserved bodies of the dead bandits were standing upright in the snow like ninepins and in the valley behind the former courthouse the mangled bodies of peasants showed that the bandits had run out of ammunition and used the chopper instead for executions'. The army despatches that month read: '1,820 guerrillas killed, 75 captured, 1,900 surrendered. 1,200 National Army killed, 62 wounded, 81 missing.' I gave the figures to *Time* in my monthly round-up.

On my weekly trips to the front I rarely found what I expected or what I had pictured a battle to be like. On one of my journeys to the front I was expecting to watch the major Greek army offensive, code-named 'Operation Coronet' against General Marcos' so-called 'Democratic Army's'* stronghold on Mount Grammos. And I did watch part of it from a brigade command post in Fort Nestorion. But what I vividly remember today is not the din of rockets and guns but the scene before me in Nestorion as I walked to the fort. The main square was packed with ambulances, trucks and jeeps. In a horse trough near the spring, peasant women were washing out used field dressings and the stained water flowed over the cobble-stones. In the church, which I peeped into, the village priest was chanting the burial service over eight soldiers who had died that morning on hill 1291. I said a prayer.

When I reached the command post I looked down on the riverbed where trucks were lumbering through a ford and up a newly bulldozed goat track. Pointing at this, an officer told me the 25-pounder guns had been hauled up this precarious slope earlier in the day and I wondered how. At about three o'clock in the afternoon the brigadier announced, 'The spaghetti is cooked and the birds are flying'. He meant that the artillery was ready and the Spitfires aloft. On the skyline, four miles across the valley the artillery opened up and the infantry jumped off.

---

* The Communist guerrillas fought under the ELAS banner but preferred the sycophantic title of the 'Democratic Army'.

For some ten minutes the shallow, dome-shaped hill was lost in smoke and dust. Spitfires swooped in wide spirals, loosing their rockets. Gradually the quick chatter of the rebels' Breda and Spandau machine-guns was subdued and the Greek army Bren guns took over. Twenty-five minutes after the attack began the green Very lights arched in a signal over the crest. The position had been taken.

Some days later when I had returned to Athens I heard that Marcos was back on hill 1291. Attacking with fresh troops who had been trained in the Yugoslav camp of Bulkes he had forced the Greek army to withdraw. When the news reached me I remembered the words of a gnarled, somewhat unfriendly peasant woman I had passed on my way up to the fort. 'The wheatfields were planted by Marcos' men,' she said, wagging a bone of a finger at me. 'They said they would be back to harvest them.' And suddenly I saw again the picture of that valley I had passed on my way home via Kastoria where the crammed, almost choked wheat-fields were ripening fast. I remembered too, that like other villages which had changed hands during the guerrilla war, Nestorion was not friendly. The women stood unsmiling in their doorways, some too frightened to be friendly in case the guerrillas should return, others – frankly hostile. About half the villagers were Slav-speaking, and this I found was the case in most of the villages in that area. It was, I must admit, something I did not know or expect since at Queen's I had not studied my country's history. A Cretan sergeant I had met at the fort referred to the women of Nestorion as 'Komitadjis'.* He had just found one carrying an anti-personnel mine in her knickers and three of his friends had had their legs blown off the day before. And when I remarked that it appeared to me that there were only shifty-eyed women left in Nestorion – the men had vanished – the garrison officer explained why. He said the men from the upper village, where there had been a small National Army garrison, had sought refuge in the neighbouring town of Kastoria. Those of the lower part had gone – willingly or unwillingly – with Marcos, many of whose followers were Slavophones. He then showed me papers taken off a dead guerrilla in the Nestorion area – a local boy – and I saw that they were written both in Greek and Bulgarian characters. There were pathetic crumpled notes on basic military training in a childish hand, and a collection of songs. One of these must have been sung to

---

* The *Komitadjis* were Bulgarian nationalists who fought the Greeks for control of Macedonia at the beginning of this century. Macedonia had been under Turkish rule since the fifteenth century. The Greek army tried to invade Macedonia in 1897, but was defeated by the Turks. After that, internal violence continued between the rival inhabitants (Turks, Greeks, Serbs and Bulgarians) until the Turks were driven out in the first Balkan War (1912–13), leaving Macedonia divided between the other three nationalities.

the tune of 'Yippee-aye-aye' for the words of the chorus ran, 'They are crazy Yankeedes who want to create chaos, who intend to send soldiers – yupee-yupee-yes-yes.' Perhaps 'yes' typified the English tongue – rhyming with 'Yankeedes'? I could not quite make out the derogatory chorus.

But I came across so many incongruous and sometimes funny scenes at the battle front. There was, for instance, that pea-green bus I met carrying a load of UN observers who nervously hung out of the windows as their determined driver bumped them up the narrow, stony mountain roads airily pointing out the huge mine craters. When they got out the soldier I was standing with gaped with amazement at the sight of an Indian press officer in black canvas over-shoes and a midnight blue homburg, a Mexican captain in green hunting costume with fur collar by Abercrombie Fitch and a London *Times* correspondent in city clothes with a rolled umbrella. The party also included a British brigadier in brand-new uniform with an impressive row of medals. He had seen fighting of this kind with the Gurkhas, with the crack 4th Indian Division, and had, I noted, visible difficulty in remembering he was a UN man and not there to give military advice.

This UN team was led up the scraggy mountainside by eager Greek soldiers who were delighted to point out the bootless bodies of dead guerrillas in Rumanian military uniform (boots were in great demand and were quickly removed by fellow guerrillas or peasants), Hungarian tins of meat and Czechoslovak hand-grenades – all scattered among the scrub, thistles and rocks. All good material for the UN officials who took copious notes. Further up towards the Albanian border the team met some Albanian stragglers who took them to be guerrillas and said they wanted to help the Democratic Army fight the Fascist Anglo-Americans. When the interpreter told them that the group were 'foreigners' one of them stepped forward and said he was trying to get to the United States. Another claimed he was a political refugee and when asked what he had expected if he had fallen into guerrilla hands – he replied snappily 'lead' (i.e. a bullet). Asked what he would have expected from the Greek army he said 'beat up and shot – it's an old Balkan custom', he added shrugging his shoulders.

On another occasion I witnessed a 'picnic' for King Paul and his eighty-year-old Prime Minister Sophoulis, who had flown for the first time in his life. After a briefing at headquarters, lunch was served on the mountain-side on garden tables with folding orange canvas chairs. As King Paul looked through his field glasses, during the National Army's attack on the rebel positions in the thick pine woods, in front of him, he caught sight of a sign which read 'D.S.E.' (This stood for *Democraticos Stratos Ellados*, the Democratic Army of Greece.) An artillery sergeant standing close by noticed the King's interest, and tapping him on the shoulder (Greeks have no inhibitions about class or status – everyone considers himself quite as good if not better than a king or a prime minister), explained that they were purposely not firing at the sign as they wanted to capture it and keep it as a memento.

I also recall a comfortable air tour of the battle scene which General Van Fleet, the Chief of the US Planning Group had laid on for some visiting American VIPs (Under-Secretary William Draper and General Wedemeyer). Beer and sandwiches were served. When the party finally touched ground – to visit the front from the divisional headquarters of the north eastern sector – alas there was nothing to be heard but the noise of crickets in the cornfields. The awkward situation was explained away by the General as a break – while the army were 'regrouping'. (But this of course gave Marcos's men time to return to their camps over the border and bring in fresh troops and supplies.) In spite of the fact that US advisers with the National Army were supposed only to advise, Van Fleet wanted the Greeks to 'get going and keep going'. The Greek officers, on the other hand, wanted more and better equipment so as to avoid heavy losses. After the visit the equipment came. But my heart was torn as I watched all these visitors and observers peering through their field glasses and – so to speak – sitting comfortably on the mountainside while the Greek tragedy was played out in front of them – with Greek blood. Often when I chatted to soldiers on the front they would make it clear to me that they felt they were fighting not only their war but an East–West war – the 'Bigs' war as they put it. 'America and Great Britain were supplying the arms,' they said, 'but it was only Greek blood that was flowing – and it hurt.'

And so while I witnessed the Big Powers hesitating, investigating, hindering or helping the Greek battle against Communist guerrillas, I also watched the stoic Greek peasants on the mountains as they continued their historically tragic lives battered between hammer and anvil. There was no clearer picture of this pain than what I saw in the village of Kalavryta (the name means 'beautiful springs') high up in the Peloponnese mountains. I remember 'Barba' as the village patriarch was called, greeting me with open arms and summing up his family's tragic history in one simple sentence, 'The blood my family has shed in Kalavryta would fill three whole barrels'.

He was referring to Kalavryta's grim past. In early times Kalavryta had twice been razed to the ground – once by the Romans who used it as a watering-place, later by the Franks and Turks. In 1821 Archbishop Germanos hoisted the holy standard from the village's ancient monastery, signalling the beginning of the Greek War of Independence. In December

1943, in World War II, German troops, who were being harassed by resistance groups in the area gathered the whole population of the village, separated the men from the women, packed the women and children into the schoolhouse and bolted the door. The men – seven hundred of them – were led to the cemetery and mowed down with machine-guns. (The operation was said to have taken three hours.) The German commander then gave orders for the schoolhouse to be set on fire. As the Germans left, the agonizing screams and wails from the schoolhouse were too much for one young Austrian soldier. He hesitated and then went back to the village and unlocked the door. Five women were saved.

On a Sunday in April 1948, Communist guerrillas consisting of fresh recruits – locally culled – struck again at Kalavryta. This time the object was loot. Word had got around that the bank held a large deposit (from payments under the Marshall Plan for reconstruction purposes and a pile of US gift parcels). The eight hundred guerrillas easily overran the garrison of 35 gendarmes and a few newly-mobilized National Guards. Some were killed, others fled. As ammunition ran out, the commander used the last bullet to end his life. When the guerrillas entered the village they called up all the menfolk and ordered them to load their mules with the loot. (The population was almost back to pre-war level. With reconstruction projects new inhabitants had moved in from surrounding villages.) And while the men were thus engaged, the women guerrillas were ordered to loot their homes. When I reached Kalavryta Giani Fotonopoulos was burying his twenty-year-old wife. She had been asked by a woman guerrilla, who had just cleared out the most prized belongings in her house, where her husbamd was. She had replied that he had been taken by the bandits. Angered by the term 'bandits', the woman guerrilla shot the six-months pregnant Eugenia in her swollen belly. I remembered how stricken Fotonopoulos looked up at me with tears streaming down his face and said, 'That this should happen to me just as life was beginning to smile'. I cannot forget him. Meanwhile I watched some of the black-clothed widows who had returned and who were scrounging in the rubble for any of their possessions. But all they found were a few hidden loaves of bread: the bank, police station and post office had been burnt to the ground. As they wept one of them said to me, '*Panagia mou* – Mother of God! I wish I had not escaped from the flames of the school house. Now I am frightened even when the wind rattles the windows and doors in my shattered house'.

There was one trip to the Peloponnese which I remember because it was going to take me away – or so I thought – from the guerrilla war I was covering. My assignment was to report on the kindling of the flame in Olympia, in July 1948, for the opening of the Olympic

Games in London. It is true that the guerrillas had been harassing the area, but like a rash they were now all over Greece and the major National Army attack in the north which I knew was taking place would, I thought, concentrate them in that area. I had never seen Olympia, I had not been able to travel there during the occupation and I longed to witness this ancient ceremony which had celebrated the truce between the warring Peloponnesian states centuries ago. With the cruel civil war in mind it seemed to me that the scene was both relevant and historic.

On the eve of the ceremony the officers of the Greek (former British) destroyer *Hastings*, which was to carry the lighted torch on to Corfu, gave a party in a taverna in the fishing village of Katakolon. Katakolon was halfway to Olympia, and while some officials who had disembarked there from the *Hastings* travelled on to Olympia, others stayed behind for the party. It was, I remember, a happy, gay gathering of British and American officials and journalists. Frank Macaskie, at that time the new *Times* correspondent, was there and so were the Sedgwicks. A rubicund, ginger-moustached British Mission officer, Colonel John Casey led the songs and we all joined in noisily. But just as he was standing, glass in hand, and singing the favourite Greek sentimental ballad *Mavra Batia* (black eyes), a burst of machine-gun fire shattered the magic of the moonlit night. And then another burst pumped shells into the building, followed by a loud wail. One of the Greek officers cut the lights, another in his haste squashed the bulbs in his hands. We all ducked under the tables. Casey, I remember went on singing to cover two of the ship's men who had sneaked out. They swam half a mile to the *Hastings*, which immediately put out a landing party on shore, and fired a star shell leaving the sky an eerie white. Then the guns were let off into the black hills – mainly for effect. The guerrillas were silent.

The next day the ceremony went off without a hitch, but under the close guard of armoured cars, guns and mortar crews. And to save time, the chanting of the chorus from Euripides by a group of schoolboys was cut. Chosen from a neighbouring village for the proud role of lighting the torch, pretty Maria Angelakopoulou – a graceful, bronzed, long-limbed Girl Guide, wore traditional white. Her dress though, as she was poor, was just a borrowed piece of cloth from her home store held together with pins. Maria kindled the flame in the age-old traditional manner – by focussing the sun's rays with a mirror on an olive branch, and with this she fired the 2,400-year-old lamp. From the lamp's flame she lit the first Olympic torch which she handed to a runner. The long relay then began to London, but this time under armed escort. The ancient lamp was later given to the British Olympic representative to take to Princess Elizabeth (which she was at that time) and Prince Philip as a gift. Handing over the present, together with a bag of earth taken from the site of Zeus's altar (which was to be strewn over the London Stadium and mixed with London earth), the melancholic tearful mayor said, 'We are sorry things are so difficult, the bandits were here only three days ago. They are bad men. They made everybody sad'.

On our way back we passed Katakolon where the church bells were tolling for the funeral of the gendarme who had been killed outside our restaurant. He was a nephew of the restaurant keeper. He had tried to protect us.

As the only woman war correspondent (I do not remember any other woman journalist covering the guerrilla war, but I could be wrong), there were moments when I knew it was a man's world. Often when travelling in military planes and trucks I would be dropped off at a village in the battle area and then had to find my own accommodation for the night. The military had tents and billets – but no room for women. One night – a night that has left me with a picture of Greek peasant hospitality that I can never forget – I was in the cold, unfriendly Grammos mountains. A US army driver had apologetically just pulled up at the foot of a mountain village, let me out and driven away. As I walked up to the main square I wondered whether I would have a roof over my head that night. Doors were tightly shut against intruders – curtains drawn. Trying my luck, I stopped at a house with a solid pine door and a bread oven in the yard. I knocked at the door. A handsome peasant woman opened it a crack. She had long black pigtails peeping out from beneath her tightly tied white embroidered kerchief; two sallow children with fair, curly hair clung to her skirt. She eyed me suspiciously and stood defiantly blocking the door and looking at me in silence. Then I realized that I was dressed in brown – brown ski-trousers and khaki war correspondent's jacket – and brown was the colour the guerrilla girls wore. I quickly explained in Greek – perhaps with a trace of an English accent – that I was a journalist working for an American paper and that women were not allowed in the army billets. 'Could you give me a bed for the night?' I asked. A smile came over her madonna-like face, she was obviously relieved. Patting her children's heads she beckoned me into her spotless, well-scrubbed home. 'My name is Anna,' she said. 'Wait, I will get your room ready.' Then she placed warm bread, cheese, olives, a hard-boiled egg and a jug of clear mountain water on a table for me, and disappeared. When she came back she led me into what I could see was the only bedroom, where the whole family usually slept at night. But now it had been cleared for 'the foreign guest' as she explained in a whisper to her children who followed my every movement as if I were a gremlin from another world. The square, white-washed room had a sloping, golden pine-beamed ceiling, and in the centre there was a raised, polished wooden platform. On this was my bed for the night. It was a large double divan with a vivid red-and-black fleece blanket and white, starched, embroidered sheets and pillow cases. Prodding the soft down pillows and fingering the delicate, embroidered roses and entwined initials Anna told me that they had been part of her dowry. In a corner I noted a framed wedding picture and seeing that I was looking at it, Anna explained that her husband was now in America. As she said this, she crossed herself, looking up at an icon wedged high up in a corner above the photograph.

I was tired that night and slept soundly. At dawn I looked at Anna's icon. The light, a wick in a glass of oil, was still burning, throwing caressing shadows on the Virgin and Child. I wondered, if the guerrillas ever took this village, what would happen to Anna and the children; they always dealt harshly with those who had relatives in the United States. When I left the house Anna was taking off my sheets and the children were dragging their mattresses back on the floor. The previous night they had all slept in the kitchen.

On another occasion a Greek army commander took pity on me. It was late at night, the villages around had been raided by guerrillas the night before, so he offered me the protection of a tent on the outskirts of his camp. I was delighted. As I lay on the army campbed that night I could just see the light of the moon peering through the flap of my tent door; and then I fell asleep. Suddenly in the middle of the night I woke with a start – there was a trampling noise outside – a figure obscured the moon and a huge black shadow appeared in the gap. I was terrified. Was it a guerrilla seeking out the army's position? I lay very still. Then the shadow withdrew. Thinking that I should report the intruder immediately to the commanding officer as the guerrillas could well be moving in on us, I got up quickly and stole out of the tent – furtively looking around on all sides and treading as carefully and as silently as possible. A few yards away the black shadow re-appeared and the shuffle came nearer and nearer. I froze. As it approached me it crossed the path of the moon and then I saw clearly what it was. It was an army mule that had broken loose – he had been my midnight visitor! I quickly went back to my bunk, realizing that I had narrowly escaped making a fool of myself to the Greek army.

But probably the most embarrassing experience I had came my way when trying to carry out New York's instructions for more and more quotes on 'the man in the street's feeling about the guerrilla war'. Back in Athens I went off to Omonia Square (Athens's Piccadilly Circus in more senses than one), and I wandered round and round, listening in and jotting down notes surreptitiously. As I was coming away I noticed that my manoeuvring had attracted the attention of a young policeman. He bore down on me and demanded, 'Your licence and card, please.' 'What licence?' I asked innocently. He blushed. My accent, it was reassuring to discover, was still too 'foreign' for an Athenian courtesan.

But if life for a woman journalist was hard, it was not exactly a bed of roses for the women guerrillas either – for the *Simoritises* – as they were called, who made up about forty per cent of the Communist-led forces. At first some were thrilled with the new life, so much more exciting than waiting at home for mother and father to marry them off. And at first they were well protected by the 'Democratic Army's' strict rules. Free love was punishable, and fiancés were separated. In the words of a pretty prisoner, Fotini Ioanidou, whom I had talked to as she was awaiting trial, 'The *kapetanios* shot any man who accosted us,' she explained and blushing coyly she added, 'They issued orders that girls should report every month to be sure they had behaved'. She also tartly boasted to having learnt 'to shoot, jump out of windows and scale walls'. Fotini had been captured by the Greek National Army after a long trek with her battalion from Albania in the snow. She recalled how they had run out of supplies and in the end had had to cut up a mule for food. Fotini did not touch it. But when asked by the judge what date she crossed the Albanian frontier – she reverted to her peasant vocabulary, 'Cherry blossom time,' she replied.

Later, as the fighting became more bitter, rules about sex went by the way – or they were manipulated by those in power, particularly by the *kapetanios*. This was sadly evident when I saw Marianthi Antonopoulou, a slim, delicate girl with a thick mop of frizzy copper-coloured hair and sad, sad, sunken black eyes. She was twenty-two. Sitting in a white-washed prison cell Marianthi, who came from the village of Mikro Hori in the Carpenissi mountain area – a village renowned for its beautiful girls and fresh springs – talked nostalgically about the exciting day when she had joined the guerrilla forces. She had slipped out of her home without her parents noticing and climbed up to the monastery, high up above the village. There she had asked the 'great Kapetanios Papouas' to take her into his battalion so that she could fight the 'Anglo-American occupation forces' and free her country. Fascist planes interrupted their conversation and she and the *kapetanios* fell side by side behind a boulder for cover. It was love at first sight.

Papouas was a former student of the Athens Academy of Physical Culture who had joined ELAS during the German occupation and had refused to surrender after the Varkiza agreement. Since then he had become the terror of Roumelia and Thessaly. He boasted seven years on mountain tops. Papouas was his proud pseudonym – adopted from wild African tribesmen who wore trinkets and gold rings on their fingers, toes and through their noses. Papouas, it is true, only wore rings on his fingers but he had a good collection of these. He was handsome. Marianthi loved him. But in line with all other guerrilla leaders Papouas had had to issue strict orders that free love was a punishable sin 'because the Democratic Army needed all its men and women for the final battle and such conduct often resulted in the Democratic Army being deprived of the valuable services of its most gallant women fighters for a consider-able time'. And as a result of these rules there was obvious whispering and gossiping in the battalion about Marianthi and Papouas. Fellow fighters looked askance – or to use Marianthi's Greek expression 'with half an eye' at the couple. And matters got worse when Marianthi needed fresh milk and Papouas gave her a goat. The guerrilla orderly in charge of the goat sulked. He complained that when the Fascist planes came over – the goat kicked and bucked and his legs were black with bruises. In an effort to stop the gossip Papouas asked the guerrilla chief, Diaman-dis, if he would grant permission for their marriage. Back like a slap came the reply, 'When ships are sinking it's no time to think of weddings'. Marianthi was desperate. Papouas tried once more to sway Diamandis and finally the chief relented and gave his consent.

The wedding was duly celebrated by a raid on a village, a grand feast, with wine, songs and dancing. Marianthi did not dance, she was five months pregnant, but she remembered the strains of her favourite song: *'Osa sidera o Truman na rixi nikitis tha eine panda o laos.'* ('However much iron Truman throws in the people will always be victorious'). She also remembered the weeks after the wedding feast when there had been marching, hiding in ditches – more marching and no food except for goat's milk in the rusty meat tin which the digruntled orderly brought her – and it did not taste good. Marianthi then fell sick, her husband too. The doctor diagnosed goat fever. A few days later Papouas was captured by the Greek National Army and Marianthi, who had at first hidden, gave herself up. I attended the Papouas trial in Larissa. It was held in a long white room, a soldiers' recreation hall. I recall the pictures on the walls of the Greek heroes of the War of Independence and a faded photograph of Truman staring down on Marianthi as she swayed, dizzy with goat fever, listening to her husband's death sentence and look-ing at him through a veil of tears for the last time. Papouas was executed.

But Marianthi had been better off than the rank and file of the guerrilla girls. In the 'Democratic Army' many of the red amazons had been left behind in the woods when wounded in action or because they had children and could not keep pace with the fleeing guerrillas. Others had been shot so that their wails would not disclose the guerrillas' positions. Not far from Marianthi's prison I saw some 600 girl guerrillas who had been abandoned, and they were highly indignant of their fate as they squatted on the stone floor of their prison camp. Some were pregnant; some had arms and legs swollen like balloons and ugly wounds where shells had cut deep into their flesh. Ages ranged from ten years to twenty-five. They all looked sullen and dazed. Some had brothers and fathers in the Greek National Army, others had mothers and fathers fighting with the 'Democratic Army'. All had been trained in the feminine martial arts of assault, booby-trap laying and ambushing. When a British officer who did not believe this asked a teenage girl guerrilla for a demonstration of rapid fire – her quick response made him blush for many a Greek army recruit!

Perhaps even more miserable than the inmates of the Larissa women's camp were the two peasant girls I had come across when I was back in Athens. They were holding hands and stood shivering outside the Grande Bretagne's swing-door; their skirts were too short, their heels too high and unsteady. The doorman who saw me looking at them told me they had been abducted by the guerrillas, debauched by the *kapetanios* and deserted by them when they had fled over the Yugoslav border. Now, he said, as they could no longer return to their villages – bathed in shame – they had become prostitutes. Or, to use his Greek phrase, 'Now they make the pavements'.

But it was not only the Communist *kapetanios* who wielded their power to satisfy their sexual lust. In the village of Klidi (Greek for key) it was the president or *Proedros* who was the villain. His story came to light at a formal Greek army court martial. And it was typical of the duplicity, the blackmail and the misuse of authority that was so prevalent in the see-saw war I covered – where power so often was thrust into the hands of the evil, small-minded bullies. Klidi was a village I had visited; it lay perched above the strategic northern supply route, it dominated or was in fact the key – as the Greek name implied – to the important Florina Kozani road junction. Its six hundred or so inhabitants lived in derelict stone farmhouses enclosed in a circle of graceful poplar trees. The population was mainly illiterate, as schoolteachers had shunned the village, fearing the guerrillas. They were politically unstable too. Only a handful of villagers had voted in the last elections and those, I was told, only did so because the village president had filled in their ballot cards for them. But there was one thing all the villagers clung to, and that was their rich cornfields. It was for these that they had refused to return to Bulgaria during the exchange of populations (1922–5) and for these that they had collaborated with the Bulgarian chief of the

Kommandantur during the German occupation while at the same time assisting the local ELAS *kapetanios*. Finally it was for the same reason that they had sheepishly obeyed the *proedros* Dimitrios Rolokos for the past three years. The *proedros* was well in with the National Army, they trusted him and supplied him with arms for his village guards. In return he denounced his Communist villagers – usually the husbands of pretty village women or fiancés of buxom village girls he had set his heart on. But the army did not know this detail.

The *proedros*, incidentally, had a nephew and niece in the ranks of the 'Democratic Army' and it was common village gossip that Antigoni, his niece, was now a brigadier. But to have relatives 'up there', or *'pano'* as the villagers called it, was as commonplace in Klidi as in all mountain villages that changed hands during the guerrilla war. The villagers of Klidi also found little reason to keep it in the dark that sixty of their friends had left for Yugoslavia after the occupation and another forty had joined the guerrillas because most of their relatives who had stayed behind could equally boast of at least one or two members of their family now fighting bravely in the National forces. Yet when the guerrillas raided the surrounding villages Klidi remained untouched. The secret behind this was simply the President's *'organosis'* – his organization of sixty villagers who, under his leadership, laid mines and acted as informers and liaisons with the guerrillas. It was a bargain struck by the *proedros* in return for which he was assured his village would not be destroyed and, it was also of course assumed by all, that the *proedros* received quite a pocketful of gold sovereigns to clinch the deal. Many of the villagers of Klidi disagreed with the *proedros*'s politics and wanted to speak out but he kept them sullenly silent with threats on their homes, their children and their fields. And then who would believe these shifty-eyed villagers when the *proedros* was held in such high esteem by the National Army – especially since he often slept on the hill outside his village at the army post?

So for three years, day and night, the *proedros*'s *organosis* was active. Wide, black-skirted peasant women lurked in cornfields hiding mines beneath their woollen petticoats. Picturesque, dreamy-eyed shepherds leant on their crooks watching (and taking note of) army convoys. To keep all irons in the fire the *proedros* kept up his denunciations of Communist villagers and many husbands found themselves in detention camps. This provided the *proedros* with his fresh supply of mistresses and there was little the villagers could do because the army believed the *proedros* was a good *ethnikophronas* – a good nationalist. After a while, though the *proedros*'s love life became complicated. He fell in love with his son's fiancée. But it was a small matter and quickly put straight when he appealed to the 'Democratic Army' to kill his wife and son who were 'collaborating with the Fascists'. The guerrillas obliged and the *Proedros* married his new love and named her Frederika after the Greek Queen. The army condoled with their nationalist hero who had borne such a severe loss – they did not know about Frederika. Then one day the army's mine-detecting team dug up several mines along the Florina–Kozani road just outside Klidi and they appealed to the *proedros*, who doubled his mine guards. A few days later the mine-detecting teams found twice the number of mines and when their truck was on its way back, it blew up. But the wounded driver had had time to notice a fieldguard hovering behind the bush and he remembered he had been there when they had gone up the road earlier. The driver arrested the guard and in an exasperated effort to make him talk, he tied him up and placed a mine at his feet. The terrified guard squeaked, 'It was the *proedros*'s fault,' he moaned, but it was 'also the army's fault for not protecting the village'. The *proedros* was arrested, the guard attempted suicide by cutting his throat with a broken bottle. A doctor sewed him up but when the doctor left, the guard tore open his wound and bled to death. The *proedros* turned king's evidence and gave the sixty names of his *organosis*. When I witnessed the court martial in Florina, the sixty villagers of the *organosis* – their heads shorn, their sunken eyes red-rimmed – pleaded not guilty. They accused the *proedros* of getting his revenge because they did not 'feed him with gold', or give him their women. When one mother heard that her twenty-year-old son was condemned to life imprisonment, she turned to me and said, 'How can one shut up fresh flowers in a box?' While a hard-looking peasant woman whose husband was to face the firing squad shouted, 'Judas has betrayed us and lives on!'

14

GREECE 1948-9

Mopping Up – Towards the End

'During the seven days ... the Corcyraeans continued to massacre those of their own citizens whom they considered to be their enemies. Their victims were accused of conspiring to overthrow the democracy, but in fact men were often killed on grounds of personal hatred or else by their debtors because of the money they owed.'

Thucydides, *History of the Peloponnesian War*, Book III

After almost three years of guerrilla warfare, as the National Army flushed out the Communist-led forces from the Peloponnese, central Greece, eastern Macedonia and Thrace as they moved up towards the final phase in the Vitsi and Grammos mountains, the peasants I met in the front-line villages still lived in fear and counter-fear; their homes had fallen first into guerrilla hands, then were captured by the National Army and then frequently recaptured by the guerrillas. On the mountain roads over which I travelled – some of them just newly bulldozed goat-tracks which had been cut out for guns, tanks and armoured vehicles, or the main highways north which had been re-surfaced with the aid of US funds – I encountered sad knots of bewildered peasants. Sitting in ditches, often with their children strapped in wooden cradles on their backs, huddled pathetically over their precious bundles and boxes – they waited. For what, they did not know. A group I stopped to talk to on the Carpenissi road, offering them a lift, gave me the true meaning of 'mopping-up operations' – in human terms. 'We left our village because we were afraid of the bandits', a parchment-faced, black-clothed grandmother croaked. 'We cannot go further because the prefect of the next village won't let us; we cannot go back because the army doesn't want us'. There was clearly nowhere in the world I could take them to. So I left them there – and drove away.

Even after the National Army's military successes, marauding bands of guerrillas would strike again. The aim of their terrorist raids was to spread fear, prevent reconstruction and stop the harvesting. After operation 'Coronet' the guerrillas recaptured a number of villages which were then retaken by the National Army. When I returned to one of these, on the fringes of what had been 'Marcos' Free Greece', although it was now once again free of Marcos' men, the villagers were dazed. They did not know what was happening to them today, or what would happen to them tomorrow. Walking round the village I found Anna Alexious bent in tears as she sat in her grey stone porch with its clinging vines. She told me – looking up through her tears – that she was sadder today than she had been a year ago. Anna had one hundred and fifty sheep which she took up to the mountains for summer grazing. Recently, fearing bandits would take them, she brought them down again. On the way down she was intercepted by a National Army patrol who seized her sheep, claiming they were bandit sheep. 'I can still hear their little bells,' she moaned. 'They did not even let me take back my little bells that I tied on their necks myself.'

Looking back on those years of civil war, it is the steadfastness and strength of the mountain peasant women that I will always remember – and can never forget. In the final assault on the main guerrilla stronghold of Mount Grammos it was the sure-footed peasant women who saved the day. I was witness to this. When the army moved into position up the mountain they would first use trucks, then jeeps and then mules, but for the final ascent they depended on the backs of the peasant women. One day as I was watching an ant-like file of women moving sturdily up the winding goat-tracks with boxes and supplies strapped on their backs, the army commander put their value to me thus, 'They can go where cats can't crawl. Only they can keep my men supplied on the mountain tops.' His men had just used scaling irons and ropes to win their position. The women followed on foot.

Peasant women too were used to repair military roads. And driving to the front I came across a group of four hundred women, grandmothers, mothers and daughters working with picks and shovels on an important military supply road. They were dressed in their traditional homespun clothing – full skirts, sleeveless coats touched up with gay embroidery and shawls tied over their long braided hair. The road they built was not exactly an autostrada, but it served its purpose as supply trucks ground dustily up it in four-wheel drive, and artillery and mountain guns were able to make their way to the front. Many of the women had taken their babies with them to work and each I was told received a daily wage from the army of 10,000 drachmas – about $1 – and a share-out of captured rebel food stocks. Though few women knew how to go about collecting their pay the abundant supplies left behind by the guerrillas in caves was what they really wanted. I also saw peasant women handling heavy military stores, and one bright-eyed girl who was working fast told me that she hoped to finish the job quickly and have time for harvesting.

At that time harvesting meant life or death to the Greek peasant women – more so than the war. And often as soon as the winter snow had melted I saw women climbing up through the craggy mountain country over sinister, twisted oak scrub to their small wheat patches which somehow sucked sustenance out of the stony, pale, sick-looking soil. On the mountain roads these peasant women went about their daily tasks – bringing in their harvest – with complete disregard for minefields. Sunken-cheeked and bent-backed, benumbed from so much war, wheat was the most important element in their lives – for them – for their children. And as the columns of army pack-mules filed through the upland fields, the peasant women stacked their tied wheat sheaves and carried them down on their backs to the valleys for threshing. A woman I watched driving her oxen round the threshing floor was working just beside the muzzle of a 25-pounder gun. Even when the salvoes blasted out – it did not check her uncanny rhythm.

I had always heard that it was traditional for Greek peasant women to do heavy manual work. In the past their husbands and menfolk often went to the United States or Australia to seek their fortune and from there they would send back money and gifts. No doubt they enjoyed their bachelor freedom before returning in later years to their villages. Almost every other cottage I visited in the poor mountain areas had a faded family photograph of 'cousin Nicko and wife' in store clothes taken in some place in the USA. And nostalgic old men in villages would often come up to me and ask for news of their relatives in Manchester, Boston or Chicago. Alas! I could not help but I was able to tell them the towns were thriving. I recall one old man walking away from me as he mumbled: 'Eh! It's good to know the places are still *there*.' And I knew what he meant – so many places in Greece were no longer 'there' after eight years of strife.

During the guerrilla war, with the menfolk either abroad, killed or fighting on one side or other, peasant women were in sole charge of their children, their families and their husband's families. And they suffered cruelly. The Communists looted their homes, if they came across a picture of a relative abroad they would mete out extra brutality. The guerrillas often seized their carefully kept cheese and salt – and in one village a distraught housewife gave me this somewhat original sequence of their barter tactics. First the guerrillas requisitioned all village goats and impounded every housewife's salt. Then they forced the village women to make cheese for them – using the milk from the requisitioned goats and the salt they had taken. Finally, they sold a slither of a ration of this cheese to the village women in 'payment' for their painfully harvested wheat. This they took to bake bread for their 'Democratic Army'.

Children were also caught up in this bewildering chaos. When the army took a village and handed out fresh white bread from US rations the children would run away. The guerrillas had taught them that 'white Truman bread was poisoned'. But there were some small boys who did accept army rations and after dark they darted into the forest to give them to the guerrillas – often local friends in hiding. And as the army moved forward I saw wary peasants piling household treasures on their donkeys and moving off downwards to the main towns for safety. They clearly feared the guerrillas would be back. An old peasant women I was watching as she and her daughter tied the last pack on their donkey explained to me, 'I must not say anything against "them" – it is dangerous – but we have to go before nightfall. The woods are still full of goat thieves.' I then recall seeing a pale-faced youth loking at us and walking towards the woods as he disappeared – clutching his army rations.

But what finally broke the backs of the sturdy Greek peasant women was when the guerrillas snatched their children. In the border mountain villages they rounded up all children from the ages of three to fourteen – promising them better food, better education and safety from 'the imperialist bombs'. Mothers who hid their children were arrested, some tortured, some shot in front of their fellow villagers. Children who hid in cellars, ditches and forests were dragged out and shot. Babies who cried on the way were shot so that their cries would not give away the frontier goat tracks used by the guerrillas to UN observers. Some thirty thousand children were taken that way. The Greek government talked of genocide. The Greek representative at the United Nations accused Greece's northern neighbours of 'intending to destroy Greece by destroying Greece's future – her youth'. Many non-Greeks thought the abduction tales were exaggerated and UNSCOB took time to work out the finer details of whether to classify this as a case of abduction or evacuation. Many of my fellow foreign correspondents disbelieved the affair. But when Marcos' radio confirmed that arrangements had been made for Greek children to be received by the 'friendly democracies', the implication of the scheme began to sink in. The rebel radio announced that Bulgaria, Yugoslavia and Albania would receive ten thousand children each, and a later broadcast from Sofia Radio gave news of the arrival of the first batch of six hundred children in Bucharest. For Greeks the sinister plan brought back memories of the horrors of Turkish rule –

the Janissaries* of the Ottoman Empire. Would these children too, one day return to fight against their parents? That was the national nightmare. Greek and foreign politicians who carefully studied the political implications of the whole 'educational' scheme — whether voluntary or forcible — believed that as a long term, forward looking Communist policy this could well be an important way of building up a highly indoctrinated hardcore for Greece whose native Communists had often irritated both the Kremlin and the Cominform with their attempts to adapt the 'faith' to their Hellenic nationalist background.

I was present at one of UNSCOB's first investigations of the Greek government's charges of child abduction — or of the *paidomazoma* — child gathering — as the Greeks called it. This took place in March 1948 in the mountain town of Kozani, in a bare city-hall library. Standing before the team was a group of peasant women wrapped in black shawls over their bulky hand-woven woollen jackets and full skirts. They were hostages, just recently released under Marcos' new amnesty,† who had lost little time in hastily hobbling down the mountain to reach the National Army's headquarters. There they were the first to break the news that Marcos' 'political men' had ordered all children between the ages of three and fourteen to be registered so that they could be taken away for their 'safety and schooling'. 'Hero Marcos', they were told, 'had successfully negotiated with the friendly Democracies of Albania, Poland, Czechoslovakia, Yugoslavia, Hungary and Rumania — to find them good homes.' Unruffled by their foreign interrogators, seemingly unconscious of their strange surroundings, the tone of these peasant women's replies was plain — matter of fact. But falling across that clarity — across those clear words which were as translucent as the water from their gushing mountain springs — one could detect the shadow of the sinister grip they had lived under.

Athena Papalexiou was the first witness to speak. She was a tall, stately woman who gave her statement in a mixture of Slav, Greek and Albanian — a patchwork language commonly used by frontier dwellers that gave the UN interpreter a hard task. Athena told the UN team that her husband

---

* The Janissaries were an elite corps of Ottoman infantry. In Greece they were recruited by the levying of the 'tribute of children' tax under which one male child in every five between the ages of ten and twenty was seized from their Christian parents, deported to Turkey and forcibly raised as Islamic soldiers to form a bodyguard for the Sultan. The Janissaries became fanatical devotees of the sultans and provided a useful cadre for Ottoman armies which wiped out the last vestiges of Byzantine culture in Greece.

† In a vain attempt to gain support and more recruits the Communist guerrilla leader General Marcos tried at times to be more lenient to peasants living in villages in the Macedonian frontier area. In 1948 he offered freedom to all hostages who in the past had supported the government and who had 'repented'.

and two of her children were in the United States. Hugging a startled, black-eyed baby wrapped peasant-fashion in swaddling clothes like a cocoon, she explained she had stayed behind to fend for the rest of the family. Asked how she knew of the order to register children between the ages of three and fourteen, her reply was simple, 'Everyone in the village of Kranies had been told and it was well known that 2 March was the date on which the list had to be completed'. 'Who was collecting the lists – a Commission?' was the UN's next query. 'It was dangerous to ask questions,' she said. And when asked if it was known whether the children would come back again, her final, flat reply was, 'It was forbidden to discuss the matter'.

Other witnesses questioned by the UN team gave similar answers. One woman referred to a 'Special Commission from Serbia* which was to make a selection for their schools'. Another woman, when asked what parents felt about sending their children away, stared unbelievingly at her interrogator and mumbled, 'Do they not know a mother's pain?' Then with cool resignation she spoke, 'Some were afraid, Mother of God, others wept openly and were greatly saddened by their evil fate'. Fate had torn three of her children from her. Fate, I remember, governed the tragic lives of the Greek peasants. They stoically walked hand in hand with it; they accepted it as the law of life.

Kranies and several other frontier villages had been in guerrilla hands for over a year and many of the women from these villages told the UN team of the threats and pressures to which they had been subjected in order to give up their children. They had been warned too that if they did not send their children away to the safety of the 'friendly republics' they would be 'killed by Fascist bombs or caught in the claws of Hitlerite Frederika'.† But few, they said, believed this tale. They did see one widower give the name and ages of his children but afterwards, when his children were gone, he sat outside his empty home and burying his head in his hands he cried, 'I have done what they asked – but who knows what it will lead to?'

The guerrillas' threats were referring to Queen Frederika's Homes – the homes the Queen had set up for over seventeen thousand refugee children and orphans who had managed to escape from the guerrillas. Daily more and more of these pathetic children sought refuge there. I visited one of the Queen's Homes and talked to a seven-year-old boy who had been in the home with another two hundred and fifty children for over a year. When I asked him how he had escaped the guerrillas

---

* Now part of Yugoslavia.
† Referring to King Paul's German wife.

he broke down and cried. Trembling all over his thin, big-boned body and burying his closely shorn head in his hands he sobbed, 'They came at night. Father was sick. He hid in the cellar but they dragged us out. They shot Father outside the village. Took Mother away and left me'. When I asked him if he was happy now or wanted to be some place else – the dazed child replied, 'Is there a better place than this?' I looked round at the clean, sparse, white-washed home – this institution was his 'castle'.

Towards the end of the war, early in 1949, I accompanied an UNSCOB team as they talked to villagers in the frontier areas. The villages we visited hung perilously over the mountain crags and could only be reached on mule-back. I am dizzy on mountain tops and unsure-footed on rocks and on this occasion I recall riding a giant mule behind the UN team. I hung on to the reins and saddle with one hand and prodded the stubborn animal with a twig I had picked up – with the other. Having had some difficulty in persuading the UN observers to take me along with them, I was desperate to cling on and not make too much of a fool of myself. When I looked down to see how my clumsy animal could manoeuvre on the narrow goat tracks which I could not manage on foot, I noticed that it moved forwards crossing its feet with the neatness of a ballet dancer, stepping first on one foot and then bringing up the other behind it in a perfect '*chassé croisé*'. Since that day I have always had much respect for mules and particularly for the ungainly animal that unexpectedly carried me so safely.

At a village called Agia Paraskevi (Greek for 'saint preparation' and later Saint Friday) we stopped and dismounted. Entering a stone cottage, which was surrounded by excited, gesticulating peasants, the UN team spoke to Thrassivolos Servinis, a bright, blue-eyed youth who had been abducted. Thrassivolos said he had first been taken to a house at Monastir – just over the Yugoslav border. He was with fifteen other boys, and spinach and beans had been their daily meal while a Yugoslav guard watched over them day and night. For a time they worked in the fields and then one day he was joined by two hundred other Greek youths, and a Yugoslav officer handed them all rifles. (When the UN team showed Thrassivolos pictures of various types of guns he picked out the new Russian tommy-gun as his.) After two days of training the Yugoslav officers gave their Greek recruits a pep talk. 'Remember you are Macedonians,'* he told them. 'Remember Alexander of Macedonia – you are going to fight the Fascists on Grammos – you must not lay down your

---

* Tito had plans for a Balkan Federation and current Cominform policy supported an autonomous Macedonia within a Balkan Federation. Macedonian peasants were of course ignorant of this scheme.

arms.' Fifteen trucks, Thrassivolos said, took them to the Greek border where they slipped across at night. After a while, Thrassivolos, who was walking at the end of the line, begged one of his friends to hold on to his gun while he went behind a tree. 'I'll catch up with you,' he remembered saying gaily. But long before the boys had noticed he was missing, he was making his way to his village through the tall grass fields and along the wild rose bushes he knew so well.

The villagers of Agia Paraskevi celebrated Thrassivolos's return and his parents wept with joy at the return of their only child. (They had two daughters too, but in Greek village language only boys are considered 'children'. Girls are something one has to bear – almost a mistake – while the boy is a prized gift.) As we were leaving the villages, Thrassivolos's father was obviously still afraid that the guerrillas would be back and he was digging a hole beneath his cart in the yard and covering it up with hay. It was there that he and his son would sleep at night. Pointing to it Servinis said, 'We work in the fields in the day-time but the whole village has to go out together with a guard and mine detectors. At night we lie in the hole waiting for the dogs to bark.'

A less fortunate boy was interviewed by the UN team when we came down to the town of Florina. Lying in a hospital bed, fourteen-year-old Nicolas Sinos had been abducted four months previously from his village of Vatohori in the Serres area. He had been taken to Bulgaria for schooling at Barkovitsa and Karlso. Then he and some one hundred Greek children were taken up to the Bulgarian–Yugoslav frontier in trucks where they changed over to Yugoslav trucks and were brought up to the Greek border in the Prespa region.

In the main guerrilla supply depot of Makrohori, he was given a rifle and told to fight the 'Anglo-American enslavers'. Like most of the one hundred children he did not even know how to use the rifle, but he was nevertheless pushed into the front-line fighting during an attack on Florina. He tried to escape but as he ran away he was shot in the back by one of the guerrilla leaders. His body lay on the rocky mountain slopes for several hours until the Greek National Army captured the position and took him to the Florina hospital. Barely able to talk, he gave his tale to the UNSCOB team in painful, jerky sentences. And when asked if the other boys wanted to escape – or were they happy? – he mumbled: 'Even the cats wanted to escape.' So much for the Communist pamphlets the UN team had collected on the frontier area where guerrillas had made a hasty retreat. These showed pictures of 'happy children in the friendly democracies, dancing, singing, awaiting the spring.'* Much truer were the pathetic notes we found in the muddy lanes of deserted villages which we passed. Written by abducted children, they had never reached their parents – now long gone with one side or other – or dead.

Looking back at that period of the Greek guerrilla war it is not UNSCOB's copious notes and their verified reports on the deportation of Greek children that come to mind, although as a journalist I reported them to New York at the time, and they are important – if forgotten – evidence. It is the faces of three Greek peasant mothers that haunt my recollections. The uncomplaining agony on the dark, oval, biblical faces beneath their tight black 'kerchieves of Calliope Gouloumi, Kleoniki Kiprou and Sofia Makri who spoke to me of their lives in simple peasant words with the cadence of an ancient Greek chorus. Calliope was a sturdy woman from a village in Epirus in northern Greece. When I met her she was still wearing deep mourning black, which she would continue to wear until her death. She gave me this account of what the guerrilla war had meant to her, 'They were in our village for a year. First they took our animals, then our food and then our children. I had three.' Wiping her eyes with her black shawl she added, 'They did not even let me say goodbye. They said they were no longer *my* children but *their* children. They handed my son a gun and said *"This* is your *mother".'* Kleoniki's description of her life was even more cruel. 'First they hanged the priest,† then they cut off his mother's hands, and then they ordered us to follow them. What could we do?' In Albania her eight-year-old girl and five-year-old son were taken from her and a rifle thrust into her hands. 'This,' the *kapetanios* had said to her, tapping the weapon, 'is your *husband, this* your *child.'* Forced into battle at Vitsi she had deserted and returned to her village. But her life, with no husband and no children, was as empty as her cold stone-built house with its shattered windows and gaping hole for a door which had been removed by the guerrillas – for a stretcher.

Sofia, I remember, had had better luck – she had managed to save her children. Though lined beyond her years and sallow-cheeked, she was proud of her village tale. 'When advance news of the guerrilla abductions had reached our village near Konitsa, mothers took their children and hid them in ditches at night, telling them that if they kept very quiet they would be handsomely rewarded with chocolates and sweets,

---

* International Red Cross investigators who saw some of the children in Communist countries after the war (no contact had been allowed by the Communists during the fighting), reported that they were not physically abused, were well fed but were being schooled as enthusiastic young Communists.

† When priests were willing to toe the political line they were not ill-treated by the guerrillas.

which they had not seen for years.' But when the frustrated guerrillas sought out the children and found none, they turned on their mothers and punished them. They took them to the mountain top and there they tortured them. 'They hung us from the pine trees,' Sofia said. 'They burned our feet with coals. They beat us. When we fainted they revived us with cold water from the spring. Fourteen of us died up there. But we did not tell. When the National Army entered our village they found the dead living, for out of the earth came our children.'

As the Greek government troops pushed up to the frontier areas in their final assault, UNSCOB had ample evidence of the Soviet Union's covert aid through the 'friendly democratic republics'. At night they watched the continuous stream of lights over the Albanian border as trucks carried away equipment and wounded guerrillas. Well inside Albania, peering through their field glasses, they could see deep trenches, mortar emplacements, pillboxes and ammunition dumps. In the woods round the former Communist headquarters of 'Free Greece', in the Vitsi area – a stretch of border territory which had been in guerrilla hands for over two years and which had been the seat of Nicos Zachariadis's 'Provisional Government' after Marcos's demise* – the *'pliatsiko'*, or loot, found by the Greek government forces was astounding. While the surrounding fields and woods were still littered with pathetic, crumpled dead bodies of teenage guerrillas and the mangled remains of mules – in the row upon row of pine-board chalets UNSCOB found everything from female underwear for the gun-toting *'andartisses'* (women guerrillas), to medical supplies, hospital equipment, contraceptives, Czechoslovak motorcycles and generator plants. In the well-stocked tailor shops there were stacks of Rumanian uniforms with three crown buttons, while alongside the row of electric sewing machines lay a number of made-to-measure British battledress jackets which had been made up from khaki cloth supplied by the 'friendly republics'. The UN team noted the plethora of German, Rumanian, British and Russian arms – artillery mortars, rifles, machine guns, anti-tank and anti-aircraft guns and ammunition. They also came across a complete propaganda and 'enlightenment' set-up, with cameras and film-processing laboratories. In a printing plant there were pages of the last news bulletin dated 14 August – the date no doubt that the plant had been removed to Albania. Scattered around the chalets, in the tall grass and thistles, were tins of Yugoslav meat, Hungarian vegetables and Hungarian cigarettes in blue-and-white boxes with a dove, the symbol of peace, on them.

* Nicos Zachariadis replaced Marcos in February 1949 as the commander-in-chief of the 'Democratic Army' as the Communist-led guerrillas called themselves. Marcos was accused of being too pro-Tito and 'defeatist'.

The '*pliatsiko*' which the Communists round the Prespa-Vitsi area had left behind kept four hundred National Army trucks constantly on the move shifting it. One convoy, which comprised entirely of goats and cattle (recently impounded by the guerrillas from the villages they had occupied), was taken down to Kastoria for distribution among the grief-stricken peasant refugees. But in one village we passed with the UNSCOB team they saw another angle to the National Army's latest victory and they faced a question they could not answer.

In the village of Vronderon, lying under the shadow of the Albanian border, a twenty-year-old private, Lazanis Nestoridis, was pinning up a pencilled notice on an unpainted front door of a two-storeyed dry-stoned house. It read, 'Please do not remove the few remaining articles from this house. It is mine. I am a soldier.' It had been four years since Lazanis last saw his house. He had fought in the first Grammos campaign and then seen the guerrillas return. This year he had attached himself to the National Army's liberating forces as a muleteer-guide, hoping finally to reach his pretty wife Melpomeni, his children and aged father and mother. But when he came to his village he found it deserted. As he sat gazing at the smouldering beehives and the upturned cheese churns in his tumbled-down yard, he asked the UNSCOB observers, '*Please, please* tell me – will they come back? Can you get them back?' UNSCOB had no answer.

I was particularly interested in following the UNSCOB team to Aetome-litsa where Marcos had lived on and off for two years – unmolested except for the occasional air attack. *Time* had published a cover story on Marcos and I was keen to see how accurate it had been. I remember at the time there had been several queries from New York – one was, 'Are his eyes brown or blue?' His brother, Cleanthi Vafiadis, who lived in Salonica, told me they were blue, but Homer Bigart, the New York *Herald Tribune*'s correspondent who had recently visited Marcos claimed that they were brown! *Time* painted them bright blue; when Homer Bigart gave Marcos a copy of the *Time* cover story he insisted on having it translated – word for word, but he did not comment on the accuracy or inaccuracy of his handsome portrait. I also remember the cloak-and-dagger game I went through to obtain a photograph of Marcos for the cover. After several 'secret' rendezvous with a shop assistant in Athens he finally handed me the picture across the counter of his crowded shop, with soldiers and policemen standing by. The 'secret' negotiations had only been a ruse to jump up the price.

Aetomelitsa was a typical mountain village of slate-roofed stone houses. Such had been the hasty guerrilla retreat that there were over two thou-sand pounds of bread left in the ovens, and the houses bulged with

Communist literature on such subjects as 'The Communist Victory in the Chicago Strikes' and 'The Ineffectiveness of the Atomic Bomb'. (Later I learnt from a captured guerrilla that in the Bulkes training camp in Yugoslavia he had been told that the atom bomb was so ineffective 'that it could not kill a goat'). But as we entered Aetomelitsa it seemed that all the villagers had fled; the streets and houses were empty – or so it appeared until I came across one old man who told me that the guerrillas had in fact warned him that if he stayed behind he would be killed by 'the Monarcho-Fascists'. 'I hid in the bushes until they left,' he said. 'I'm an old man, done my years, don't mind if I die. Lived here all my life. Want to die here.' He was trailing round the village, carrying out the platoon commander's orders and with a paintbrush and a pot of whitewash he was painting over the Communist slogans, splattered like blood on all the buildings. These read, 'Men are judged by their deeds' on the courthouse, 'Long live Marcos! Knowledge is light – ignorance is darkness' on the school building, and 'Cleanliness is strength and civiliz-ation' splashed across another wall. 'They have all come and gone – many of them – they didn't bother me,' the old man said philosophically. 'But they kept everyone *working, working, working* – why, I haven't sat at a *cafenion* for two years!'

Still trying to check my facts about the colour of Marcos' eyes – it had obviously become an obsession – and generally what he looked like and what he said – I wandered round the village hoping to meet someone else who had managed to slip away from the guerrillas. Just as I was giving up my search I stumbled across a crippled old woman lying on the ground like a sack. Had she seen Marcos, I inquired. Fixing her gaze on me through a film of bloodshot, ageing eyes, she replied, 'He was here my child. But no one saw him. The sun did not shine on him by day nor the moon by night'.

15

Athens as Far as the Moon

'... And in the end it was only because they had destroyed
themselves by their own internal strife that finally they were forced
to surrender ...'

Thucydides, *History of the Peloponnesian War*, Book II

When I was in the mountains I seemed to live and share the
suffering I witnessed as if it were my own pain. Often I felt
guilty that I was only on the perimeter of this tragedy – that
my home was in a country at peace and that I could go there whenever
I chose – and not be shot in the back. I was torn by the stories that
the captured teenage guerrillas told me – and as the National Army pushed
forward to victory there were more and more sad, desolate young prisoners taken. In my mind I was always searching, probing and wondering
what had made these children join the Communist guerrillas. What was
it they had gone in search of and whose fault was it? Who had deceived
them? One day I got some of the answers from a pathetic group of
about a hundred prisoners as they were sitting in a chicken-wire cage
in a make-shift courtroom – the radio concert hall – in Salonica. Their
average age was around twenty. The boys, with their heads shorn and
well-scrubbed faces, looked like naughty children; the girls, trussed-up
in their unflattering, ill-fitting brown uniforms, were sullen. On the ele-
vated platform, against a grand piano, was the military court's 'evidence'
– rifles, machine guns, grenades and a mountain howitzer – most of
them of Hungarian, Yugoslav, Czech and Russian origin.

I first approached some of the girls and asked them why they had
joined the Communists? Two of them – one a weather-beaten brown
skinned girl of twenty and the other, her friend, an eighteen-year-old
girl who fiddled with her long black pigtails and whose traditional delicate
gold peasant earrings were strangely out of place beneath her brown
military cap – giggled nervously at my question and then, shrugging
her shoulders, one replied, 'It was the fashion,' and the other nodded
assent. Then they gave me this description of their schooling with the
'Democratic Army': 'At dawn we did Swedish drill. After the first meal
we had shooting practice and lessons on how to read and write, and

all about politics. In the evening we were taught 'Athenian dancing' – foxtrot and tango – by a captured Athenian officer (i.e. instead of traditional peasant dances). Before the evening meal we learnt singing.' Their favourite song they said was called, 'Never give up my Tommy-gun' and it had a line which went, 'High up on the mountain there is a shady well where the *andartes* (guerillas) drink the clear water, but which to the Fascists is poison'. Both girls had tried to escape when forced into battle. One of them had fallen into a muddy ditch and, when the *kapetanios* saw her, he pointed his gun at her ready to shoot. Pleading that she was too tired to go any further she added blushingly: 'Begging your pardon to mention such a thing – but he told me to hang on to his donkey's tail.'

Another group of girls I spoke to said they were still Communists and were proud of it. They had joined the Communist youth organization EPON (National Panhellenic Organization of Youth) because it had both a meeting place and a dancing hall. 'We wanted to live a better life than our parents. At home we all sit in one crowded bedroom,' they told me. But one of them admitted that although 'Communism on paper looks good – the way they practised it up there where the *kapetanios* chose a new wife every day – was not what we expected.' Finally it was a tearful peasant girl, Chrysoula (Greek for 'golden') in tattered brown trousers, her bleeding, swollen feet protruding from her torn boots, who gave me the most simple yet vivid picture of her disillusionment with the 'Democratic Army'. At home,' she said, 'I was kept like a jewel. Up there the *kapetanios* took everything. When we ate macaroni the *kapetanios* took the top of the pot.* They told us that in the water it is dry† and that we must believe this.'

The young boys and men I talked to often had joined the Communists for personal reasons. One, for instance, was afraid that he would be arrested and charged with a murder he had committed in his village; another was told he could get free medical treatment in Yugoslavia and was suffering from tuberculosis (after a short spell in hospital he was pushed into the front line, where he deserted); another was interested in the theatre and had joined EPON because they organized amateur dramatics. But all the prisoners I talked to had found the war in the mountains too arduous and Communism as practised there by the *kapetanios* unlike the theory they had embraced. 'Why, no two people can talk together, and brothers are separated,' young, balding George Molivitis said to me, and added, 'When we found

---

* In Greece, macaroni is usually served with a thick topping of cheese sauce – this went to the *kapetanios*.

† The expression in Greek means that black is white.

newspapers in a village the *kapetanios* would read them – we were forbidden the monarcho-Fascist press'. Molivitis and his friends 'wanted Greece to join up with the other Balkan countries and overthrow capitalism. But,' he added, 'I now see that this whole plan is leading to the destruction of humanity as a whole as well as Greece. Up there we were certain we could win but we knew we had to wait for the big war.* Our *kapetanios* said the big war was coming very soon and after it we would be victorious. We were told Russian planes would drop bread and clothes. But they never came.'

I found that a number of the boys liked the initial treatment they had received in the 'Democratic Army'. 'We were proud of our uniforms and they made us officers,' a student from Salonica, Stavros Ionidis, told me. 'Ninety per cent of the villagers we took with us would weep. But our *kapetanios* had promised us that when the war was won and capitalism overthrown, Russia would set up a Balkan Federation and since we Greeks were the most intelligent – the other states being far inferior – we would be the leaders.'

Mulling over these words – over and over again in my mind – I realized that there was no doubt that for the girls it appeared to be progress indeed to join EPON and the 'Democratic Army', since traditionally, at that time, peasant women and young girls could not share the company of men. For the boys – just as a small child grabs his first toy weapon – so they too were thrilled as they reached out for their first **real** guns. And they, like so many Greeks, had wanted a better world. The Communists had promised them this. It was the broken promises and Communist theory as practised by the bosses – the *kapetanioi* – that had destroyed their youthful illusions. 'Zacharia-dis told us we *must* win. They *poisoned* us with words,' was how a village carpenter, recently released from an Albanian hospital and pushed into battle put it to me. He was reeling with fatigue and misery.

Towards the end of 1949 the long drawn out war in the mountains was coming to a close. Perhaps historians would say that this was largely thanks to British support, US aid, UN intervention and the Cominform break with Tito which also resulted in General Marcos' demise and the change of guerrilla tactics.† But looking back, for me, the strongest force had been the will and spirit of the Greek

---

* Presumably the 'big war' was an East–West conflict.
† Faced with the increase in numbers of trained Nationalist forces, the new Communist leadership had decided to move from guerrilla tactics to a more disciplinary military strategy. They also openly supported the formation of an autonomous Macedonia.

peasant population and the determination and strength of the Greek soldier.

I had nursed Greek soldiers during the Albanian war and I had met them during my frequent visits to the front during the guerrilla war. Most of these young men had been fighting non-stop. They had suffered the Italians, the Germans and the Communists. They had known little and had no faith in peace. They had had no family life. Yet they always greeted me with a smile, and a ready joke when off duty. As far as I could see there was no reason for their high spirits – it was just their miraculous will to survive. Greek privates were usually peasant boys who could not return to their villages until the guerrillas had been beaten – so they had decided to fight to the end. Dressed in a variety of different bits of different origin, a typical group of men in a mountain brigade displayed an unusual patchwork spectacle. Some had been issued with new GI shirts, which they wore either inside or outside their trousers, others still wore British battle-dress. Some wore old Greek army peak caps, others the British beret, and others the brand new GI cap.

When in action a Greek private lived on bread and tinned beef – but his favourite food was a mess-tin full of meat and beans cooked with garlic and swimming in oil. For fresh fish he would sometimes hurl a grenade in a stream and pick up a couple of fish. Often he would hold up a whole convoy in a dangerous area to pick a branch of striking pink Judas-tree blossom or wild apple blossom to decorate his jeep or truck. In his spare time he read magazines, or, if billeted in a village, he would listen to the villagers' antiquated gramophone with its large, pink horn. On feast days – at Easter for instance – soldiers would dance national dances. The *Kalamatiano* from the Peloponnese or the *Kretiko* from Crete were favourites. I remember watching Cretan General Manidakis skip lightly through the intricate steps of his national dance as his men linked up, holding hands and breaking the monotonous repetition of the steps with wild leaps and shouts of '*Hopa*!'

Greek soldiers also loved to 'tell them' – as the Greek expression goes for singing. When resting behind the lines they would sing the melancholic 'Kleftic'* ballads which the guerrillas had sung during the War of Independence (1820–32) or new songs like 'The Black Crows' (the guerrillas) 'who wound the nation'. Jokes were an essential part of these soldiers' lives and there are two I particularly remember. One referred to guerrilla tactics and was about a doctor called in

---

* See Appendix II.

to examine a pale-faced soldier. On inquiring where his pain was the private pointed to his heart. When the doctor examined his heart and asked where *exactly* the pain was, the private said the pain had now moved to his stomach. On examining and prodding his stomach the private said the pain had now moved again. Finally the harassed doctor gave his diagnosis – '*Andarticopono*' – guerrilla pain. The second story made fun of UNSCOB and was about a mule that had strayed over the Albanian border. When the Albanian border guards asked for its return the Greek guard firmly replied that this was impossible as the mule had violated the territorial integrity of Greece and was at present being interrogated by UNSCOB.

In the field hospitals I visited and in the military hospitals in Athens I was always amazed at the high morale of the wounded soldiers. They sang patriotic songs, listened to the radio blaring nationalistic music; they played tric-trac, a form of backgammon. It was all so reminiscent of my days in the military hospital in 1940. One day as I was leaving a hospital ward, musing over those early war days and my nursing experiences during the civil war in Athens, a soldier, a young peasant boy whose legs had been blown off by a mine, waved me goodbye and shouted: 'Tell America we've done our bit!'

General Van Fleet,* the head of the Joint US Military Advisory Planning Group (JUSMAPG), was very conscious of that 'bit', and he greatly admired the Greek soldier. 'I love him', he had once remarked. 'I get mad when he is not trained and used properly.' Just after a major National Army victory on Mount Grammos, I found the General in an unusually expansive mood, and when I remarked that it was good to see that US equipment had finally reached the front – punching the air with his fist he said, 'It's the *Greek soldier* who did magnificently. He's tough and hardy. I'd like to have had some with me in the Battle of the Bulge.' The Greek soldier though – who often pronounced Van Fleet's name as 'Van Flit' – a pun referring to the 'flit' guns he had given them to fight the 'black crows' (guerrillas) – had had a particularly hard time during the guerrilla war; he had had both to train and fight at the same time. When the war against the Communist-led guerrillas started, Greek troops had had no experience. The army had been disbanded during the occupation and BMM, the British Military Mission, had had to start from scratch. There were no officers except for veterans of the Albanian and Balkan wars. But General Van Fleet and his US advisers by 1949 had moved the Greek army – which only at the bitter end

---

* A Statue of General Van Fleet was unveiled in Kastoria in 1951.

outnumbered the guerrillas – from the defensive to the offensive, using modern methods. And after much persuasion – first by the British training mission and then by the US advisers – young Greek officers had been promoted and operations had changed radically from the old-fashioned Maginot Line tactics practised by some revered but out-of-date ageing Greek generals. Van Fleet, a keen footballer since his West Point days and a football coach, realized as he once put it to a Greek commander – forgetting that he was only there to advise, 'You must not relax, for if you do you can't get started again – you must *keep going.*'

After years of hard mountain warfare, much of the final successes of the revitalized National Army were due to its new commander-in-chief, General Papagos, the hero of the Albanian campaign whom the Germans had kept in a concentration camp. Papagos, as I remember him, was a tall, majestic man with huge, sunken, rather sad eyes. He had only agreed to accept the leadership in 1949 with the understanding that he would have a free hand and no political interference (a point Van Fleet strongly supported as he too had little time for Athenian politics). Papagos's strength lay in that he managed to win the respect of Greeks whatever their political leanings and, perhaps more important he had won the trust and admiration of the Greek soldier. It was under Papagos' leadership that the early seesaw gains and losses by the National Army were not repeated and it was he who led them in the final assault that ended the war.

When in Athens General Van Fleet and his wife Helene (whom he had met at West Point when she was studying at Columbia) lived in the Grand Bretagne Hotel. Their apartment was not far away from mine and I often joined them in their sitting room which overlooked Constitution Square with the Acropolis in the distance on one side – and the Giannakis *cafenion* on the other. At that time, although I was working for an American magazine, I had not met many Americans and I was struck by Van Fleet's enthusiasm, his sincerity, friendliness and generosity. He had a youthful quality of openness and frankness which amazed the Greeks; they marvelled at his simple, direct approach and often referred to it as *'san paedi'*, as a child's – but in no derogatory sense.

In his own words, Van Fleet was 'first and foremost a combat soldier'. In World War II he had served under General Patton and among his imposing collection of medals he pointed out to me his Infantryman's Badge as being the one he was most proud of. Born in 1892 in Coytesville, NJ of Dutch stock, he had an uneventful childhood in Florida where his parents settled when he was a baby.

In 1915 he had graduated from West Point – his star-spangled class included such names as Eisenhower and Omar Bradley. In World War II he served in the 4th Infantry Division; his regiment was the first to hit Utah Beach on D-Day but in the heavy fighting he was wounded. After a brief spell in hospital he took over the 90th Division and soon shaped it into one of the best on the Western Front. He led the drive to the Rhine from the Remagen bridgehead and by VE Day he had crossed Germany and was right up against the Austrian border. He obviously believed in – 'keeping going'!

But Van Fleet, like most foreigners in Greece, preferred to talk about Greece and Greeks rather than reminisce about his past. His job in Greece was to advise the military and supervise the flow of US arms and supplies to the Greek army. This he did, but I knew that he had given Greeks more than that – he had given them hope and courage when they had needed it most. He was understanding too, and knew that the Greeks felt that they were really fighting 'World War Three'. The US was supplying the arms but Greeks were giving their lives – a point Van Fleet always emphasized when briefing his US staff on their arrival in Greece. It was true that US arms and supplies had been slow in arriving and Greece's charismatic orator, George Papandreou (father of the present Prime Minister) had complained that US aid was 'coming through a medicine dropper'. But eventually, when US tanks had replaced the obsolete British tanks which I had seen stuck in the mud on mountain goat-tracks and being pushed into position by cranes, when the overworked Spitfires had been replaced and backed up by newly arrived Helldivers, when the Greek army had been supplied with the latest US rifles (seventy-five millimetre recoilless guns) – Van Fleet became the most popular man in Greece after '*Barba*' (uncle)* Truman who had saved the Greeks from fighting Communism alone. In Athens one morning as I was walking past the Tameion building which was the US military headquarters, I noticed an old peasant woman staring at the towering US General coming down the stairs. Turning to me she asked who he was. When I told her it was Van Fleet, she crossed herself and muttered, 'God is with him'.

But Van Fleet had his critics too. He was not much of a diplomat, his relations with the US relief missions were strained; and he often became impatient with Athenian politicians. Once, looking from his hotel window at the Greeks sitting out at the Giannakis pavement café – watching them propping up their extended limbs over three

* '*Barba*' can mean 'uncle' but is also used as a general term of endearment for an old man.

or four extra chairs – the theory being that with a prop for each limb and the body completely relaxed, the mind functions best – and watching them sipping their *vari glico*, the heavy, sweet coffee, chased down by glasses of cold water as they argued, gesticulated – made and broke governments – Van Fleet remarked 'Only Greeks could get so much out of a cup of coffee and a glass of water'. I think he shared, and certainly understood the view of a Greek soldier I had met once during the Grammos campaign. He was I remember, bent over a map of Greece which was marked with two blood-red circles – one around the Grammos area and the other round Athens. 'When I've finished here,' he said to me, pointing to the Grammos area, 'I will move down there and finish off the politicians.' His finger remained stuck some time on the circle round the capital. Perhaps he was waiting for my reaction – or perhaps he knew the political battle would be a long drawn-out one too.

The Communists had attempted to murder 'Butcher' Van Fleet as they called him (and Papagos too). They had a carefully worked out plan which envisaged watching the General's driver unfurl his flag and, just as Van Fleet was about to enter his car, he was to be gunned down. But the Athens police chief, Evangelos Evert, who had saved so many Greek and British lives during the occupation – had discovered the Communist cell. He nipped the plot in the bud and made widespread arrests. This was a major coup for the British-trained police force, now unarmed and respected after the disastrous events of 1944, and for the head of the British Police Mission (BPM), sixty-nine-year-old Ulster police chief Sir Charles Wickham. Wickham, a wiry, six-foot tall, upright figure, had a first-class staff which included senior British police officers from the Metropolitan Police and members of Scotland Yard's 'Big Five'. He was a sincere Evert fan and lost no time in congratulating the Greek police chief on his swift action; the two men respected and understood each other well. 'Evert's strength,' Wickham once said to me, 'lies in the fact that he knows everything about everybody and what's more important, nobody knows what he knows about them'. When the British Police Mission arrived in Athens the police bore the marks of the war. They were badly clothed, ill-equipped and down-at-heel. They also needed some careful purging of collaborators – not many it is true. The British Mission began by getting new uniforms made. An attempt to fob off the force with discarded British battledress was quashed by Sir Charles on grounds that good policemen could not go around in 'reach-me-downs'. I saw quite a lot of Sir Charles who also lived in the Grande Bretagne Hotel. I was always glad to get his well balanced, sensible reactions to Greek affairs and I remember he did much to prevent Communist prisoners in the various island prison camps receiving harsh treatment at the hands of some of the reactionary guards. But what was highly amusing for me was when he would sally forth into Constitution Square during a noisy political meeting to check that his trained men were 'behaving'. This he did 'incognito' – or so he thought. But I remember clearly that the only sign of his 'disguise' was that he wore no tie and allowed the top button of his shirt to be undone. Otherwise he was impeccabbly dressed, in an elegant well fitted tweed jacket and cavalry twill trousers. In the square, amid the excited, gesticulating Mediterranean crowd he stood out like a rare northern migratory bird.

The attempt to murder Van Fleet in Athens did not worry the General as he was never happy in the capital and spent as much time as possible at the front. When *Time* planned a cover story on him and discussed how he should be portrayed he suggested 'riding a donkey with a mountain in the background'. The General, like many a Greek soldier, had found that the 'four-legged Greek jeep', performed better on a goat track than the American version with its four-wheel drive. In the end, *Time* printed a portrait of the General emphasizing his heavy build, wooden features and piercing blue eyes. They left out the donkey and instead painted a torch up in one corner – 'Operation Torch' was the code name for the final assault on Mount Grammos. But Van Fleet's favourite quotation was one I knew he kept in his desk drawer. It was about donkeys; those he had seen being lashed and kicked up the mountainside during the war, and it read 'It is to be hoped that if there be a paradise it be full of Greek donkeys and if there be hell the generality of Greek donkey-drivers are roasted for ever'.

On my last visit to the front, General Van Fleet gave me a lift in his plane – something that generated quite a bit of jealousy and a great deal of leg-pulling from my fellow correspondents. When we arrived in the north Van Fleet asked me if I would interpret for him – briefly and unofficially – while he was interviewing some captured guerrillas. 'Please ask them,' he said very earnestly, 'How they think we can end this war.' I found the question rather naïve but put it to the sullen young prisoners with their heads shorn like lambs as they sat on the stone floor of the local police station. Much to my surprise their reply came back like a happy school chorus, 'Give us all visas for the United States and we will stop fighting,' they said. The General smiled. Communist indoctrination, like the trajectory of a bullet, had left no imprint.

During the guerrilla war Athens – once described to me by a gnarled old peasant woman as being 'as far as the moon' – was my base and I returned there between journeys to the front. It always struck me though how different the atmosphere in the capital was to the battle-torn mountainside. Morale in Athens would soar when the National Army was victorious and sink when the Communists struck again. Political scandals, economic chaos, the problem of carrying out long-standing death sentences, crammed prisons, detention camps and the murder of the Minister of Justice were a few of the daily problems in the capital. The postman who brought my letters from home – from England – and who, like all Greeks liked to dally and discuss politics, once expressed the mood of Athens more clearly than I could ever have done. His words, which are still true today, not only des-cribed the feeling in Athens at that time but also the permanent, the recurring dilemma facing all small nations. 'What happens to us,' he said, 'depends on what America will do to help us. Greeks have always got to do things which do not make Russia angry, which Britain does not mind and which America wants.'

When I was in Athens my mind would often turn back to my other home – to London; or sometimes I would indulge in my favourite pursuit of day-dreaming – unconsciously perhaps I was searching for warmth, friendship and love. How was it, I often wondered, that flowers grow, people fall in love and the moon shines down so brightly on the Acropolis – all in spite of the tragic war being fought in the mountains and the death, tears, desperation and destruction it brought in its train? Rather non-sequitur, confused and random thinking – but perhaps it was because I was falling in love.

My war-time life in the capital was pleasant. Sometimes though, it made me feel guilty that it was so pleasant. One day, after an unusually cold winter spell was over – and which Athenians had blamed on Russia – the blossom on the orange trees which lined the streets snapped open, filling the air with their heavy scent. As I was sitting out in a pavement café enjoying the balmy air and warm sunshine a large bus swung round Constitution Square, brimful of wounded soldiers waving their crutches and little bunches of flowers and singing gay peasant songs. When they passed by I felt almost ashamed of being well, healthy, strong – and in love. But during much of the guerrilla war life in Athens, with its modern apartment blocks, its packed shops displaying the latest Paris fashions, its crowded cinemas and cafés, and its elegant embassy receptions, was comparable to any international capital. It is true that there were no masked balls by order, and no dancing,* but in the evenings I dined out at tavernas with friends or sat in pavement cafés. Often friends would buy me bunches of flowers from peasant vendors as they passed by with their donkeys weighed down with bulging baskets overflowing with hyacinths, stocks, narcissi, violets and almond blossom. At weekends I looked forward to picnics with delicious crisp lettuces, olives, tomatoes and feta cheese. Sometimes we would light a fire and grill lamb on a spit, turning it slowly and coating it in the Greek manner with lemon, oil and thyme. There were always sticky cakes from Giannakis or Zonars and cool resin wine to wash it all down.

It was towards the end of the war, on one of these picnics at the temple of Sounion, that I met Nicko my husband. Half-Scottish, half-Irish, he was a friend of George Jellicoe's. George had written asking me to 'look after him' and added that Nicko 'had been much spoilt by American hostesses, but was nicer than he seemed'. (He had been a Junior Secretary at the British Embassy in Washington.) Nicko was tall, very tall and thin with an easy, natural, untidy chic – a white silk scarf wound three – or was it four – times round his neck in the heat of the summer; a crumpled US seersucker suit and a copy of Thucydides' *History of the Peloponnesian War* stuffed in his pocket. I remember thinking that night at Sounion that it was all too perfect: the setting, the warm, caressing air blowing gently off the sea – mixing the dizzy scents of thyme, cistus and sun-baked earth. The silver waves lapping on the white sandy shore and the moon – that same moon that had shone through the bars in Haidari – but now twice as large – or so it seemed – and smiling. From that day I knew I was in love but at the same time I was terrified that everything would collapse around me again. I was terrified of happiness and decided to run away – and go home to London.

Some time later, when Nicko took me to Athens airport, he handed me a small, badly wrapped parcel in an offhand way. I hastily pushed it into my bag. I did not dare to look at him – or it – as I was afraid of showing my feelings; Nicko, I think felt the same. We parted almost in silence. On the plane I slowly unwrapped the parcel – inside there was something that looked like a giant Allen Hanbury's lozenge. But on closer inspection I saw it was a deep red ruby – an antique Greek oval stone with the goddess Athena carved on it. I wrapped it up again and carefully put it back into my bag. My eyes were so

* The official reason for the ban was to remind Athenians of Greece's plight, but what was more to the point, the head of the Athens police, Evert, feared that masks and festivities were too good a cover for Communist activities in the capital.

full of tears – I could have bitten into the stone as if it were a sweet!
I laughed at the thought, then picked up my book. It was to be the
stone of my engagement ring.

Some time after I had returned to London Nicko came back too.
He had told me he would be back but I did not believe him – or
was afraid to believe him. We were married in the Greek Orthodox
Church in Moscow Road – under the mosaics I had gazed on as
a child when my mind was wandering during the service. There was
one – to the right of the altar – of Jesus with His hands on a child's
head, calling the children to come unto Him – that caught my eye
once again. The mosaic halo round Christ's head glittered like pure
gold in the candlelight and the children suddenly reminded me of
those tattered, spindly-legged village children in Greece who had clustered round my jeep hoping for sweets or chewing gum.

As I walked round the altar three times behind the priest, my hand
in Nicko's, my orange blossom crown linked to Nicko's by a white
satin ribbon, the candles, the incense, the chanting of the choir, made
me recall the words of a Greek peasant girl who had fled from the
guerrillas, 'They wanted us to marry ... but not in church ... you
know what I mean,' she had said blushing coyly. I knew well what
she meant: I had seen village churches desecrated, holy pictures white-
washed and saints defaced, with pipes and moustaches scrawled on
them. How lucky I was to be safely home – my other home – and
to be happily married.

My parents were now old and frail. Life in London after the war
had been hard, and both Father and Mother believed that they would
be happier, that life would be easier, if they went back to Greece.
Rather like my visions of happiness in the past, they had built up
in their hearts and minds an illusion of Greece – a warm, fragrant,
friendly paradise where the sun shone every day and where one was
never cold or unhappy. They went back. It was a traumatic experience
– physically they were too old to do it. A few years later they were
both dead.

I flew out to Athens when my mother was dying. I found her
in the hospital that had been my father's years ago – the Evangelismos.
In my hastily assembled travelling bag I had brought a bottle of Yard-
ley's lavender water, which I knew Mother loved and I poured a
little out on my hand and gently wiped her warm, damp brow. She
looked up and smiled – it must have reminded her of London and
of me – she recognized me. As I tucked her bedclothes in I noticed
that her nails were split and jagged. I had a nail file in my travelling
bag – so I filed them into shape; I knew how much Mother minded

what her pretty white hands looked like. A nurse who was sitting in a corner watched me, smiled wryly and left the room.

I slept alongside Mother that night, in an iron cot that was wheeled in for me. Early the next morning I noticed her breathing was heavier, a sort of throaty, hoarse snore. I knew – as a nurse – but I did not want to know what it meant. Later, I tried to give Mother a little liquid – I brought a spoonful of milk to her mouth. 'For my sake do try darling Mother,' I said, as if speaking to a child. She opened her eyes, she looked at me with such love – a Mother's possessive love. I can never forget that last look. Then it was all over – one huge sigh, the milk trickled out of the corner of her mouth and down her chin, her eyes gazed upwards – to heaven? They stayed there.

I remained pinned to the floor until the doctor and nurse came into the room and asked me to wait outside. Then I stood in the corridor motionless, afraid to breathe, waiting for minutes or longer, I cannot remember – and then what did it matter? Time had lost its meaning. But finally the nurse came out of Mother's room and handed me her wedding ring and her brooch and, as she bustled busily past me, she said, 'Bring a dress, stockings and shoes and the usual. We will put her in the chapel.' Once again I suffered the nightmare of not knowing what *was* the usual in Greece. But happily the nurse had indicated the shop where it, whatever it was, was obtainable and luckily it was a shop I knew well as it was close to my childhood home. I walked into that shop feeling that it was not me but that somebody else was there and that my real self was elsewhere crying my heart out, but, pulling myself together, I addressed the man behind the counter in a somewhat abrupt fashion roughly like this, 'Mother has died. I require the usual.' The man mumbled condolences and after disappearing to the back of the shop he brought out a roll of thin white muslin which he carefully measured. So that was the usual. I took it to the hospital, together with Mother's clothes, and handed them all to a man who, in his own words, was 'preparing' Mother and promised 'to arrange her and put everything in'. I was dazed. I did not understand what he meant – what was there that one could possibly keep back from the dead and not 'put in'?

Later, when I visited Mother in the chapel I found her 'arranged' – lying in an open coffin, dressed in the dress I had chosen with her little black-laced shoes and her hands clasped round a painted tin picture of the Virgin and Child. The coffin was lined with the white veiling – the usual shroud. On my way to the chapel I passed the morgue where corpses were lying awaiting burial. I felt guilty but relieved that Mother had received special reverence and had been put in the chapel. Earthly details still seemed to matter – I did not know why. I said a prayer as I stood by the coffin, and I tucked a small bunch of lilies-of-the-valley which I had bought on my way, under Mother's stiff fingers. Crossing myself, I tiptoed away as if afraid to wake her.

Father died two years later. When I arrived in Athens he was already in the intensive care unit of the Red Cross hospital. As a Red Cross nurse I was given a white gown and mask and was allowed to stand by his bed. I think that through the maze of plastic tubes Father recognized me – but I shall never know. I held his hand and talked to him – hoping that he would know I had come to be by his side. I kissed his hand, and exhausted emotionally and from the hurried flight, I left the hospital to get a few hours rest. No sooner had I fallen asleep in the hotel where I was staying that night, than the phone rang and a nurse from the hospital announced over the crackling line that Father had died. I knew that all that really meant was that they needed the life-support machine – possibly for someone younger – and had switched it off. I was too tired to cry. Instead, I went back over the last sad years my parents had spent in their former native land, missing England where they had lived for most of their lives. In Athens Father missed his medical work, his friends, his clubs and his Saturday walks down Charing Cross Road choosing books for his library. But what seemed really odd – but then they must have forgotten – was that the flat my parents had bought in Athens was in Merlin Street – just where the Gestapo headquarters had been, and where Mother and I had been imprisoned. I could hardly believe it, how could they have done such a thing? To me the street was haunted by the wails and the agonizing cries that pierced the barred windows of the ss gaol. Of course now the building was new and modernized and sweet-scented jasmine hung in festoons over the white marble balconies. And it was, after all, in a very fashionable part of Athens – Kolonaki.

The phone went again. This time it was an undertaker. He gave his name and said he could offer me a 'good price'. I hung up. The next morning Mother's brother, my dear Uncle Aleko, took me to another undertaker to choose a coffin. A roller-blind across one of the walls of the undertaker's shop was lifted to exhibit coffins of different woods – more or less ornate, according to status – I was told. I felt sick – but happily my uncle helped me. I had to choose, and in the end I did – I chose plain, solid wood. Then came the decision on the burial service. For 'important' people the service was 'different', there should be more singing and it should be more elaborate – and it would be more expensive. Father was a highly respected man in his country and in England too, but did one really have to pay one's way to heaven? Once more I felt a foreigner.

At the funeral service in the small chapel facing the sea on a hill outside Athens the singing was beautiful – unforgettable. It was not a lament, nor a sad dirge – the rhythmic chanting was more like a Byzantine dance being performed by a chorus of bearded, gold- and silver-robed priests holding a thousand candles. I do not remember who was there – I just remember the walk up the pine-scented alley to the family tomb. I noted the names of grandfather, uncle and mother engraved on the marble slab. I threw three tuber-roses into Father's open grave. My last link with Greece was severed.

'An earthquake opened up a deep chasm
Which filled at once with flowers.'*

* Lines by the National Poet Solomos, quoted on a poster designed by Constantine Doxiadis, the dedicated coordinator for the reconstruction of Greece after the liberation. He had been an Allied agent and had sabotaged much of the work which he was later to reconstruct.

Some Dates

1924   King George II of the Hellenes is deposed. The Greek monarchy is replaced by a republic.

1935   King George II returns to Greece.

1939   Outbreak of World War II.

1940–1 Greco-Italian War in Albania.

1941–4 German occupation of Greece.

1944   Liberation of Greece by British forces; Civil War in Athens.

1946–9 Communist Guerrilla War in Greece.

Historical Notes 1920–49

▣ CHAPTER 1 (1920–4)

Between 1920 and 1924 Greece was rocked by successive coups and counter-coups, by schisms, manipulated plebiscites and elections. The main antagonism was a personal one, between the Cretan politicians Elefterios Venizelos who had supported the Entente Powers (a term used for the collaboration of Britain, France and Russia between 1907–17) and King Constantine who had supported the Germans or preferred to keep Greece neutral. But even more traumatic – and with far-reaching consequences – had been the humiliating defeat of the Greek armed forces in Asia Minor where the Turks had refused to accept the 1920 Treaty of Sèvres. To force the issue the Greeks launched a major attack on the Turks in March 1921 but received little support from the ambivalent Allies who decided to remain 'neutral' (Britain refused to sell arms to the Greeks; the Italians and French sold them to the Turks.) Taking advantage of Greece's weakening position, Mustafa Kemal launched a devastating counter attack in August 1922. His forces overwhelmed the Greek army's over-extended positions and the fighting ended in a Greek rout, the massacre of thirty thousand Christians and the influx into Greece of half a million destitute, mainly Turkish-speaking, Greek refugees. Although Venizelos had instigated the campaign – ever since the Versailles Peace Conference he had demanded the annexation of Smyrna – the blame fell on King Constantine who had nominally led the Greek forces. A revolutionary committee called on King Constantine to abdicate and those responsible for the débâcle to be brought to trial. The king abdicated in favour of his eldest son George II; and five senior ex-ministers and the former commander-in-chief were executed. This political murder of six of Greece's leading politicians caused an even greater rift between Venizelists and Royalists. After endless political strife King George left Greece for London pending a plebiscite which resulted in an overwhelming vote for a republic in 1924.

▣ CHAPTERS 2–7 (1924–41)

The period of republican rule in Greece (1924–35) was merely an extension of the instability which had preceded it. It was punctuated by military and political coups, by the suspension of the constitution and the introduction of electoral 'reforms' brought in to suit one or other political party. Venizelos, who returned to power in 1928, concentrated on external affairs and improved Greece's relations with her neighbours (the Balkan Pact in 1934 included such unwilling bed-fellows as Turkey, Yugoslavia and Rumania). But the endemic ill was economic. This had been exacerbated by the compulsory exchange of population after the Asia Minor débâcle and the influx of refugees from Russia and Bulgaria. In all over a million refugees had to be resettled; many of them, in their disgruntled state of poverty, were later to form the nucleus of the Greek Communist Party.

A manipulated plebiscite in 1935 brought King George II back to Greece. Those who actually voted for him, and there were quite a number, hoped that with the end of republican rule there would be no more politicking and some form of stability. But more political pressures followed – this time joined by left-wing labour unrest, angry strikes and Communist threats. Finally the King took the measures recommended by his new Prime Minister, General Metaxas – he suspended Parliament – handing Metaxas the powers he had wanted to become Greece's dictator.

Initially, General Metaxas' regime appeared to be paternalistic, but with the pressures caused by Germany's strong hold on the Greek economy and Hitler's and Mussolini's grip on Europe, Metaxas became more autocratic – some would say – Fascist.

In September 1939 at the beginning of World War II, Greece (like Turkey) firmly declared her neutrality. But after the fall of France, and Italy's declaration of war against the Allies in the summer of 1940 Metaxas began a partial mobilization; he realized, as most Greeks did at the time, that Greece would inevitably become embroiled in the war. Yet even when Italy was inventing incidents to prove that Greece was siding with Britain, flying her planes over Greek territory and harassing Greek ships, Metaxas continued to affirm Greek neutrality.

Then on 15 August, the Feast of the Holy Virgin, an 'unidentified submarine' – clearly an Italian one – torpedoed a Greek cruiser off the island of Tinos during the official religious ceremonies. Later, on 27 October, after a reception at the Italian Legation in Athens, which Metaxas had attended, he was handed an ultimatum at the very moment that Italian troops were crossing the Albanian border. Metaxas replied with what has in Greece become the legendary '*Ochi*' – Greek for 'No' – and, with the whole country united and without weighing the consequences, Greece entered the war on Britain's side. (She was at that time Britain's only ally and Churchill referred to this act of defiance as 'Greece's finest hour'.) Throughout Greece there were no doubts, only an almost superhuman driving force to throw the enemy out – reminiscent of the spirit of the Greek rising against the Turks. But as winter set in the Italians held a line cutting the Greeks off from the Albanian port of Valona which they needed for bringing in supplies and reinforcements. Britain – hard pressed at the time – offered Metaxas an expeditionary force, but fearing that it would be too small to be effective and only provoke the Germans, he refused it.

Metaxas died after a short illness and in January 1941 the new government accepted a joint battle plan which was drawn up by the British High Command

and which included the dispatch of a British expeditionary force, Australian and New Zealand troops and a Polish brigade. The actual plan, however, was never successfully carried out as there was a misunderstanding between British and Greek military commanders as to what each was to do. The Greeks were expected to withdraw to a safer line and Yugoslavia's support was to be sought. But none of this took place.

The Germans attacked Yugoslavia and moved swiftly on to Greece. The Greeks and the expeditionary force fought heroically but could not stem the advance. After a vain last attempt to hold Crete, the Greek King, the Greek government and as many of the men of the British expeditionary force as could get away, were evacuated to the Middle East. By May 1941 the occupation of Greece was complete; an occupation shared with Italy and Bulgaria.

CHAPTERS 8–11 (1941–4)

During the first few months of the occupation British agents had to organize the escape of the large number of British and Commonwealth forces who had been left behind after the evacuation. Meanwhile, a number of Greek resistance movements had been formed, the most effective of these being the Communist-dominated EAM (the National Liberation Front) which operated in the towns, and its military arm, ELAS (the National Popular Liberation Army), which operated in the mountains. Under the Metaxas dictatorship Communists had been imprisoned and many had been driven underground. Their clandestine cells, which had sprung up in towns throughout Greece during that period, proved to be a great advantage to EAM as they formed a ready-made resistance network. At first the politics of EAM/ELAS were not evident and a number of Republicans who had suffered under the dictatorship joined their ranks as did many pro-British patriots who wished to fight the enemy. Both EAM and ELAS were directed by Moscow-trained Communists, some of whom had been released from prison by the Germans. (The Germans did however keep the Secretary General of the Communist Party, Nicos Zachariadis, in a concentration camp throughout the war.)

The main right-wing organization was EDES (the National Republican Greek League), led by General Zervas. Other liberal and right-wing organizations were formed but these were rapidly destroyed by the Communist forces. Although ELAS did harass the occupying forces, it also attacked, murdered and blackmailed the right-wing resistance groups and their supporters. The only joint operation which ELAS and EDES undertook was the destruction of the Gorgopotamos viaduct in 1942. This was designed to cut off German supplies to North Africa during the 8th Army offensive and was executed under the direction of British agents who had flown in from GHQ Middle East.

Greek material and human losses during the occupation were tragic and the poor suffered most. Hundreds died during the famine which was caused by the requisitioning of existing food supplies by the occupying forces and the

Allied blockade. Hundreds more were brutally tortured and killed in their homes, and villages burnt by the Germans as retaliatory measures against the resistance guerrilla operations. Finally hundreds were murdered as a result of internecine strife between the various resistance organizations.

Greece during those years was irreparably torn by Communists, Republicans and Monarchists who all fought for power. The enmity between the various factions was fanned by both the Germans and the British. On arrival the Germans released the Communists from jail, then later, in 1943, formed the brutal anti-Communist security battalions. The British both supported the King and the Greek government in exile and at the same time supplied the Communist ELAS forces in occupied Greece. Further, Britain's continued support for the monarchy was something the Communists were able to exploit since the overriding feeling in occupied Greece was in favour of the Republicans, this mainly because of the King's unconstitutional role during the dictatorship. When Churchill and the British Foreign Office eventually realized that EAM/ELAS's aim was to take over the country after liberation it was too late. Arms supplies were stopped for a brief period but ELAS obtained all the arms it wanted from the Italians after their surrender. An attempt was made to form a Greek government-in-exile which was more in keeping with the political feeling in occupied Greece. And after two Prime Ministers had resigned, a government 'of National Unity' was formed. But the Communist-inspired mutiny among the Greek forces in the Middle East and ELAS's murder of Psaros, a prominent leader of a right-wing resistance force infuriated Churchill, who came to an agreement with Stalin (and Roosevelt) to give him a 'free hand' in Greece in return for Stalin's 'free hand' in Rumania and Bulgaria. (The Percentage Agreement of 8 October 1944)

For a very brief time – possibly because of Russian pressure – the resistance forces were united and in February 1943 'The National Band of Guerrillas' was formed under Allied command. But this was very temporary since the Communists, who had already extended their grip over most of Greece, had a plethora of splinter organizations which they were ready to use when they took over the country – either from within or by force. (These organizations included a naval unit, a youth movement, a trade union organization and a secret police.) However the Communists missed their first chance when the Germans unexpectedly withdrew in October 1944 without a major battle, for by then, small, specialized British and American commando-type units had already landed. These were followed by the arrival of more British forces, the Greek crack Rimini Brigade, who had fought so gallantly in Italy, and the Greek Commandos of the Sacred Squadron.

Though most Greeks were deliriously happy to be liberated, the hard-line Communists were not. They demanded power and the rapid execution of collaborators and the 'Monarcho-Fascists'. Tension rose in Athens, and in November the British commander ordered the disbanding of all guerrilla forces. EDES agreed but the Communists refused. Instead a major Communist-led demonstration was called for 3 December. The Greek government first allowed it to go ahead and later banned it. As the shouting mass of demonstators got out of hand

and surged towards the main square, shots were fired. Was it the police who had panicked or did the shots come from the crowd? It was never proved, but at least five people were killed, many injured and fighting broke out.

The Communists must have expected this since their forces, which had done little to harass the German retreat, had already ringed Athens and were moving out to cut off the airport and port of Pireaus. A six-week bitter battle for the capital ensued.

CHAPTERS 11–13 (1944–6)

As the shells from the Communist 75 mm guns lobbed into the centre of Athens, Churchill and Eden flew into the capital on Christmas Eve 1944. At the British Embassy they held a secret meeting with Archbishop Damaskinos, the head of the Greek Church (who had taken an active part in the resistance), and representatives of the Communists. Although no agreement on the immediate end of hostilities was reached a decision was taken to delay the King's return until after a plebiscite had been held. Meanwhile, Archbishop Damaskinos was to be regent. These moves, together with the arrival of British reinforcements (which Britain could ill afford at the time) changed and strengthened the military and political scene. On 11 January the Communists, who had begun their retreat, agreed to a cease-fire and this was followed by a political settlement. (The Varkiza Agreement signed on 12 Februrary 1945, see p. 221.)

The new Prime Minister who took over was General Plastiras, the titular head of the Republican resistance movement, EDES.* In return for the arms which the Communists handed over, he promised that collaborators would be brought to trial and that an amnesty would be granted to those who had 'committed political crimes'. (An ambiguous description, the interpretation of which was to cause much trouble later.) He also agreed to a plebiscite which would be held under international supervision to decide on the return of the King, to be followed by free elections.

Throughout the fighting in the capital Russia had not intervened and Stalin kept his agreement – reached in Moscow in October 1944 – allowing Britain freedom of action in Greece. The Americans remained neutral – hostilely neutral, to be correct. They accused Churchill of colonialism, their Mission personnel and reporters wore stars-and-stripes armbands and moved in and out of the Communist-held area of the town while their Ambassador refused to allow the hard-pressed British troops to drink from his well in the Embassy garden.

In spite of the cease-fire and the amnesty, both right-wing and left-wing thugs continued their reign of terror. Atrocities were carried out by both sides. These were stepped up after the full horror of the ELAS atrocities had been discovered – the mass graves and the murder of some eight thousand civilian hostages whom they had taken with them during their retreat from the capital.

* Plastiras was in exile in France during the occupation, having fled there after the abortive coup of 1933. EDES was led by General Zervas.

CHAPTERS 13–15 (1946–9)

Hatred and political schisms continued well after the 1944 battle for the capital, and Greece became ungovernable. Premiers came and went as accusations were hurled at them for being either pro-ELAS or collaborators; for being right-wing supporters and not bringing the collaborators to trial or being left-wing and supporting those who had plundered and murdered and sought revenge. Coalition governments did not fare any better. In an attempt to bring some form of political order, Archbishop Damaskinos arranged for general elections to be held on 31 May 1946 under international supervision. At this point the US became involved in Greece for the first time and sent observers. The Communists boycotted the elections, claiming that the country was in such chaos that free elections were a farce. However, sixty per cent of the population did go to the polls and the right-wing Populists won a clear majority. On 1 September a plebiscite was held which resulted in an overwhelming vote for the King's return; the King to most Greeks at that time seemed a lesser evil than Communist rule.

When King George II returned in September he found that two-thirds of the country was in ELAS hands and that a strong Communist Party under the leadership of Nicos Zachariadis (who had been liberated from Dachau by the British) was active in the major towns. A year later, when he died and was succeeded by his brother Paul with his German wife Frederika, the situation was unchanged and steadily became worse. The occupation and civil strife had left Greece with a black-market economy, mounting inflation, total economic and political chaos and the breakdown of security throughout the countryside – a natural breeding-ground for Communism. In the villages in northern Greece and the Peloponnese ELAS Communist guerrillas swooped down on right-wing villages and murdered the inhabitants and the right-wing supporters, many from the former security battalions set up by the Germans to mete out similar punishment to left-wing supporters. In the towns the jails bulged with Communists and collaborators awaiting trial. To add to this tragic scene, Russia had changed her policy and in January 1946 demanded the immediate withdrawal of British troops from Greece. When this motion failed at the UN she supplied and assisted the Communist guerrillas indirectly through Albania, Yugoslavia and Bulgaria. As a result a much-strengthened Communist guerrilla army was formed in October 1946 under the leadership of the former ELAS commander Marcos Vaphiadis: it called itself the 'Democratic Army'. With large areas under its control and with assistance from neighbouring Communist countries civil war broke out in earnest in the winter of 1946.

Early in 1947 Britain, with its post-war economic problems, could no longer shoulder the added burden of Greece and dumped it on the US's lap. America responded with the Truman Doctrine on 12 March – a pledge to support 'the free peoples who are resisting subjugation by armed minorities'. The Senate voted emergency funds to the tune of $400 million which put an end to the US policy of non-intervention.

The Civil War continued until 1949. During these years over eighty thousand Greeks were killed, some thirty thousand children were abducted – forcibly taken from their parents to neighbouring Communist countries to be brought up as 'good Communists'. Thousands of Greeks lost their homes or fled in terror. The special UN Committee (UNSCOB) which was sent to Greece to investigate the Greek government's claims that the guerrillas were receiving aid from neighbouring Communist countries, and the fact that the Greek children were being abducted confirmed the truth of both of these complaints. Even though UNSCOB had its hands tied and could only investigate on Greek soil in border areas it did collect all the evidence it needed. But in the end it was the massive US assistance that turned the tide. With better-equipped government forces, better led – in 1949 by General Papagos, the hero of the Albanian campaign who had been imprisoned by the Germans – and with the assistance of US military advisors under US General Van Fleet, the military situation changed. On the Communist side, the Democratic Army's terror tactics were turning the rural population against them. Militarily they were never able to take any major town and had twice failed to set up their 'Free Government' in Konitsa, a town on the Albanian border. In 1949 their leadership was split; Marcos was deposed and Zachariadis took his place. But by then the Tito-Stalin rift had resulted in the closing of the Yugoslav frontier with Greece and in July that year the guerrillas were cut off from this important route for supplies and reinforcements. In August the Greek National Army successfully flushed out most of the guerrillas from their mountain strongholds and the Communists were finally defeated. By mid-October the Communists publicly admitted their defeat and agreed to end hostilities, bringing the Greek Civil War, the first armed struggle in the Cold War, to an end.

Appendix I

1 Open letter from Georges Vlachos, editor of the *Kathimerini*, to Adolf Hitler, published 8 March 1941, on the eve of the German invasion.

To His Excellency, Adolf Hitler, Chancellor of the German Reich

Excellency

Greece, as you know, wished to keep out of the present war. When it broke out she had barely recovered from the wounds that she had suffered from various wars and dissensions at home. She had neither the strength nor the intention, nor any reason to take part in a war, the end of which, no doubt, would be of great importance to the whole world, but at the start did not offer any direct threat to her integrity. Let us ignore her declarations on this point, let us ignore the official documents published in the White Book, let us ignore the speeches and articles which bore witness to her permanent desire to keep out of the war. Let us take into account one fact only. When, after the Italian sinking of the *Elli* in the port of Tinos, Greece found the remains of torpedoes, when she had proof that these torpedoes were Italian, she kept silent. Why? Because if she had disclosed the truth she would have been forced either to declare war, or to see war declared against her. Greece never wished for war with Italy, neither by herself nor with allies, whether these be British or Balkan. She wished only for her small part of the world to live as quietly as possible, because she was exhausted, because she had fought many wars and because her geographical position is such that she could not have as an enemy either the Germans on land or the English on sea.

At the moment of the sinking of the *Elli*, Greece, apart from her pacific longings, had a guarantee as well, bearing two signatures. The Italian signature, which had guaranteed her against all aggression on the part of Italy, and that of England, which was a spontaneous guarantee of Greek integrity. Nevertheless, when, some time after the sinking of the *Elli*, Italy had shown clearer signs of her future aggression, Greece, convinced that the first signature was valueless, did not turn, as she should have turned, towards the country which had given her the second. She turned – do you remember, Excellency? – towards yourself, and she asked for your protection. What was the reply we were given then? What was said I do not know exactly, but this I know, because I heard it from the lips of our late President himself, that Germany replied to our request by advising us not to offer any pretexts – that is to say, not to mobilize – and to stay quiet.

We did not offer any pretexts, we did not mobilize; we slept quietly, or rather we were sleeping quietly – for that evening the Italians had invited us to dinner – when the Italian Minister appeared with his ultimatum. To whom and where then would you have liked us to turn? Towards Italy, whose valueless signature we had in our pocket with the remains of the torpedoes? But it was the Italians who had declared the war. Towards yourself? But unfortunately that very morning of 28 October, you were at Florence. To remain alone? We had no air force, no material, no money and no fleet. We turned then to the signature that was left, to the English. And those whose own homeland was in flames, those were keeping anxious watch and ward on the Channel, those who, they said it themselves, had not sufficient material for their own defence, they came, and they came immediately. Without haggling, without excuses, they came, and a few days later on the front in the mountains of Epirus, where the brutal Italian aggression had begun, fell together the Greek troops and the first English airman.

What happened after that you know well, you and the whole world. The Italians have been thrashed. They have been thrashed there man to man by us, the weak and feeble Greeks. Not by the English, because no English soldier has set foot in Albania. The Italians have been thrashed. Why? Because they had no ideals, because they had no heart in the fight, because – but that is another story. In the face of this victory, it is sure because we have been told so, you have remained a spectator. 'This affair,' you said, 'does not interest me. It concerns the Italians only. I will only interfere when the English army land at Salonica in numbers.' We could have asked your Excellency: 'Florence? Is it a fact that on the very day that the Italians attacked us you were meeting them on the banks of the Arno, and you handed over to them the Greeks?' But we did not wish to ask. Hidden away with the remains of the Italian torpedoes we hid Florence also, and when indiscreet people brought it to our notice we said, 'They were not in agreement, the Italians deceived them.' Why? Because that is what we wished to believe. That is what it was our interest to believe. So at the same time as we were advancing in Albania, our relations with Germany went smoothly on their way. The swastika flew from your Legation on New Year's day, it came to half-mast when Metaxas died, and your Minister paid his respects to the new President of the Council. Commercial dealings were renewed, and you yourselves protested strongly on one occasion when an American paper announced that German tanks had appeared in Albania. Everyone was happy at the results in Albania. You as spectators, and the English, our allies, with their air force and their fleet. Only that. You know how we tried to keep that 'Only that' a reality. Enough to say that when an English aeroplane crashed at Salonica we asked the English not to salvage it themselves, in order that not even ten British soldiers should appear there, in order that there should be no misunderstanding, no pretexts. You laugh? How right you are.

But all the time that our relations were like this, while a certain calm due to the German attitude remained, you had begun to concentrate forces in Rumania. But the first contingent was to teach the Rumanian army, the second to protect the oilfields, the third the frontiers. The fourth ... but the fourth contingent was 300,000 men. The writer went as a journalist to Bulgaria, covering the road over which now pass your soldiers. And when he came back he said to the late President, 'The road to Sofia has just been widened. The wooden bridges have just been strengthened, the shavings of the carpenters are still lying on the ground. It is clear that the Bulgarians have got ready hastily the road on which an army passes.'

And after that what was Greece to do? To see the Germans on the frontiers of Bulgaria? To count their ships on the Danube, to see them entering Sofia and allying themselves with the Bulgarians? To hear the Bulgarians talking of their national claims, and to keep calm in the knowledge that the Germans are at Koula to guard the Rumanian oilfields?

But enough. Forget the past. Come to facts. According to every wireless station in the world it appears that the Germans wished to invade Greece. Why? If an attack on Greece was from the beginning essential to the interests of the Axis, M. Grazzi would not have been alone four months ago at three o'clock in the morning. Germany and Italy would have been there together. From the beginning, therefore, the attack on Greece does not seem to have been necessary for the Axis. Apparently now it is. But why? Is it an order that a front was not to be created in the Balkans against Germany? But this comes out of a fairy story. Neither the Greeks nor the English – this was stated officially in a communiqué of 6 March, and is shouted from the housetops by logic – nor Serbia nor Turkey have any reason for spreading the war. The war as it has been is big enough for all these countries. Is it, then, in order to save the Italians in Albania? But what sort of salvation is this? The Italians have been thrashed openly and for all eternity, and will not the public opinion of the world be certain of this thrashing as soon as a single German soldier steps on to the soil of Greece? Will not the whole world shout that forty-five millions of Italians after having attacked our poor eight millions, have now to call for help to another eighty-five millions? But if the Italians wish to be saved, why should others come to their help in a way which is particularly humiliating for them when we could save them ourselves with pleasure and without exposing them to ridicule? Let the Italians evacuate Albania, let them shout from the housetops that they are tired of chasing us and are satiated with glory and have decided to retire. We will help them. But, Excellency, perhaps you are going to say to us, 'This is all very well, but what about the English?'

But it is not us, your Excellency, who made the English come to Greece. It was the Italians. And now you wish us to say farewell to those whom the Italians brought here. So be it. Let us say it. But to whom? To the living.

But how can we throw out the dead? Those who died on our mountains. Those, who, wounded, fell to earth in Attica and drew their last breath. Those who at a time when their own country was in flames came to Greece and fought there, died there and there found their graves. Listen, your Excellency, there are deeds which cannot be done in Greece, and that is one of them. We cannot throw out either the living or the dead. We will throw out no one, but we shall stand here upright by their side until the day when the sunshine breaks through the storm.

Everyone is saying that you intend to invade Greece. But we do not believe it, and we are an ingenuous people. We do not believe it of your army, with its history and its traditions which even its enemies do not deny. We do not believe that your army is willing to disgrace itself by such an action. We do not believe that a great power armed to the teeth, with a population of eighty-five million fighting to create in the world a 'New Order', an Order which we thought to be founded on right, we do not believe that this great power wishes to attack on the flank a little country which already struggles for its liberty against an Empire of forty-five million men.

What would your army do, your Excellency, if instead of horses and artillery we sent to receive them on the frontier our twenty thousand wounded in their bloody bandages? But no, that cannot be. Small or great, that part of the Greek army which can be sent there will stand in Thrace as they have stood in Epirus. There they will await the return from Berlin of the Runner, who came five years ago to light the torch at Olympus. We shall see this torch light a fire, a fire which will light this little nation, which has taught all other nations how to live, and will now teach them how to die.

*   *   *   *

2 Message from King George VI of Great Britain to King George II of the Hellenes, after the fall of Crete

Telegraphed to Sir Michael Palairet on 10 June 1941 with instructions to explain to His Majesty that it would be appreciated if permission were given for full publicity.

COPY
NO. R 5939/4488/19.

The loss of Crete must be to Your Majesty and to all Greeks as it is to us, a bitter blow. We share Your grief but we also share Your hopes. News reaches this country daily to prove that the tragedy of Greece has left unbroken the spirit of Your gallant people who have shown and continue to show a heroism and a disregard for odds unsurpassed in history. Your country has indeed been overwhelmed, but the spirit of the Greek people remains high and the fame of their resistance will outlast the transitory conquests of the enemy. Fortified by the Greek example we shall continue the struggle proud to have at our side those units of Your Fleet which survived the battle, the nucleus of a new Hellenic Air Force, and the cadres of a new Army. Meanwhile my Government learn that Hellenic communities overseas are expressing their determination to pursue the struggle for victory and asking how best they can help.

I greet through Your Majesty all who fought in the valiant Hellenic armies on the mainland, those who fought in Crete, and particularly the injured and bereaved; and I thank you one and all each individually, for your co-operation; for the battles which you won, for the help you gave My soldiers; for the tremendous moral blow which you have struck for our common cause. To You and Your people we are for ever grateful and in our gratitude we do not forget that great soldier statesman John Metaxas who said to the Italians 'You shall not pass', nor his successor, Alexander Koryzis, who said 'No', to a yet more powerful foe.

10–11 June 1941.

*   *   *   *

3 Evacuation figures of British and Commonwealth Forces

Churchill gives the following evacuation figures of the Expeditionary Force (*Second World War*, III).

Forces	In country at time of attack	Evacuated to Crete	Evacuated from Crete and direct to Egypt
UK Forces	19,206	5,299	7,301
Australian	17,125	6,451	7,706
N. Zealand	16,720	7,100	7,354
Total	53,051	18,850	22,361

Note: These figures explain the number of British and Commonwealth troops who were left behind and had to either surrender to the Germans or hide until some form of evacuation was possible.

Appendix II

Some favourite Kleftic ballads*

DIAKOS

(Young Diakos was training to be a priest when he heroically threw in his lot with the Klefts or guerrillas who fought against the Turkish occupation.)

Three birds sat on Diakos' camp betwixt the dawn and noon:
One looks towards Livadhia, one looks towards Zetoun.
The handsomest spoke drearily (he was as black as black could be):
'Is it Kalyvas marching there? Is it young Soldier John?'
''Tis not Kalyvas marching there; it is not Soldier John,
But Omer Vriones there, with all his host comes on.'

Diakos heard the bruit of it, and ill it seemed him then,
He shouted loud, he called to him the chief of all his men.
'Gather the lads,' Diakos said, 'and marshal all my bands,
Deal out the powder without stint, and shot to fill two hands:
We'll hold the Alamana Bridge – be swift – far down below,
Where we have made good stone redoubts and cover from the foe.'

They took their long guns in their hands, they took their swords so fine,
And at the Alamana Bridge they manned the battle line.
'Courage, my lads,' Diakos cried, 'nor fear the invader's band;
Think of the old Hellenic name, the Grecian fame, and stand.'

But they were sore afraid; they fled, they scattered up the glen.
And brave Diakos faced the fire with eighteen valiant men.
Three hours 'gainst eighteen thousand Turks Diakos made his stand:
He fired until the musket burst and splintered in his hand.
He drew the good sword by his side and at the foe he flew:
Seven captains fell before his blade; past count, the foes he slew;
Then snapped the good sword at the hilt, down fell the broken blade,
And he was prisoner ta'en alas, alive, but undismayed.
A thousand guards before him marched, two thousand more behind;
And Omer Bey, beside the way, spoke to him with accent kind:

* Translated by A.R.Burn *The Modern Greeks* (Thomas Nelson & Sons Ltd). The words of
these ballads are often changed by the singer to fit his mood or the occasion.

'Diakos, friend, now change your faith, and live, a Turk, with me,
And leave the Church, and in the Mosque with Moslems bend the knee.'
But brave Diakos shook his head and angered made reply:
'Not so: a Grecian I was born; a Grecian I will die.
But ah' – he said – 'how fair a time death chooses for my doom,
In Spring, when all the woods are green and all the world in bloom.'

THE MAID AT ARMS

(is the tale of the fair Amazon maiden)

O who has seen fish climb a hill, or corn grow in the sea?
O who has seen a maiden fair in warrior's finery?
– But Diamanto ten long years among the warriors stayed,
Soldier or bandit, and none guessed or knew her for a maid.

But one fair morn of festival, a summer's holy-day,
The outlaws bold at swordsmanship and hurling stones did play.
They fenced, they ran, great stones they threw, and as they sported there,
The brooch upon her shoulder burst and showed her breast so fair.

Then shone the sun, the silver moon, as after dark eclipse!
'What ails you now, you outlaw boy, to stare so hard at me?'

'O the golden sun, the silver moon unclouded I did see!
For I did see your breast so fair, your breast as white as snow.'

'O keep my secret, outlaw boy, that nobody may know!
– I'll take you for my squire-at-arms, I'll give you wealth untold,
I'll give to you my gun so fine, all damascened in gold.'

'I willna be your squire-at-arms, I want no wealth untold;
I willna take your gun so fine, all damascened with gold;
But I would have ye as my wife, the damsel I hae found' –

With that she seized him by the hair and hurled him to the ground.
'O maiden fair, let go my hair and take me by the hand!
I'll work for you, your squire so true, and always by you stand.'

STERYOS

(This comes from Thessaly and typical of the Kleft ballads it repeats the
will not 'to bow the knee' to the invader. The refrain 'While springs outflow
...' is repeated.)

The foe has won the mountain pass, they hold the vales so fair,
But Steryos lives; though Pashas rage, for them he will not care.
While snows are white on mountain height, while flowers are fair on lea,

(i) Maintenance of law and order in the territories where their forces are operating.

(ii) Prevention of civil war and the killing of Greeks by Greeks.

(iii) Prevention of infliction of any penalty whatsoever and of unjustifiable arrest.

(iv) Assistance in the establishment of the legal civil authority and the distribution of relief.

(A map showing the operational boundaries was issued to both commanders.)

*   *   *   *

2 Varkiza Agreement

The articles in the Varkiza Agreement, signed at the end of the civil war in Athens on 12 February 1945 were as follows:

ARTICLE i – Liberties

The Government will secure in accordance with the Constitution and the democratic principles everywhere recognized, the free expression of the political and social opinions of the citizens, repealing any existing illiberal law. It will also secure the unhindered functioning of individual liberties such as those of assembly, association and expression of views in the Press. More especially, the Government will fully restore Trade Union liberties.

ARTICLE ii – Raising of Martial Law

Martial law will be raised immediately after the signature of the present agreement. Simultaneously with this action there will be brought into force a Constitutional Act similar in all respects to Constitutional Act No. 24, whereby the suspension of those articles of the Constitution to which reference is made in Act 24 shall be permitted.

Articles 5, 10, 12, 20 and 95 of the Constitution shall be suspended forthwith throughout the country. This suspension shall continue until the completion of disarmament, and the establishment of administrative, judicial and military authorities throughout the country. As regards Article 5 in particular, this suspension shall not take effect in the cities of Athens and Piraeus and their suburbs. Especially, however, as regards persons arrested up to the present day it is agreed that Article 5 of the Constitution is not in force, and that they will be liberated within the shortest possible period of time, the necessary orders to this effect being given to the competent authorities.

Followers of EAM who may be held in captivity by other organizations shall be set free as soon as possible.

ARTICLE III – Amnesty

There shall be an amnesty for political crimes committed between the 3 December 1944, and the publication of the Law establishing the amnesty. From this amnesty shall be excluded common-law crimes against life and property which were not absolutely necessary to the achievement of the political crime concerned. The necessary Law will be published immediately after the signature of the present agreement. From this amnesty will be excluded any persons who, being under obligation to surrender their arms as being members of the organizations of ELAS, the National Civil Guard or ELAN*, shall not have handed them over by the 15 March 1945. This last provision concerning exclusion from the amnesty shall be annulled after verification of the fact that the disarmament of ELAS has been effected, since there will then be no further cause and justification for it. Guarantees and details of the amnesty to be provided are contained in the draft law attached to the present agreement.

ARTICLE IV – Hostages

All civilians who have been arrested by ELAS or by the National Civil Guard (EP), irrespective of the date on which they were arrested, shall be set at liberty immediately. Any who may be held on the charge of collaboration with the enemy or of commission of any crime shall be handed over to the justice of the State for trial by the competent Courts according to law. (See draft law of amnesty attached.)

ARTICLE V – National Army

The National Army, apart from the professional officers and NCOs, shall consist of the soldiers of the classes which shall from time to time be called up. Reserve officers, NCOs and other ranks, who have been specially trained in modern weapons, shall remain in service so long as there is a formation requiring them. The Sacred Squadron shall remain as at present, since it is under the immediate orders of the Allied High Command, and shall thereafter be merged in the united National Army in accordance with the above principle. The effort will be made to extend regular conscription to the whole of Greece in accordance with the above principle. The effort will be made to extend regular conscription to the whole of Greece in accordance with the technical facilities existing and the necessities which may arise. After the demobilization of ELAS those men who belong to classes which are to be called up in accordance with the attached protocol shall report for enrolment in the units already existing. All men who have been enrolled in the units now existing, without belonging to the classes being called up, shall be discharged. All members of the permanent cadres of the National Army shall be considered by the Councils for which provision is made in Constitutional Act No. VII. The political and social views of citizens serving in the Army shall be respected.

* ELAN was the EAM/ELAS navy (National Popular Liberation Navy).

ARTICLE vi – Demobilization

Immediately on the publication of the present agreement the armed forces of resistance shall be demobilized and in particular the ELAS, both Regular and Reserve, the ELAN and the National Civil Guard. The demobilization and surrender of arms shall take place according to the detailed provisions of the protocol drawn up by the Committee of Experts which, duly initialled, is attached hereto.

The State will settle all questions arising out of requisitioning carried out by ELAS. The goods requisitioned by ELAS, including beasts, motor vehicles, etc., which will be handed over to the State according to the detailed provisions of the protocol which has been drawn up and is attached hereto, will be regarded thereafter as having been requisitioned by the Greek State.

ARTICLE vii – Purge of Civil Service

The Government will proceed, by means of Committees or Councils, to be established by a special Law, to the purging of the personnel of the public services, officials of public companies, local Government officials, and those of other services dependent on the State or paid by it. The criteria of which the purge will take account will be either professional competence, or character and personality, or collaboration with the enemy or the utilization of the official as an instrument of the dictatorship. Officials of the above services who, during the occupation, joined the forces of the resistance will return to their positions and will be considered in the same manner as other officials. The above-mentioned Councils will also consider the cases of officials who have taken part or collaborated in the manifestations which have taken place between the 3rd December, 1944, and the date of signature of the present agreement. Those of them who are found to have been concerned may be placed at the disposal of the State as provided by Law. The final disposal of such officials will be decided by the Government which shall result from the elections to the Constituent Assembly. Officials who have already been placed *en disponibilité* by decisions of the Ministers will be submitted to the decision of the Council above mentioned. No official will be dismissed solely on account of his political opinion.

ARTICLE viii – Purge of Security Services

The purge of the Security Services, the Gendarmerie and the City Police will be carried out as soon as possible by the special purge committee on the same basis as the purge of the Civil Service. All officers and other ranks of the above Corps who fall under the provisions of the Amnesty Law, who, during the period of the occupation, joined the ranks of ELAS, ELAN or the National Civil Guard, will return to their positions and will be considered by the purge Councils in the same manner as the rest of their colleagues. All the officers and other ranks of the above Corps who left their positions between 3rd December, 1944, and the date of signature of the present document shall be placed *en disponibilité*, their final disposal being left for the decision of the Councils to be constituted by the Government arising from the elections.

ARTICLE ix – Plebiscite and Elections

At the earliest possible date, and in any case within the current year, there shall be conducted in complete freedom and with every care for its genuineness a plebiscite which shall finally decide on the Constitutional question, all points being submitted to the decision of the people. Thereafter shall follow as quickly as possible elections to a Constituent Assembly for the drafting of the new Constituent of the country. The representatives of both sides agree that for the verification of the genuineness of the expression of the popular will the great Allied Powers shall be requested to send observers.

Of this present agreement two similar copies have been made, whereof the one has been received by the Government Delegation and the other by the Delegation of ELAN.

In Athens, at the Ministry of Foreign Affairs, 12th February 1945.

Resumé of Draft Law of Amnesty referred to in Article 4 of the Act of Agreement:

ARTICLE 1

Para. 1. An amnesty is granted to the political offences committed between 3 December, 1944, and the date of publication of the present law. Common offences against life and property connected with the political offences but not absolutely necessary for its accomplishment are excepted from the amnesty.

Para. 2. Are excepted from this amnesty all those belonging to ELAS, ELAN and the Civil Guard who, though obliged to hand in their arms, have not done so before the 15 March, 1945.

ARTICLE 2

The Court of Appeal will settle any doubts as to the interpretation of Article 1.

ARTICLE 3

Those who do not receive the amnesty cannot be prosecuted for the excepted offences after six months in the Athens area and after the end of 1945 in the rest of Greece.

ARTICLE 4

These same persons who do not receive the amnesty cannot be held in custody pending trial for more than six months. After that they must be released.

(Articles 5 and 6 concerned technical details of procedure.)

Bibliography

Authors I have drawn on:

C.M.Woodhouse, *Apple of Discord*, Hutchinson & Co Ltd; 1948
                 The Struggle for Greece, Hart Davis MacGibbon Ltd; 1976
                 Modern Greece, A Short History, Faber & Faber Ltd; 1968
W.Byford Jones, *The Greek Trilogy*, Hutchinson & Co Ltd; 1945
Richard Capell, *Simiomata*, Macdonald & Co Ltd; 1945
W.Stanley Moss, *Ill Met by Moonlight*, Harrap & Co Ltd; 1950
X.Fielding, *Hide and Seek*, Secker & Warburg Ltd; 1954
S.Casson, *Greece against the Axis*, Hamish Hamilton Ltd; 1941
P.Leigh Fermor, *A Time of Gifts*, John Murray Publishers Ltd; 1977
Sir Reginald Leeper, *When Greek Meets Greek*, Chatto & Windus Ltd; 1950
N.Clive, *A Greek Experience*, Michael Russell; 1985
Olivia Manning, *Friends and Heroes*, William Heinemann Ltd; 1965

I have also consulted:

John Colville, *The Fringes of Power: Downing Street Dairies, 1939–55*, Hodder
   & Stoughton Ltd; 1985
Winston Churchill, *The Second World War*, Cassell Ltd; 1954
Harold Macmillan, *War Diaries*, Macmillan Publishers Ltd; 1984
A.R.Burn, *Modern Greece*, Thomas Nelson & Sons Ltd; 1944

Index